Nial Osborough was born in Belfast
in 1939 and went to school in Bango
County Down and also in Edin
He graduated in law from Q
University, Belfast in 196
subsequently spent two years
Tulane Law School in New Or
He taught law at Belfast until 19
before taking up an appointment
with University College Dublin,
where he is now dean of the Faculty
of Law. He is editor of *The Irish Jurist*.
Nial Osborough is married
with two children.

BORSTAL IN IRELAND

Borstal in Ireland

Custodial Provision for the Young Adult
Offender 1906-1974

NIAL OSBOROUGH

INSTITUTE OF PUBLIC ADMINISTRATION
DUBLIN

© Nial Osborough 1975

Institute of Public Administration
59 Lansdowne Road
Dublin 4, Ireland

ISBN 0 902173 66 9

Set in Monotype Bembo

Made and printed in the Republic of Ireland
by Task Print and Packaging, Naas, Co Kildare

For Margaret

For Margaret

Contents

The Arthur Cox Foundation

Arthur Cox, classical scholar, senator and former President of The Incorporated Law Society of Ireland, was associated with the foundation of many industries which have become great enterprises. He was a specialist in company law and was chairman of the Company Law Reform Committee. He made many outstanding contributions to our community. When he decided to retire from practice, a number of his clients, professional colleagues and other friends thought that a fund should be established as a tribute to him to subsidise the publication of legal textbooks. There was a generous response to our appeal.

After his retirement, he was ordained a priest and went to Zambia to do missionary work. He died there as the result of a car accident.

He had often spoken to me of the importance of having textbooks on Irish Law published. The Foundation has already subsidised two books. Mr Osborough's study of Borstal in Ireland is the third, and the trustees of the Foundation, Mr Charles Russell Murphy F.C.A., The Incorporated Law Society of Ireland, and I am glad to have been able to assist in the publication of his book.

JOHN KENNY

The High Court
Dublin
June 1975

Preface

Little has been written on the administration of the penal systems in either the Republic or Northern Ireland. The aim of this book is to present an account of custodial provision for young adult offenders in Ireland since 1906 and thus to go some way to remedy the deficiency. The main emphasis is necessarily on borstal, but included, too, is a portrait of St Patrick's Institution which, from 1956, effectively superseded borstal in the Republic. In the circumstances, I trust that no one's sensitivities will be offended by the choice of title.

Late adolescence to early manhood marked off the age-group for which borstal was designed to cater; it likewise isolates those in custody with whom this study is concerned, whether in borstal or elsewhere. There is one exception. I have purposely omitted from consideration provision for youngsters detained in what were formerly termed reformatory schools: the "intellectual neglect" of penal administration to which I have referred has been least obvious in the cases of the training school system in the North and the equivalent reformatory and industrial school systems in the South.

Sources have presented a problem. Independent assessments of any aspect of Irish penal administration are rare. In the case of borstal prior to 1950, only one such assessment came to light: Edward Fahy's article in *Hermathena* in 1941 (traced, I am glad to acknowledge, through the medium of the O'Higgins *Bibliography*). In the result, I was forced to rely heavily on the information contained in the various series of official prisons reports. Some lack of balance was inevitable. The reports themselves suffered from two further defects: a dearth of desirable detail and the patently simplistic conclusion occasionally offered on some aspect of administration.

Extraordinary legal complexities surround the day-to-day operation of the penal system in the contemporary Republic. In attempting to describe these, I have often had to borrow extensively from reports in the press; I trust my confidence in the accuracy of these reports has not been misplaced.

Early drafts of two small sections in chapters III and V have previously appeared in print, in the *Dublin University Law Review* and *The Irish Jurist*, respectively.

I am endebted to a number of people and organisations: to Kevin Boyle, the late Frank Connolly, and John Parkes, for their kind criticism of early drafts of portions of chapters II, III and IV (any remaining errors are, of course, my responsibility); to John Bruton, TD, Alan Hewitt, the Honourable Mr Justice John Kenny, Matthew Russell, Kevin Waldron, Jonathan Williams, and the various governors of institutions and civil servants North and South, for their assistance; to Francis Murphy and his wife, for their hospitality in Clonmel; to The Arthur Cox Foundation, The Incorporated Law Society of Ireland, the Northern Ireland Association for the Care and Resettlement of Offenders, and University College Dublin, for their financial support of publication.

NIAL OSBOROUGH
Dublin, 18 August 1975

Table of Cases

Table of Legislation

Table of Statutory Instruments

ABBREVIATIONS

C. & Y.P. Act	Children and Young Persons Act
Clonmel Notes	The Borstal Institution at Clonmel: Notes by the Visiting Committee 1948 (R.I.)
Cussen Report	Report of Commission of Inquiry into the Reformatory and Industrial Schools 1936 (R.I.)
Home Office Services Report	Report on the Administration of Home Office Services (N.I.)
Kennedy Report	Report of Committee on Reformatory and Industrial Schools Systems 1970 (R.I.)
Lynn Report	The Protection and Welfare of the Young and the Treatment of Young Offenders: Report of the Committee appointed by the Minister of Home Affairs 1938 (N.I.)
Moles Report	Report of the Departmental Committee on Industrial and Reformatory Schools in Northern Ireland 1923
Molony Report	Report of the Departmental Committee on the Treatment of Young Offenders 1927 (England and Wales)
1908 Act	Prevention of Crime Act 1908
1914 Act	Criminal Justice Administration Act 1914
N.I.	Northern Ireland: the six-county area
Prisons Board Report	Report of the General Prisons Board Ireland
Prisons Report	Annual Report on Prisons (and, since 1972, of Detention Centres) (R.I.)
Prisons Report (N.I.)	Report on the Prisons Northern Ireland
R.I.	Republic of Ireland: the twenty-six county area

CHAPTER I

Origins of Borstal in Ireland

I looked up,—a wild unearthly looking creature stood on the cliff above, in the very act of launching a huge stone at me ! Just then a female figure rose beside him, and with threats and blows drove him from the rock. It was my fair friend of the curragh, who seeing me take the lonely path I did, hastened after me to warn me of the danger. She told me that the assailant was a dangerous lunatic; he was treacherous beyond description, and his antipathy to women and strangers was remarkable . . . To my inquiry 'Why this dangerous being was not removed to some asylum?' my protectress replied with a smile, 'He was but a poor natural, after all; he was born in the island, and God forbid that they should send him among strangers.'
W. H. Maxwell, *Wild Sports of the West* (London, 1850 ed.), p. 110.

The borstal system introduced into Ireland in 1906 was consciously modelled on the celebrated system evolved a few years earlier in England. This system, though English in immediate conception, was, in turn, derived from a tradition in penal reform which earlier innovations in Ireland (not ordinarily thought of as a pioneer) and elsewhere had helped to shape. Distinctively Irish antecedents are thus at hand, though their importance must not be exaggerated: while they help to explain the emergence of borstal in England, they had little influence on the eventual decision to introduce the system in Ireland.

These earlier innovations in Ireland took place during the phasing out of the transportation of convicts in the years immediately before its final abolition in the eighteen fifties. This transitional era was to produce an important change in the philosophy of penal treatment, though no one would then have predicted it. The particular incentive was provided by the fears, publicly expressed, of the consequences of an end to transportation, especially of the risk to the community presented by the eventual release into it of large numbers of convicts.[1] Nonetheless, the change itself would not have occurred had not penal administrators appreciated the need to allay these fears and set out to do so.

In Ireland, the responsibility for the administration of the new convict prisons lay with the Board of Directors of Irish Convict Prisons set up in 1854 under the chairmanship of Walter Crofton. In response to the apprehensions of the public and in accordance, at the same time, with its conviction as to what was right, the Board pioneered an approach to penal treatment which was later to win fame both on its own account and for Crofton, the prime mover. The innovation was 'the progressive stage system', a variety of prison discipline consisting of four stages: solitary confinement at Mountjoy prison in Dublin, employment on public works at Spike Island in Cork harbour, trade training at Smithfield prison in Dublin and Lusk in County Dublin, and finally conditional release.[2] Crofton himself placed special emphasis on the 'intermediate prisons' of the third stage. "These establishments", the Board wrote in its *Second Report*,

> will act as filterers between the prisons and the community; but to enable them to be *really* such, the system pursued in them must be of such a character as to test the reformation of the prisoner, and throw him more on himself; hard work and coarse fare must be the rule . . .
> We consider that the community will have greater faith in such a test than they would in a character earned merely under prison discipline.[3]

The system provided for promotion based on marks for good behaviour and hard work, and depended on a scheme of classification.

With the possible exception of the judicially invented suspended sentence, Crofton's 'progressive stage system' is the single major Irish contribution to penal reform. At this remove of time, evaluation of the system's immediate apparent success is difficult: the proportion of former

---

[1] Jasper Ridley, *Lord Palmerston* (London: Constable, 1970), chapter 29.
[2] Max Grunhut, *Penal Reform* (Oxford: Clarendon Press, 1948), pp. 83–88.
[3] *Second Annual Report of the Directors of Convict Prisons in Ireland 1855*, p. 14 (C. 2068), H.C. 1856, xxxiv, 18.

convicts who emigrated was always substantial and the effectiveness of the system in relation to those who stayed in Ireland seems to have owed much to the assiduous supervision of Crofton's remarkable protégé, James Organ.

The system earned praise both on the Continent and in the United States where, indeed, a new penal institution was established, based on the progressive stage system, which was the next phase in the origins of borstal. This institution was the Elmira Reformatory, opened in New York State in 1876. Elmira provided a special form of prison discipline for offenders between 16 and 30 and thus represented the first attempt to offer a distinct régime in separate premises for a proportion of offenders over 16.[4]

Establishment of some similar institution was in the minds of members of the British Departmental Committee on Prisons, the Gladstone Committee, which reported in 1895.[5] However, the main concern of the members was not so restricted; it was, rather, generally to find ways of reducing the number of habitual criminals. The age group within which the majority of criminals was formed, the committee thought, was that between 16 and 21. For offenders in this group it recommended two changes. The first was to raise the age of admission to reformatory schools from 16 to 18; this proposal was not accepted and nothing more is heard of it. The second was the establishment of a special penal reformatory under government management. The courts, it was envisaged, would have the power to commit to such an establishment "offenders under the age of 23, for periods of not less than one year and up to three years, with a system of licenses graduated according to sentence, which should be freely exercised."[6] This special institution, the committee said,

> . . . should be a half-way house between the prison and the reformatory. It should be situated in the country with ample space for agricultural and land reclamation work. It would have penal and coercive sides which could be applied according to the merits of particular cases. But it should be amply provided with a staff capable of giving sound education, training the inmates in various kinds of industrial work, and qualified generally to exercise the best and healthiest kind of moral influence.[7]

In 1900 effect was given to the committee's second recommendation.[8]

---

[4] Grunhut, *Penal Reform*, pp. 91–92.
[5] *Report from the Departmental Committee on Prisons 1895* (C. 7702), H.C. 1895, lvi.
[6] *Report from the Departmental Committee on Prisons 1895*, p. 30.
[7] ibid.
[8] Roger Hood, *Borstal Re-Assessed* (London: Heinemann, 1965), chapter 1.

Early that year eight young adult prisoners were transferred from London prisons to the prison at Bedford where they were separated from the other adult prisoners and subjected to a special system of discipline. The experiment was repeated the following year. This time a portion of the convict prison at the Kent village of Borstal was adapted for the reception of further young prisoners from London prisons, all of whom had been given sentences of at least six months. The name 'Borstal' was henceforth associated with the system of discipline inaugurated there.

Borstal can be seen as the practical implementation of the philosophy that lay behind the progressive stage system. In so far as it provided a special régime in a separate penal establishment for offenders of a younger age group, it is important to set it beside other developments which had as their aim the securing of the complete segregation of younger offenders with custodial sentences. A brief survey of these developments in Ireland will provide this extra perspective.

A significant breakthrough was the legislation which sanctioned the establishment in Ireland of reformatory and industrial schools, in 1858 and 1868 respectively. Pressure for the introduction of identical legislation in England had earlier come from a small group of campaigners, foremost among whom was Mary Carpenter,[9] and, as was to be the case with borstal, the Irish development was both derivative and later in time. The efforts of Crofton and his colleagues on the Convict Prisons Board were nonetheless equally instrumental. When the Board was set up in 1854, it had at its disposal no special accommodation for juvenile convicts. For a few years before 1841, Smithfield in Dublin had been used as a juvenile prison,[10] a development which was contemporary with the establishment of Parkhurst in England,[11] and the Board at once set about securing new premises for this purpose. The juvenile convicts, it reported in 1855,

. . . can at present be scarcely treated as satisfactorily as could be wished. Further contamination is prevented, and education and industrial occupations, as far as trades are concerned, are promoted as much as possible; but we have no land attached to the prisons, and cannot expect really satisfactory results until the erection of the 'Juvenile Penal Reformatory', when prison construction, and the various occupations of farm labour, will aid properly selected officers in bringing about the reformation we seek to produce.[12]

---

[9] Grunhut, *Penal Reform*, pp. 371–73.
[10] *Second Annual Report of the Directors of Convict Prisons in Ireland 1855*, p. 69: report of the governor of Smithfield government prison.
[11] Grunhut, *Penal Reform*, p. 370; Erica Stratta, *The Education of Borstal Boys* (London: Routledge & Kegan Paul, 1970), pp. 3–5.
[12] *Second Annual Report of the Directors of Convict Prisons in Ireland 1855*, p. 5.

The penal reformatory referred to by the Board was one for which legislative sanction was in the process of being obtained. The later enactment in 1858 of legislation providing generally for the establishment of reformatory schools in Ireland caused the Board to change its plans and, in the event, the first Irish reformatory school was opened at Glencree, County Wicklow; the site secured for that purpose at Lusk was earmarked instead, along with Smithfield, for use as an intermediate prison under Crofton's progressive stage system.[13]

Neither the introduction of reformatory schools for offenders between 12 and 16 nor that of industrial schools which provided a home for various categories of deprived children, including offenders under 12, ended the use of prison for juveniles. Indeed, for a while, a fortnight's imprisonment was the necessary prelude to detention in a reformatory school. A more serious defect was the absence of segregated facilities in local prisons, even though the provision of such facilities was compulsory for boys transferred from reformatory school to prison. In 1896 Irish prison rules insisted on the provision of these facilities for all under 16.[14] Over a decade later, in the Children Act 1908, the legislature finally prohibited sentences of imprisonment for offenders under 14,[15] a measure directed mainly at a few intransigent magistrates; the same legislation also restricted the use of the power to send 14- and 15-year olds to prison.[16] In retrospect, the provision of specially segregated premises for those over 16 can be seen as a natural progression.

---

[13] *Reports of the Royal Commission on Prisons in Ireland 1884, Vol. II, Minutes of Evidence*, p. 156 (C. 4233-1), H.C. 1884-5, xxxviii, 418: Sir John Lentaigne.
[14] *Prisons Board Report 1900-01*, p. 11.
[15] Children Act 1908, s. 102.
[16] ibid., and see *The State (Hanley)* v. *Governor of Mountjoy Prison*, High Court, 12 January 1973.

CHAPTER II

Borstal before Partition 1906-1921

The extension of the Borstal System in this country . . . is a great blessing.
Catholic chaplain at the Clonmel borstal, 1906.

The borstal system reached Ireland in May 1906. "Following the lines of the scheme known in England as the 'Borstal System'," the *Prisons Board Report* for that year relates,[1]

> a new departure has been made in this country during the year in the treatment of male convicted criminal prisoners between the ages of 16 and 21 years with a view of bringing special reformatory influences to bear on them before they have become hardened in a course of crime.

At first, the new treatment was applied to offenders sentenced to nine months and upwards but, with the alteration in the legal basis of borstal in 1908 and a further modification in 1914, treatment became restricted to a group rather differently described. Nevertheless, the object behind the system remained constant: it continued to be that of "bringing special reformatory influences to bear."

---

[1] *Prisons Board Report 1906–07*, p. x.

There was only one Irish borstal, at Clonmel in County Tipperary, in the period before 1921. Its problems were not unique but it is of interest to learn that they occurred—and were confronted—at so early a date. It is a familiar list: unpredictability of judicial sentencing practice, inadequacy of training facilities and difficulties in after-care are all prominent. The list would doubtless have expanded had administrative experience lasted longer. The period from 1906 to 1921 is short, but circumstances, unconnected with matters penological, make it a coherent whole. In 1906 the Clonmel borstal served all Ireland. Between May 1906 and March 1907, for instance, the eighteen boys transferred there comprised four from Derry, three each from Dublin and Belfast, two from Cork and one each from Waterford, Galway, Kilkenny, Castlebar, Tullamore and Clonmel itself.[2] After 1921 this was no longer possible. Political turmoil also made the administration of the borstal unusually difficult after 1919, as it did that of all penal institutions in the country. And this was an inauspicious precedent for the new Free State government when faced with worse difficulties in 1922 and 1923. It is worth remembering, however, that a world war also occurred in the same administrative period and that it is only in half of these first sixteen years that the borstal experiment in Ireland can be said to have been operated in an atmosphere which was entirely normal.

Law

Between 1906 and 1909 the selection of boys for inclusion in the borstal at Clonmel was the responsibility of the Irish Prisons Board which made its selection from among the young prisoners in the various local prisons. This system was replaced in 1909, when the Prevention of Crime Act 1908 came into force, by the new procedure under which the prime responsibility for deciding who would be sent to borstal was transferred to the courts. Power in the executive to transfer from prison to borstal was nonetheless reserved by the 1908 Act and a few inmates continued to arrive in this way. On a number of occasions, too, as the *Prisons Board Report 1911–12* makes plain, sentences of penal servitude on juvenile adults were commuted by royal prerogative to borstal detention, and such persons were sent to Clonmel as well.

Section 1 (1) of the Act conferred power on the courts of assize and quarter sessions to send offenders direct to borstal. It said:

> Where a person is convicted on indictment of an offence for which he is liable to be sentenced to penal servitude or imprisonment, and it appears to the court—

---

[2] ibid., p. 86: report of the governor of Clonmel prison.

(*a*) that the person is not less than sixteen or more than twenty-one years of age; and

(*b*) that by reason of his criminal habits and tendencies, or associations with persons of bad character, it is expedient that he should be subject to detention for such term and under such instruction and discipline as appears most conducive to his reformation and the repression of crime;

—it shall be lawful for the court, in lieu of passing a sentence of penal servitude or imprisonment, to pass a sentence of detention under penal discipline in a Borstal Institution for a term of not less than one year nor more than three years.

The Act went on to require the court (i) to consider reports from the Prisons Board on the suitability of the offender for borstal treatment, and (ii) to be satisfied, from evidence of the offender's character, health and mental condition, that he was likely to benefit from borstal. It also stipulated that offenders were to be given "such industrial training and other instruction, and be subject to such disciplinary and moral influences as will conduce to their reformation and the prevention of crime."

Further legal changes were introduced by the Criminal Justice Administration Act 1914, an Act which, like that of 1908, was common to England and Ireland. This measure extended the powers of courts to sentence to borstal. Magistrates' courts could still not sentence to borstal directly, but for the first time they were allowed to commit suitable offenders to quarter sessions to be sentenced to borstal there, but only in limited situations. Under section 10 (1) (*b*), it had to be proved that the youth (i) had been convicted of an offence for which the court had power to impose a sentence of imprisonment for one month or upwards without the option of a fine, and (ii) had been previously convicted of an offence, or, having been previously discharged on probation, had failed to observe a condition of his recognisance, and in addition, as under the Act of 1908, that he had criminal habits or tendencies or was associating with persons of bad character.

The shortness of the sentences passed on many of the Clonmel boys was a common complaint in the early years. Even before the reforms of 1909, the Prisons Board was far from happy. In its *Report* for 1907–08, for instance, it bewailed the fact that thirteen of the thirty-three receptions for that year, receptions it itself had selected, had received the minimum of nine months imprisonment. The report for 1910–11 of the after-care body, the Borstal Association for Ireland, regretted that so many committals under the 1908 Act were for only eighteen months. The Association thought that the period imposed should usually be the maximum of three years and pointed out that, in an appropriate case, discharge could take place long before. (It was possible after six months in fact). The Association's support of the three-year sentence was the consequence of difficulties in dealing with unruly lads sentenced for the minimum period:

> There are cases in which less than three years' detention cannot be of much service. In these latter the youths are generally of unruly and depraved character. At large they are under no control, and will not acknowledge any authority; they live idle, vicious lives, unamenable to discipline in any shape or form, and to think that a sentence of 12 or 18 months will cure them is altogether a mistake. These terms are too short to make them perfect in a trade or get them to forget the vagabond life they had been leading, and they have to be discharged just at the time they are beginning to understand that they must be more self-respecting in manner and appearance, and more submissive to authority after they leave the Institution.

The Association, in consequence, urged the judges of assizes and county courts to consider the wisdom of imposing longer sentences.[3]

The plea was not at first heeded. In its *Report* for 1911–12, the Prisons Board objected that more offenders had not been given the maximum three-year sentence and once again reminded the judges that a boy could be released on licence as early as six months. The 1914 legislation increased the minimum sentence to two years, and this, coupled with the Board's relentless pressure, appears to have had the desired effect. Until 1921, with the single exception of 1918, a majority of the annual committals received the maximum three-year term. That the 1914 Act refused to set the minimum at three years undoubtedly reflected the attitude of judges who continued to maintain that a three-year sentence was too long, even for the laudable purpose of attempting reformation.

The continued possibility of discharge after six months, alongside the increase in the minimum term to two years, emphasised the indeterminate nature of the borstal sentence. In 1901 Sir Evelyn Ruggles-Brise, the English Prison Commissioner behind the borstal experiment, had noted that the indeterminate sentence was "at variance with two of the most sacred principles of the English criminal law—(1) the free discretion of the judge in awarding sentence, (2) the prerogative of mercy vested in the crown."[4] Ruggles-Brise, nonetheless, was a staunch advocate of the indeterminate sentence in the case of young offenders.[5]

---

[3] Quoted, *Prisons Board Report 1910–11*, at p. xvii.
[4] Quoted in Hood, *Borstal Re-Assessed*, pp. 10–11.
[5] Rupert Cross, *Punishment, Prison and the Public* (London: Stevens, 1971), p. 24.

In 1914 no critical voices were raised in London; it was unlikely they would be in Dublin.

Criticism of the judiciary's sentencing practices continued. Before 1914 the Board had complained that sentences were too short and, after 1914, that magistrates were not employing their new powers. There was considerable variation in the annual numbers of committals and in the proportion of first offenders among those sentenced: just before 1921 first offenders formed a majority. There is no information on sentencing policy for this period which might provide the clue to the reasons behind such variations. The explanation for this lies principally in the absence of an Irish court of criminal appeal; this, of course, deprived the convicted offender of a forum in which he could contest the sentencing decision.[6]

Accommodation

When the Irish authorities decided to copy the English experiments at Bedford and Borstal, premises had to be found and the No. 2 prison at Clonmel was chosen. It was a dubious choice. The building had been unoccupied for many years [7] and the accommodation, by modern standards, was far from ideal. Edward Fahy, a Dublin barrister, who later surveyed the penal systems in Ireland, was unimpressed: the prison was the oldest in Ireland and "built at a time when the prevailing idea was to make jails as poky, uncomfortable and forbidding as possible."[8] The noise of heavy locks being turned, the effect of iron bars on the windows, stone flags in the yards and the total absence of grass in the main square [9] were all in striking contrast to the charm of the town itself and its attractive setting in the Suir valley.

Accommodation for fifty-four boys was provided before the first transferees arrived. At the time it was not expected that the daily average would exceed twenty,[10] a rather conservative estimate. "A schoolroom, recreation room and a large and commodious carpenter's shop" were also fitted up.[11] When the 1908 Act came into operation in 1909, the premises were thereafter treated as an official borstal. At the same time, work was started on converting the entire prison, and the necessary

[6] English case-law from this period is considered by Hood in *Borstal Re-Assessed*, pp. 28–30.

[7] Report of the governor of Clonmel prison, quoted, *Prisons Board Report 1906–07*, at p. 86.

[8] Edward Fahy, "Borstal in Ireland", *Hermathena*, LVIII (1941), 70. For earlier prisons in Clonmel, see William P. Burke, *History of Clonmel* (Waterford: for the Clonmel Library Committee, 1907), pp. 58 and 170–71.

[9] These conditions continued at Clonmel until 1947: *Prisons Report 1947*, p. 12.

[10] *The Nationalist* newspaper, Clonmel, 11 August 1906.

[11] Report of the governor of Clonmel prison, quoted, *Prisons Board Report 1906–07*, at p. 86.

arrangements, including the transfer of ordinary prisoners to other institutions, were concluded by 12 August 1910, the date when the prison was legally named a borstal institution.[12] The increase in numbers required an extension of the day-time accommodation first provided in 1906 and the boys themselves helped to convert several small single cells into larger rooms for training, education and recreation.

The Gladstone Committee of 1895 had recommended that the reformatories be located in the country. This had not been done in either England or Ireland; instead, existing buildings in centres of population had been converted—a policy presumably explicable in terms of cost. The English Prison Commissioners recognised the objections to such a policy and as early as 1914 urged the creation of special *ad hoc* establishments which offered possibilities of land cultivation and strenuous manual labour.[13] In 1911 a field adjacent to the borstal at Clonmel was acquired for instruction in gardening, but this was no answer and the continued absence of adequate facilities for training in agriculture was repeatedly criticised by the Prisons Board.[14] The deficiency was perhaps met, to a limited extent, in 1917 and the succeeding year, by the practice of hiring out boys as farm labour, but by 1922 nothing had been done to secure permanent improvements. The time was not favourable. In the same way as the war prevented the adoption of changes in England, so the war[15] and also the political situation interfered in Ireland. However, there were some signs that improvements would soon have been effected, had British administration continued.

In 1895 the Board had been given permission to acquire a thirty-four acre farm for the convict prison at Maryborough (Portlaoise)[16]; this was an encouraging precedent. Secondly, the tone of the Board's reports became more optimistic. In 1918 the Board was hopeful that, with the end of the war, finance would be forthcoming to enable facilities to be provided in new surroundings for agricultural training as in England and Scotland,[17] and by 1920 it was able to disclose that remedial proposals were then under active consideration by the executive.[18]

In the year 1914–15, at one stage no less than ninety-eight boys were in custody; the crisis forced adoption of the temporary expedient of

[12] 1910 S.R. & O. No. 821.

[13] Hood, *Borstal Re-Assessed*, p. 31.

[14] See *Prisons Board Report 1912–13, 1914–15, 1917–18* and *1918–19*.

[15] The war forced a reduction in the staff of the Prisons Board: *H.C. Debates* (5 series), Vol. 78, col. 891, 24 January 1916.

[16] *Prisons Board Report 1895–96*, p. 12; R. B. McDowell, *The Irish Administration 1801–1914* (London and Toronto: Routledge & Kegan Paul, 1964), p. 160.

[17] At Borstal itself, from the beginning, there had been considerably more space available than there ever was to be at Clonmel: Hood, *Borstal Re-Assessed*, p. 98.

[18] As they were in regard to education. Compare the fate of the Education (Ireland) Bill, dropped on 13 December 1920: T. J. McElligott, *Education in Ireland* (Dublin: Institute of Public Administration, 1966), pp. 63–64.

halving the size of each cell. The Criminal Justice Administration Act, passed the same year, threatened to make things worse: the Act, it will be recalled, permitted magistrates to forward offenders to quarter sessions for sentence to borstal, and the Board feared that quarter sessions would become a "clearing house of young offenders." By the following year, however, it was clear that the Act was going to pose little threat at all; it risked, rather, becoming something of a dead letter. In fact, numbers committed in the immediately succeeding years fell significantly. The years 1920 and 1921, on the other hand, saw an increase in numbers committed and fresh accommodation difficulties arose. The reason was the political situation which affected the number of committals and also delayed discharges.[19]

Régime

Between 1906 and 1921 two different sets of regulations governed the régime at Clonmel. The Prison Board's rules of 14 May 1906[20] applied from 1906 to 1909. Further rules, made in 1909,[21] applied, with only minor adjustments, between then and 1921.

Under the 1906 rules, boys were divided, according to age, character, and nature of offence, into two classes known respectively as the 'star' and the 'ordinary'. This division was independent of the grading system and was not continued by the 1909 rules. Before 1909 the selection of boys to be committed to Clonmel lay, in theory, with the Prisons Board and, in practice, with the governors of the various local prisons. The Board instructed the latter to remember that any candidate for selection must have received a sentence in excess of nine months, be between 16 and 21 years old and not possess "any special features . . . which would render his transfer to Clonmel Prison undesirable; e.g., exceptional incorrigibility, or exceptional tendency to corrupt others."[22] In 1907, the first complete year of operations, receptions totalled thirty-three. Twenty-two of these had one or more previous convictions, information regarding the remaining eleven was "unsatisfactory", and no boy was placed in the 'star' class.

From 1909, power of selection was transferred to the judiciary.[23] The Prisons Board had still some role to play, for the courts were required by the enabling legislation to take into account suitability reports furnished by it. Moreover, delay was inevitable before final removal to Clonmel

---

[19] *Prisons Board Report 1920–21*, p.v.; *Prisons Board Report 1921–22*, p. v.
[20] Set out in the *Prisons Board Report 1906–07*, at pp. 2–4.
[21] Rules of 29 July 1909, confirmed, as required under the 1908 Act, by an order in council on 6 October 1909: 1909 S.R. & O. No. 1371.
[22] Directive of 17 May 1906: *Prisons Board Report 1906–07*, p. 4.
[23] 1908 Act, s. 1.

could take place and rule 15 of the 1909 rules spelt out the course of action to be followed in such cases: boys were to be kept segregated in the prison of the district in which they had been committed and were to be subject to the rules for offenders sentenced to imprisonment without hard labour.

Under the 1906 rules, the boy at Clonmel was not only 'star' or 'ordinary' class; he was also one of three grades: 'penal', 'ordinary' or 'special'. This latter classification was the only one recognised by the 1909 rules. Under both sets of rules the procedure was identical. On arrival, all boys were placed in the 'ordinary' grade where they remained until, by industry and good conduct, they earned promotion to the 'special' or were demoted for misconduct to the 'penal'.

A boy might advance to the special grade once he had earned a certain number of marks: 600 under the 1906 rules, or marks representing at least five months detention under the 1909 rules. Marks were awarded for good conduct and industry and for special merit. The boy's attention to instruction counted, as did his evinced desire "to profit by the reformatory influences by which he was surrounded." Promotion was not automatic: a committee, called the 'Institution Board' under the 1909 rules, reviewed every case.

A system of privileges was an inevitable concomitant of the division into grades, and the rules of both 1906 and 1909 are especially informative about it. Boys in special grade were entitled to a variety of extras. As regards food, other grades had to make do with the "'C' Local Prison Diet, with one pint of milk added to the dinner on Wednesdays and Fridays", but those in special grade were allowed, in addition, two ounces of golden syrup or jam at supper on Sundays and Thursdays. This particular dietary privilege appears to have disappeared by 1909.[24] Boys in ordinary were obliged to wear brown clothes and those in penal grey; boys in special wore blue. Under the 1906 rules, boys in special enjoyed unique rights in regard to the furnishing of their cells: they were entitled to a special iron bedstead, a strip of carpet, a looking glass and approved small pictures or photographs. Boys in both ordinary and special were allowed to write and receive letters and to receive visitors, but the permitted frequency of incoming and outgoing letters and of visits varied: the stipulated interval was six weeks for boys in ordinary and one month for those in special. The rules of 1906 also laid down a different allowable duration for visits: twenty minutes in the case of a visit to a boy in ordinary and thirty for a visit to a boy in special. However, this particular distinction was not preserved in the rules of 1909.[25]

---

[24] The Prisons Board prescribed the dietary: 1909 rules, rule 11.
[25] Rule 16 of the 1909 rules makes no reference to the duration of the visits.

By these, boys in special were permitted to have a light in their cells for half an hour longer than other grades and to be in association in the reading room for an hour after each day's work.[26] They were also entitled to wear a good conduct stripe for every three months spent in the grade. Boys in both ordinary and special were permitted to work in association and "to attend instruction in a useful industry": boys in the latter grade could also qualify for employment on parole on the premises or elsewhere.[27] Boys in penal grade, on the other hand, were required to work separately on unrewarding manual tasks.

Any boy in special or ordinary grade could have his privileges removed "for idleness and misconduct." Relegation to penal grade was a tough sanction; it was to occur only when a boy was reckoned to be an unwholesome influence and was to last only so long as was thought necessary.[28] The principal disadvantage of the penal grade was that, whilst in it, a boy could not earn any gratuities which were awarded to others for industry. Special gratuities could also be earned by boys for exemplary conduct. The system of awarding gratuities was altered slightly by the 1909 rules. First, for every good conduct stripe which a boy obtained, i.e. for every three months spent by him in special grade, he might receive a money payment which could be used to buy extra food.[29] Secondly, other gratuities, based on the number of marks earned according to the prescribed scale, were to be placed to the credit of each boy and expended on assisting him when he was discharged.[30]

In 1907, the day at Clonmel began at 5.45 a.m. and ended with 'gas turned off' at 8.30 p.m. It is not clear whether before 1922 there was any change in this basic timetable, but it seems unlikely. During this long day, time was set aside for meals and for exercise. Otherwise, borstal being what it was, training of sorts was prescribed.

Work

This training was of the classical kind. Schooling for those of poor educational attainments, and instruction in a 'trade' for everyone.[31] The reports say little on the nature of the schooling, but fortunately there is more information about the system of trade training. In 1907 classes were receiving instruction in carpentry, tailoring, painting, gardening and general jobbing.

---

[26] "To play such games as chess, draughts and dominoes. This they thoroughly appreciate, and the privilege had not been abused, so far, on any occasion": report of the governor of Clonmel prison, quoted in *Prisons Board Report 1906–07*, p. 86.

[27] An innovation introduced by the 1909 rules, rule 9.

[28] 1909 rules, rule 3.

[29] Rule 8.

[30] Rule 17.

[31] To equip the boy for employment on release, a requirement spelt out by the 1909 rules, rule 10.

Among criticisms of the system, the first general complaint was that, since sentences were too short, the boys were not given a proper chance to learn a trade. As we have already seen, the Act of 1914 was designed in part to meet a criticism[32] heard in England as much as in Ireland. The dominant complaint of the Irish Prisons Board, however, related to another matter: the absence of proper facilities for training in agriculture. In its *Report* for 1912-13, the Board regretted that no farm was attached to the institution to train the boys in looking after stock and cows; securing such facilities and providing such training were a high priority.

> The present institutional industries of shoemaking and tailoring, while of service as calling for the exercise of intelligence and industry, are mere 'blind alley' employments, so far as equipping a boy with the means of earning a livelihood on discharge. The Board hope in the future to be able to give a training to these boys better adapted to produce intelligent and skilful farm labourers, and so secure for lads desirous of taking up agricultural work not merely certain employment but good wages.

The fact was that agricultural employment was the easiest to arrange for any boy nearing discharge. "Owing to the peculiar labour conditions in Ireland," wrote the Borstal Association in 1914, "the continual drain of young people through emigration, and what might be called the fastidiousness of those who remain at home as to the work they engage in, there is no difficulty in obtaining employment for Borstal juveniles—the fact is that the demand for their services exceeds the supply."[33]

In urging their case, the Board and the Association stressed three arguments. It was said, first, that better training facilities would have a rehabilitative effect—many of the lads were from Dublin, Belfast and Limerick and had no knowledge or experience of farm work. If there was farm training, it would be possible to change "a city 'corner boy' into a decent farm labourer."[34] It was claimed, next, that there would be a higher rate of employment if training within the institution could be improved. "One of the first questions", the Association wrote in 1912-13, "usually put by a farmer when he proposes to employ a licensee is whether he can milk cows. In the vast majority of cases the reply is in the negative and often the boy selected is unable to obtain a situation."[35] Thirdly, the Association warned against prolonging indefinitely a state

---

[32] By increasing the minimum length of detention.
[33] Quoted, *Prisons Board Report 1913-14*, at p. xiii.
[34] Report of the Borstal Association, quoted, *Prisons Board Report 1912-13*, at p. xii.
[35] ibid.

of affairs where the institution produced unskilled farm labourers. These labourers could only receive low wages, and that bred discontent and trouble.[36]

In 1917 Major Dobbin, the governor at Clonmel, introduced a scheme which provided some kind of remedy: he arranged for selected groups of boys to be hired out to local farmers. The boys left the institution in plain clothes in the care of a warder each morning at 8 a.m. and were back at 5.30 p.m. During the day they worked at harvesting and threshing, tasks which they would have to perform should they go into farming when they were released. The experiment was short-lived: local labour troubles ended it in 1918.[37] While it lasted, the farmers paid the borstal for the services of the boys. In 1917, the sum came to £111 10s. and, in 1918, to £219 15s. 6d.

Contemporary English records examined by Roger Hood disclose that, in England, observers were not always impressed by the work performed in borstal.[38] Too much of it, all pretensions to the contrary notwithstanding, was unexciting manual labour. Doubt was also expressed about both the wisdom of entrusting administration to officers of military type and also the usefulness of whatever trade instruction was imparted. The absence of comparable records for Ireland is a pity, but the general position is unlikely to have been any better than in England.

Recreation

Recreational facilities at Clonmel were limited. Physical training was possible but outdoor team games were not. Facilities indoors steadily improved. A gramophone was presented in 1914; band practice in 1918 and 1919 was an advance on the chaplain's choir practice of 1906 and 1907.[39] Another welcome innovation was the gift of a cinema machine in 1914, used, as it was put, "whenever possible for the entertainment and education of the inmates."[40] In 1907 there had been chess, draughts and dominoes[41] and a library consisting of "suitable . . . books . . . most calculated to assist in the moral improvement of young prisoners." There were histories, biographies and travel books,[42] and the boys

---

[36] Report of the Borstal Association, quoted, *Prisons Board Report 1913–14*, at p. xiii.

[37] The introduction of regulated agricultural wages may have had some connection; they certainly accentuated difficulties for placement on discharge: see below.

[38] Hood, *Borstal Re-Assessed*, p. 103.

[39] Standing orders of 14 May 1906; see *Prisons Board Report 1906–07*, at p. 3.

[40] *Prisons Board Report 1918–19*, p. x.

[41] Report of the Clonmel Discharged Prisoners' Aid Society, quoted, *Prisons Board Report 1907–08*, at p. ix.

[42] R. R. Cherry, "Juvenile Crime and its Prevention", *Journal of the Statistical and Social Inquiry Society of Ireland* (64 session) XII (1907–12), 435 at 444. The provision of books was considered at length in the *Report of the Departmental Committee on the Supply of Books to the Prisoners in H.M. Prisons and to the Inmates of H.M. Borstals 1911* (Cd. 5589), H.C. 1911, xxxix.

of the time were said to be fond of reading and constantly changing their books.[43] Nonetheless, the attraction of the cinema must have been considerable[44] and, significantly, the film shows were referred to appreciatively in a letter from an ex-borstal boy.[45] Some boys would not have seen films before, though others, in the view of certain critics, would perhaps have seen more than was healthy for them.[46]

Lectures were at one period given by members of the Royal College of Science from Dublin,[47] and there were appropriately uplifting addresses too from the institution's chaplains.[48]

Discharge

Both the 1908 and the 1914 Acts made provision for a possible release on licence after six months and for supervision after final release (lasting six months under the 1908 Act and one year under the 1914). Prior to 1909, remission of part of the remaining sentence might be ordered after six months. In general, information is scarce about both the average length of detention and the factors influencing release in individual cases. In 1911 the Prisons Board reported that the then average period of detention was seventeen months and that some boys had been detained for a mere seven or eight; how many precisely is not specified.

The general rule was that discharge took place when the Board decided that a boy merited his release. It acted on the report of the borstal visiting committee who, in turn, acted on the recommendation of the Institution Board composed of borstal officers.[49] Rule 18 of the 1909 rules laid down the procedure to be followed: the Institution Board might recommend a boy for discharge if, having examined his character and conduct and discussed the case with any society or person interested, was satisfied both that the boy would lead a useful and industrious life and abstain from crime and that employment would be found for him.

In the period up to the end of 1921, outside factors could, and did, influence the timing of decisions to release boys. War hastened the moment of discharge for some: the *Reports* for the war years tell of several inmates

---

[43] Report of the governor of Clonmel prison, quoted, *Prisons Board Report 1906–07*, at p. 86.

[44] Compare Maurice O'Sullivan, *Twenty Years A-Growing* (London: Chatto and Windus, 1933), chapter 23.

[45] *Prisons Board Report 1917–18*, p. x.

[46] The recorder of Belfast, for example, attacked "the attractions of cinema houses and the attractions of ice-cream shops augmented by gaming machines": *Irish Law Times and Solicitors' Journal*, L (1916), 244. For modern interest in borstal boys' passive leisure pursuits, such as cinema-going, and their relevance for education programmes in borstal, see Stratta, *The Education of Borstal Boys*, pp. 106 ff.

[47] *Prisons Board Report 1914–15*, p. xiii. The lectures were authorised by the 1909 rules, rule 13.

[48] For such regenerative lecturing in England, see Hood, *Borstal Re-Assessed*, p. 100.

[49] This Board, as we have seen above, also considered promotions.

who were discharged, with the consent of their parents, to enable them to join up.[50] The moment of discharge for others was delayed by one consequence of the introduction of regulated agricultural wages. The *Prisons Board Report* for 1918–19 explains:

> Increasing difficulty is . . . experienced in placing inmates out on licence with farmers, the latter being naturally reluctant to employ at the rates fixed by the Wages Board lads whose farming experience has been limited to what can be taught in the small plots of ground attached to the Institution. As a result, a considerable number of the youths have to be retained until the expiration of their sentences, and have then before them nothing but the unpromising prospect of returning to the surroundings and associations to which in many cases they themselves attribute their lapse into crime.

Further factors contributed to delays in discharges in 1920. "The difficulties", the Prisons Board reports for 1920–21,

> met with in administering the Borstal system due to the restricted space and unsuitable buildings at Clonmel were increased during the year by the abnormal conditions existing in the country and the prevailing unemployment. It was difficult to obtain suitable work for inmates released on licence and the releases of many youths who had shown by their conduct and industry that they might be placed out on licence had to be postponed. This combined with an increase in the number of committals and a reluctance on the part of the Military Authorities to accept inmates who had volunteered for service in the Army led to an increase in the number in custody.

When a boy was discharged on licence, he had to proceed immediately to a fixed destination and could not move from there without the approval of the person or society that had undertaken his supervision. His life was circumscribed in other ways too. He was to be regular and punctual in attendance at work, report as required, abstain from violating the law and associating with bad characters and lead a sober and generally industrious life.[51] If it came to the attention of the Prisons Board that a boy had escaped from supervision or had been guilty of a serious and wilful breach of the conditions of his licence, he was to be cautioned. If this proved unavailing, his licence might be revoked.[52] If it were,

---

[50] In England, on the eve of World War II, two-thirds of those then in borstal were prematurely discharged, and many of the institutions were taken over by the War Office or for use as prisons: Hood, *Borstal Re-Assessed*, p. 63.

[51] 1909 rules, sch. A (slightly modified by 1910 S.R. & O. No. 842, sch. A).

[52] 1909 rules, rule 20.

the boy was to be readmitted to borstal and detained in the penal grade for as long as the Institution Board thought fit. He could, it is true, also be placed straightaway in the ordinary grade but, if he were, the consent of the Prisons Board had to be sought before gratuities could be earned or the privileges of the special grade awarded.[53]

The maximum length of recall was set at four months under the Act of 1908 and one year under that of 1914.

After-care

Section 5 of the Act of 1908 made after-care an integral part of the borstal system. It had been anticipated by the standing orders of 1906:

> Special provision will be made for the discharge of each prisoner by arrangement with benevolent societies or persons who may be willing to assist the case on discharge. Full information will be afforded and help given to such societies or persons, with the object of securing a continuous and well-directed supervision of the case, both at the moment of discharge and afterwards at the home or place to which the prisoner goes. Every encouragement shall be given to preliminary visitation in prison before discharge, in order that the society or individual may have a personal knowledge of the prisoner, and be in possession of the views of the Prison Authorities concerning him.[54]

From the early years, a variety of persons and societies helped in the work of after-care. In its *Report* for 1908–09, the Prisons Board paid tribute to a number of local priests and policemen, the Borstal Association in London, discharged prisoners' aid societies in general, Salvation Army Homes and the conferences of St Vincent de Paul, as well as to the local after-care association.[55] This association had been founded in 1906, shortly after the foundation of other provincial after-care associations in Waterford and Limerick. It was originally called the Clonmel Discharged Prisoners' Aid Society, the name given to it at the public meeting in the town hall in Clonmel on 18 May 1906 which brought it into existence.[56] At this meeting R. Bagwell, DL, was elected chairman, Lord Donoughmore, vice-chairman, R. Bradley, JP, treasurer and W. M. Casey, CPS, secretary; other founder members included local

---

[53] Rule 21.

[54] See *Prisons Board Report 1906–07*, at p. 4. The wording is almost identical in rule 19 of the 1909 rules.

[55] For the early history of borstal after-care in England, see Hood, *Borstal Re-Assessed*, pp. 162–73.

[56] *The Nationalist* newspaper, Clonmel, 19 May 1906.

clergy, visiting justices, magistrates, professional men and merchants.[57] As was to be expected, the main burden of after-care fell on this society and on its successor, the Borstal Association of Ireland, which was established in 1910. The Society's first report, that for 1906–07, gives details of its earliest achievements:

> In each instance before the discharge of a boy, careful inquiries were made in the locality from which he came, and such assistance was afforded to him as the Committee deemed most suitable. One boy was assisted to emigrate to friends in America upon the strong recommendation of his parish Clergyman. The Committee considered this an exceptional case, and would prefer, when possible, to give aid in some other direction. Two other boys were provided with employment, and, so far, appear to be doing well. In a fourth case an offer was made to the prisoner to procure work for him away from his native place, as the information received by the Committee as a result of their inquiries showed that there could be very little hope of his amendment there. He refused, however, to avail himself of this offer, and was then informed that if upon his return home he showed a disposition to conduct himself well in future he would receive assistance. Up to the present, unfortunately, the Committee have not been justified in affording him aid, but the case is still receiving attention. A fifth boy was re-arrested on discharge, and of course in this instance the Society could do nothing.[58]

On discharge, a boy could count on two sources of finance: gratuities earned by him in the borstal and money made available to him by after-care societies or interested individuals. The 1906 standing orders inform us about the level of gratuities earned—primarily, for industry. The basic rate was one penny for every day on which two marks were obtained. However, gratuities could not be earned on Sundays, and the total amount, in any event, could never exceed £2. Special gratuities also existed. These could be recommended, again with a £2 limit, in any case where, in the opinion of the borstal visiting committee, "the general demeanour of the prisoner has been exemplary, and such extra gratuity can be usefully employed in his behalf on his discharge."[59] Modified arrangements were introduced in 1909.[60]

In 1906–07 the Prisons Board obtained Treasury sanction for the making

---

[57] Report of the governor of Clonmel Prison, quoted, *Prisons Board Report 1906–07*, at p. 86.
[58] Quoted, *Prisons Board Report 1906–07*, at p. 149.
[59] *Prisons Board Report 1906–07*, p. 3.
[60] 1909 rules, rules 8 and 17.

of special supplementary grants of money in deserving cases. This small Treasury grant was made available to the boy through the after-care body which was responsible for his supervision.[61] In 1908 these special grants varied from fifteen shillings to £2; there was some increase in the amounts in 1912.[62]

Lack of finance posed difficulties for the local after-care association.[63] In time it became entitled to support from the Treasury, but, for ordinary running expenses, it was forced to depend on the philanthropy of individuals. It is significant that many of the earlier *Prisons Board Reports* go out of their way to solicit support for the work of the after-care association at Clonmel;[64] the implication is that it had a struggle to survive.

---

[61] *Prisons Board Report 1906-07*, p. x; *Prisons Board Report 1908-09*, p. ix.
[62] *Prisons Board Report 1912-13*, p. xii. Authority for the making of these grants was provided in the 1908 Act, s. 8 and the 1914 Act, s. 7.
[63] Cherry, "Juvenile Crime and its Prevention", *Journal of the Statistical and Social Inquiry Society of Ireland* (64 session), XII (1907-12), 435 at 446.
[64] See below, chapter 8.

CHAPTER III

Borstal in Northern Ireland 1921-1974

The new borstal will be more or less on all fours with the borstal institutions in England.
Sir Dawson Bates, Minister of Home Affairs, May 1926.

Ireland was partitioned in 1921. Any account of subsequent administration must thus concern itself with two separate jurisdictions.

In Northern Ireland, administrative experience was not continuous as it was in the Free State; indeed, until 1926, no borstal institution was physically sited within the six counties. Nevertheless, despite this hiatus, developments in Northern Ireland after 1926 display an affinity with what had occurred before partition. British experience was readily to hand and there was both the inclination and the will to copy it.

In the rest of Ireland, the story of borstal after partition was to be quite different.

The start to a borstal

On 1 December 1921 the responsibilities of the Prisons Board, so far as Northern Ireland was concerned, were transferred to the Northern Ireland Ministry of Home Affairs.[1] The new ministry was presented

---

[1] For a few months before, there existed a General Prisons Board for Northern Ireland: *Prisons Report (N.I.) 1921-23*, p. 3.

with a unique situation. Legislation carried over from before the passing of the Government of Ireland Act provided for the committal of offenders by the Northern Ireland courts to a number of custodial institutions, not one of which was physically present within the six counties. The Irish inebriate reformatory at Ennis had closed in 1918 and did not matter. The other all-Ireland institutions did and they were sited in the South: the criminal lunatic asylum at Dundrum, the convict prisons at Mountjoy and Portlaoise, and the borstal at Clonmel. What partition meant to these four institutions was that committals from Northern Ireland could not continue. The new Northern Ireland government, in turn, had to look elsewhere. In the case of boys sentenced to borstal after December 1921, section 9 of the Act of 1908 fortunately provided the temporary solution: it enabled borstal boys to be transferred from Britain to Ireland and vice versa. 'Ireland' could be interpreted as 'Northern Ireland'. The English borstal at Feltham was willing to accept such boys, and the Northern Ireland government was prepared to pay for their maintenance there.[2]

Up to the end of 1926, more than sixty boys sentenced to borstal in Northern Ireland, who did not have their sentences commuted to imprisonment, were transferred in this way to England.[3] The solution, while clearly legal,[4] could be objected to. First, the judge could say that he ought to be able to exercise his sentencing discretion uninfluenced by the consideration that any borstal sentence passed by him would be served 'abroad'. Secondly, visits by family and friends to boys transferred to England were both inconvenient and expensive, and there was always the risk that links with home would be cut, which, as a senior Northern Ireland civil servant remarked, was unlikely to be in the boys' interests.[5] Inevitably, the authorities came to face the question: should Northern Ireland open its own borstal?

Early in 1923, nine resident magistrates replied to a circular in which they were asked whether they were in favour of borstal detention for those over sixteen.[6] Two did not express an opinion, but six were in favour and only one was hostile. Their answers were contained in an appendix to the report of the Moles Committee which had been appointed

---

[2] *Prisons Report (N.I.) 1921-23*, p. 6; *Moles Report*, p. 25.

[3] December 1921 to March 1923: nine; April 1923 to March 1924: five; April 1924 to March 1925: twenty-two; April 1925 to March 1926: twelve; April to November 1926: eighteen.

[4] Because of a similar lack of proper premises, Northern Ireland convict prisoners were transferred to British convict prisons and, in judicial proceedings, this form of transfer was held to be legal, although it took place under less clear statutory authority: R. (*ex parte Maguire*) v. *Governor of Maidstone Prison* (1925) 59 I.L.T.R. 63, 101; *Prisons Report (N.I.) 1924-25*, p. 7.

[5] A. P. Magill, quoted in the *Moles Report*, p. 25.

[6] *Moles Report*, p. 53. The replies are on pp. 54–65.

to consider, amongst other matters, the issue of a local borstal. The committee proceeded on the assumption that the borstal system had to be continued. It had no option: the administration of the Supreme Court was, as a constitutional matter, reserved to Westminster and, in consequence, the power of assize courts to impose borstal sentences could not be removed by legislation enacted by the Northern Ireland Parliament.

The Moles Committee explored three courses of action. First, and perhaps unexpectedly, it appears to have contemplated the possibility of entering into an arrangement with the government of the Irish Free State.[7] Apart from any constitutional difficulties, this step did not commend itself: the committee found the cost of maintenance to be marginally higher than in England and were not impressed by borstal facilities in the South anyway. A second possibility was to continue the arrangement with the English Prison Commissioners whereby Northern Ireland boys were maintained at Feltham. The committee rejected this option on two grounds: the undesirability of geographical separation of boys and their families, and the inability of the Prison Commissioners to confirm that the arrangement could be continued indefinitely.[8] The committee felt that it had no alternative to recommending that a borstal institution be opened in Northern Ireland, but acknowledged that this solution was not ideal. There was the cost of administering a local borstal system. If a suitable building already in existence could not be obtained, the committee reckoned that this cost, in view of the small population of Northern Ireland, was unlikely to be as low as £123 per boy per year. On penological grounds, there was the further objection that an average annual population of fifty boys, contrasted with Feltham's 200, would limit the variety of training available. On the other hand, relatives would not be inconvenienced by having to travel across the Irish Sea and "the probable higher cost per head might be set off against the decided advantage of spending the money at home and having ample accommodation for the numbers that might be committed." As a means of reducing the cost per head, the committee recommended the provision within the new institution of accommodation for short-term offenders who qualified for modified borstal treatment.[9]

A second report by Lord Polworth, chairman of the Scottish Prison Commissioners, and Colonel Rogers, surveyor to the English Prison Commissioners, likewise advised the Northern Ireland government to

[7] pp. 22, 25, 26.
[8] pp. 25 and 26.
[9] p. 26.

open a local borstal. Eventually, the government announced its agreement.[10]

However, it was one thing to support the establishment of a second local penal institution so soon after convict prison facilities had been made available in Belfast, and another to find money for the undertaking. Members of Parliament were certainly impatient with the existing arrangements. In the House of Commons on 9 April 1924 Mr McGuffin queried the cost of maintaining Northern Ireland boys outside the province. In reply, Sir Dawson Bates, the Minister of Home Affairs, referred to the possibility of money for a local borstal being provided out of the Colwyn award.[11] The Colwyn Committee had been appointed to deal with financial readjustments in the relationship of Northern Ireland to the United Kingdom consequent on partition, and one of its tasks was to make an award to Northern Ireland following its loss of all-Ireland permanent assets. Early in 1924 the committee awarded Northern Ireland a sum of £400,000, which it considered "would provide all that Northern Ireland can reasonably claim in respect of training colleges, police depots, prisons, asylums and higher scientific teaching." No conditions were to be attached to the application of the grant to particular items of the Northern Ireland claim.[12] The Colwyn award was funded under the terms of the Exchequer and Financial Provisions Act (N.I.) 1924, but no call was made on the amount set aside for the borstal for some time to come. Some MPs might not have minded if the call had never been made. Mr Crawford's reaction to Sir Dawson Bates's speech of 9 April 1924 was to oppose the building of "palatial places" for offenders.[13] Two years later, Mr Kyle was similarly critical: inmates cost £2 a week to maintain; most boys would be delighted if £2 per week were spent on their education and upbringing.[14]

In the end, it was decided to establish a dual purpose institution. The Northern Ireland cabinet adopted this plan towards the end of 1925 as a solution to two problems: a site for the borstal, and the financial difficulties of the Protestant male reformatory school at Malone.[15] The Malone school, founded in 1860, had experienced financial problems before, but these became especially acute after World War I. Courts then began to make greater use of the Probation of Offenders Act 1907 as an alternative to committal to a reformatory school, and the fall in

[10] *Prisons Report (N.I.) 1923–24*, p. 5; id., *1924–25*, p. 7; id., *1925–26*, p. 4.
[11] *H. C. Debates (N.I.)*, Vol. 4, col. 626; compare *Prisons Report (N.I.) 1924–25*, p. 7.
[12] *First Report of the Northern Ireland Special Arbitration Committee* (Cmd. 2072, 1924), p. 6.
[13] *H. C. Debates (N.I.)*, Vol. 4, col. 630, 9 April 1924.
[14] *H. C. Debates (N.I.)*, Vol. 7, col. 443, 13 April 1926.
[15] *The Roots of Rathgael* (Bangor, Co Down: Spectator, n.d. (1968)), p. 18.

numbers resulted, in turn, in a reduction in the financial support provided out of both local rates and government funds.

In May 1924 the authorities at Malone notified the government that, in view of the parlous state of the school's finances, they intended to surrender their certificate at the end of the year. Temporary provision was made to prevent the school's closure but a long-term solution had to be found. At this point the government drew up its plan for a joint borstal and reformatory school institution. In May 1926 the trustees of the Malone reformatory transferred their interest to the government in accordance with an agreement providing that part of the premises was to be used as a Protestant reformatory school as before, but that the rest should be designated a borstal institution.[16] The Malone Training School Bill, introduced later in the year, gave effect to this agreement, and on 19 October, during the bill's second reading, Sir Dawson Bates repeated, as the principal justification for setting up the borstal, the undesirability of the practice of transferring boys to England.[17] The premises at Malone were formally transferred on 1 December 1926 but it was not until April of the following year that the borstal was in full operation.

Law

Between 1921 and 1953 the only courts that could sentence to borstal were assize courts and quarter sessions (county courts).[18] Magistrates' courts (courts of summary jurisdiction), under the power conferred in 1914,[19] could forward an offender to quarter sessions to be sentenced to borstal there, and from 1933 these same courts were also enabled to forward such offenders to assizes[20] (as had been allowed in England under its Criminal Justice Act 1925). The Government of Ireland Act 1920, with its rigid prohibition of legislation by the Northern Ireland Parliament touching the local Supreme Court, had prevented the step being taken any earlier.[21] In 1953 magistrates' courts were given the power to sentence directly to borstal,[22] and, as a result, the power to forward offenders for sentence was abolished. This reform had been officially advocated in 1938 on the grounds that committal to assizes or quarter sessions to await sentence could mean a delay of several weeks or even months.[23] Its adoption signalled an important extension of

[16] Malone Training School Act (N.I.) 1926, sch.; *Prisons Report (N.I.) 1925–26*, p. 4.
[17] *H. C. Debates (N.I.)*, Vol. 7, cols. 1752–53, 19 October 1926.
[18] 1908 Act, s. 1.
[19] 1914 Act, s. 10.
[20] Criminal Justice Act (N.I.) 1933, s. 1.
[21] The particular obstacle was removed by the Northern Ireland (Miscellaneous Provisions) Act 1932, s. 1(2).
[22] Criminal Justice Act (N.I.) 1953, s. 7.
[23] *Lynn Report*, pp. 161–62.

the sentencing powers of magistrates' courts. Their English counterparts do not yet possess a like power despite the fact that both the Molony Report of 1927[24] and an abortive reform bill of 1938 suggested that they should.[25] The explanation for this variation may be found in the traditionally broader jurisdiction possessed by this level of court in Ireland and in the fact that the Irish courts are now manned exclusively by professional lawyers. In the Republic, the district court has, since 1960, possessed the same power of imposing the direct sentence.[26]

Appeals may be taken against borstal sentences imposed at any level. The Criminal Appeal (Northern Ireland) Act 1968 (a Westminster Act which replaces an earlier Act of 1930)[27] enables appeals against borstal sentences passed following conviction on indictment at assizes or county courts to be heard by the local Court of Criminal Appeal.[28] (Special provision had been made by the earlier Act of 1930[29] and by the Criminal Justice Act (N.I.) 1933[30] for the hearing of appeals against borstal sentences imposed by quarter sessions and assizes, respectively, under the now defunct procedure whereby offenders could be referred to these courts to receive sentence). A right of appeal to the county court against a borstal sentence imposed by a magistrates' court is now provided for in the Magistrates' Courts Act (N.I.) 1964.

There is a short legislative history. When magistrates' courts were given power to impose borstal sentences themselves in 1953, it was assumed that the Summary Jurisdiction and Criminal Justice Act (N.I.) 1935 enabled appeals against such sentences to be heard by county courts. Section 24 of that Act provided for appeals "by any party against whom an order is made for any term of imprisonment." County court judges handled a number of borstal appeals on the assumption that a person sentenced to borstal was the same as one sentenced to imprisonment. The assumption was far from unreasonable. In 1917 an Irish court held that detention within a reformatory school fitted within an equivalent category;[31] the Prison Rules in force also employed the term 'prisoner' to embrace an inmate of a borstal.[32] In 1963, however, the recorder of Belfast chose to differ, in a judgment in which he held that he had no

---

[24] *Report of the Departmental Committee on the Treatment of Young Offenders* (Cmd. 2831, 1927), pp. 101–02.
[25] Criminal Justice Bill 1938; Hood, *Borstal Re-Assessed*, pp. 42 and 59.
[26] See chapter 5.
[27] Criminal Appeal (Northern Ireland) Act 1930.
[28] Criminal Appeal (Northern Ireland) Act 1968, s. 8.
[29] Criminal Appeal (Northern Ireland) Act 1930, s. 19 (4).
[30] S. 1.
[31] R. (*Higgins*) v. *Justices of Dublin Metropolis* [1917] 2 I.R. 45; Michael V. O'Mahony, "Legal Aspects of Residential Child Care", *The Irish Jurist* (*new series*), VI (1971), 228.
[32] See rule 175 of the Prison Rules (N.I.) 1954. In the South, for constitutional law purposes, detention in St Patrick's Institution has been treated as synonymous with imprisonment. This is discussed in chapter 5.

power to entertain a borstal appeal: 'imprisonment' was not the same as 'borstal'. The outcome was the Summary Jurisdiction (Appeals from Borstal Training Orders) Act (N.I.) 1963.[33] This measure has since been replaced, and the power of a county court to hear an appeal against a borstal sentence is preserved in a general provision on the appellate jurisdiction of county courts in section 140 of the Magistrates' Courts Act (N.I.) 1964.

In the two sets of legislation which have governed borstal sentences, nomenclature has varied. In the Acts of 1908 and 1914, the term borstal 'detention' was employed; in the Criminal Justice Act (N.I.) 1953 and the Treatment of Offenders Act (N.I.) 1968, borstal 'training'. The qualifying conditions have varied too (those introduced by the 1908 and 1914 Acts have been set out previously).[34] The qualifying conditions at present in force are those contained in the Act of 1953, as modified by the Act of 1968. Section 7 of the 1953 Act stipulates three conditions, each one of which must be fulfilled:

(i) the offender must have been convicted either summarily or on indictment of an offence punishable with imprisonment (or which would be so punishable were he not a child or young person);

(ii) the offender must be between 16 and 21 years of age;

(iii) the court must be satisfied, having regard to the offender's 'character and previous conduct, and to the circumstances of the offence, that it is expedient for his reformation and the prevention of crime that he should undergo a period of training in a borstal institution.'

The section also requires the court before whom the offender appears to consider a report on his suitability for borstal.

Removal of the reference to proof of 'criminal tendencies' is less significant than might appear. It may merely have been designed to encourage courts to forego insistence on proof of previous convictions. Brian Maginess, the Minister of Home Affairs in 1953, indicated that that indeed was the purpose.[35] It is plain that from the end of World War II, fewer first offenders were being sent to borstal, and if it was thought desirable to make the resources of borstal available for such offenders, a change in wording was certainly called for. Nonetheless, it is arguable that the change has made little, if any, difference. In this

[33] *Northern Ireland Legal Quarterly*, XV (1964), 296.
[34] Chapter 2.
[35] During the second reading of the Criminal Justice Bill (N.I.) 1953: 37 *H. C. Debates* (N.I.), Vol. 37, col. 322, 12 March 1953.

area, the conventional view of sentencers on who should be sent to borstal matters more than what the words of a statute imply. This can be easily demonstrated. In Northern Ireland between 1929 and 1940, and in the whole island between 1917 and 1921, sentencers showed themselves capable of committing first offenders to borstal despite the fact that the legislation then in force demanded evidence of 'criminal tendencies'.

Section 7 of the Act of 1953 must now be read subject to sections 10 and 11 of the Treatment of Offenders Act (N.I.) 1968.[36] In the wake of English findings that the length of a borstal sentence had no appreciable effect,[37] section 11 reduces the minimum period for a borstal sentence to six months and directs the sentencing court to have regard to the circumstances of the offence and the offender's character and previous conduct. In addition, section 10 forbids the passing of a borstal sentence in the case of any person—

(i) on whom such a sentence has previously been imposed and who has served more than nine months thereof;

(ii) on whom such a sentence has previously been imposed and who has already served that sentence; or

(iii) where the court considers that a sentence of imprisonment of three years or more is appropriate.

The principal purpose of this last change is to stop the committal to borstal of offenders with a history of institutionalisation.[38] For them, and for offenders who are thought to need a period of incarceration in excess of three years, a young offenders centre is planned. Power to set up such a centre was conferred by section 2 of the Act of 1968. No such centre has yet been opened and young offenders who can no longer be sent to borstal are being given ordinary terms of imprisonment. It is hoped to open a centre at Purdysburn, south of Belfast, by 1977.[39]

Only one case on sentencing has found its way into the law reports, Hayes, [40] decided by the Court of Criminal Appeal in 1939. Hayes, aged 19, had, together with seven others, pleaded guilty at the Belfast Recorder's Court to a charge of breaking and entering and stealing articles worth 7s. 5d. The fact that Hayes had been placed on probation seven years earlier was treated as proof of 'criminal tendencies' and he

---

[36] Brought into force in 1969: Treatment of Offenders Act (N.I.) 1968 (Commencement No. 2) Order 1969.

[37] Hood, *Borstal Re-Assessed*, pp. 83–87.

[38] All borstal recalls will be sent, not to borstal itself, but to the young offenders centre mentioned below.

[39] *The Irish Times*, 3 July 1974.

[40] (1939) 73 I.L.T.R. 29.

was sentenced to borstal. On appeal, counsel called a probation officer and Hayes's employer to give evidence. The latter stated that Hayes was "trustworthy, honest and most satisfactory and that his firm would not hesitate to take him back if there should be a vacancy." The Court of Criminal Appeal decided that Hayes's lapse in 1932 could be forgotten, quashed the borstal sentence and bound Hayes over to keep the peace for two years.[41]

Under the 1908 Act, sentencers considered suitability reports prepared by the Ministry of Home Affairs before an offender was sent to borstal. A disturbing feature of *Hayes* was that the pertinent report stated baldly that Hayes was a fit subject for borstal treatment "on account of his criminal tendencies" despite the fact that his only previous conviction was seven years before when he was 12. The risk of committal based on an unfair or incomplete assessment still remains, but is guarded against to an extent, for the Act of 1953 now provides that a copy of every suitability report officially prepared must be made available to each boy or to his legal representative.[42] A further improvement in the initial screening procedure was introduced in the same legislation: the court is empowered, after conviction but before sentence, to remand the offender in custody for three weeks or until the next sitting of the court.[43] That the court should possess this power had been officially recommended in 1938.[44]

Children and Young Persons Acts have also made provision for young offenders to be sent to borstal. The legislation currently in force enables any absconder from a training school who is over fifteen years of age to be brought before a magistrates' court and sentenced to borstal.[45] This arrangement is an alternative to the remedy of an increase in the period of detention in the training school. Boys at training school who are guilty of serious misconduct there may likewise be transferred to borstal by court order.[46]

The usual method which has been employed to commit to borstal has been the judicial sentence. Committal in Northern Ireland is possible— as, indeed, it was at Clonmel[47]—under a power residing in the executive

---

[41] A comparable decision from the South is *Carolan* [1943] Ir. Jur. Rep. 49, discussed below, chapter 4.

[42] Criminal Justice Act (N.I.) 1953, s. 7(3).

[43] S. 7(2). On pre-sentence inquiry, see *Report of the Interdepartmental Committee on the Business of the Criminal Courts* (Cmnd. 1289, 1961), part B, and F. V. Jarvis, "Inquiry before Sentence" in Grygier, Jones and Spencer (eds.), *Criminology in Transition: Essays in Honour of Hermann Mannheim* (London: Tavistock Publications, 1965), pp. 43–66.

[44] *Lynn Report*, pp. 162–63.

[45] C. & Y. P. Act (N.I.) 1968, s. 140, replacing C. & Y. P. Act (N.I.) 1950, s. 110, where the critical age was 16.

[46] C. & Y. P. Act (N.I.) 1968, 5 sch., para. 11; changing C. & Y. P. Act (N.I.) 1950, 4 sch., para. 8, where the critical age was 16.

[47] Chapter 2.

to transfer an offender from one penal institution to another. Judicial intervention is required in the case of a transfer from a training school to borstal, but this is not so where the transfer is from prison[48] and will not be so in the case of a transfer from a young offenders centre (when one is opened); in both instances, the relevant legislation requires the executive, where practicable, to consult the sentencer responsible for the original sentence.[49] Intra-United Kingdom borstal transfers are made possible by Westminster legislation of 1961.[50] A final form of committal by the executive is possible where a young offender, found guilty of murder or other serious indictable crime, is ordered to be detained at the pleasure of the Secretary of State (formerly the Governor of Northern Ireland). The offender is then liable to be detained wherever and on whatever conditions are directed.[51]

Accommodation

Even before boys were committed to the Malone institution, the prospect of their mixing with the younger reformatory school boys gave rise for concern[52] and steps were immediately taken to guard against the eventuality. In 1929 reformatory school and borstal were structurally separated, the front of the building being reserved for the former and the north-west end for the latter.[53] Complete segregation of the two inmate populations could not always be guaranteed and this continued to be a preoccupation until 1956. In 1938 the Lynn Committee, whose mandate included general reform of the law on juvenile offenders, advised against the adoption for Northern Ireland of the English decision of two years before to raise the maximum age for committal to borstal to twenty-three, specifically because of the situation prevailing at Malone.[54] Ten years later, the government's White Paper, *The Protection and Welfare of the Young and the Treatment of Young Offenders*,[55] urged that the borstal section at Malone should be divorced from "the existing reformatory side" still housed in the same premises.[56] Behind the

---

[48] Prison Act (N.I.) 1953, s. 17, replacing the 1908 Act, s. 3. Once a young offenders centre is opened, prison sentences will be a rarity for those between the ages of 16 and 21. It may be noted that s. 14 of the 1968 Act provides for prison-borstal transfers, consequential upon the legislation coming into full force.

[49] Prison Act (N.I.) 1953, s. 17 (1); 1968 Act, s. 7(1).

[50] Criminal Justice Act 1961, s. 26, replacing s. 9 of the 1908 Act (under which transfers of boys to British borstals prior to 1927 was effected). S. 9 was also employed rather later in regard to girls: see chapter 6.

[51] C. & Y. P. Act (N.I.) 1968, s. 73, replacing C. & Y. P. Act (N.I.) 1950, s. 55. S. 73 must now be read subject to the Northern Ireland (Emergency Provisions) Act 1973, s. 8(1).

[52] H. C. Debates (N.I.), Vol. 7, col. 1753, 19 October 1926: Sir Dawson Bates.

[53] *The Roots of Rathgael*, p. 20.

[54] *Lynn Report*, pp. 163–64. The English decision was reversed in the Criminal Justice Act 1948, s. 20. Power to increase the age to 23 had been contained in the 1908 Act, s. 1(2).

[55] Cmd. 264, 1948.

[56] p. 21.

decision to move the borstal to an altogether different site lay the same continuing anxiety about the presence in one building of the two inmate groups. It is true that in 1956 there was yet another consideration. The administration of a joint borstal-training school establishment became much more difficult once it was decided to set up a separate board of management for the Malone and Whiteabbey training schools.[57] (These had previously been the responsibility of the Ministry of Home Affairs).

Unlike the buildings which were to house the comparable institutions in the South, those at Malone had not been designed as a prison, and in the years when the Northern borstal was there, considerations of security, though present, were never permitted to dominate.[58] This was illustrated in 1931 when the building was fitted with steel frame windows and the bars on the outside of the windows were removed; the change, it was said, both improved the building's appearance and gave extra light and ventilation. However, in the same year some thought was given to security when it was decided to install special locks for the cubicle dormitories. The need to provide against the risk of fire underlay further development in the early years. In 1929 new fireproof cubicles were erected and a new emergency system installed under which all doors could be simultaneously unlocked by the officer on duty. To reduce the number of open fires in the building, a central heating system was introduced. Staircases and exits were also adapted and it was reported in 1931 that the risk of fire had been eliminated.

Improvements to the premises were made gradually. In 1929 both the bootmaker's and the tailor's shops were resited. The old tailor's shop had been located in the borstal section and the space released enabled further cubicles to be built. In 1931 an extra wing was added. On the upper floor it included twenty-two additional cubicles; on the ground floor a large schoolroom, four isolation rooms and bathrooms. Two years later pressure on space led to the temporary reallocation of rooms for dormitory use and in the following year to the erection of a makeshift wooden hut, adjacent to the main building, again for use as a dormitory. The critical problem of accommodation in 1934 was due directly to more borstal sentences being imposed. The annual *Home Office Services Report* attributed this to "a wave of juvenile crime spreading over the country." This, "in the opinion of those best qualified to judge", was the result of a "lack of parental control, . . . lack of employment, and . . . the effect of crook films and plays."

---

[57] Malone and Whiteabbey Training Schools Act (N.I.) 1956. The schools had previously been the responsibility of the Ministry of Home Affairs.

[58] All further detail contained in this chapter, unless otherwise indicated, is based on the contents of the appropriate year's *Home Office Services Report*.

Other developments took place over the years. In 1934 showers were installed in the swimming baths and a new tomato house was built— a tribute, so it was put, to the boys' training in carpentry. A two-year programme of workshop construction was completed in 1938; the *Report* for that year claimed that the new workshops building had "an appearance of spaciousness and design in keeping with present-day standards of a borstal institution run on modern reformative lines." Some years before, the general appearance of the grounds had also been improved. New entrances had been built at both front and rear, and the Great Northern Railway Company had been successfully persuaded to make repairs to the access road. In 1936 the Company leased further land which enabled more agricultural activities to be undertaken.

On the outbreak of war, a large underground shelter was built but further improvements had to wait until 1945 when the kitchen was enlarged and new equipment was supplied. There was considerable activity in 1947: the surgery was re-equipped, the old workshops converted into recreation rooms, a new gymnasium completed, playing fields improved and other ground levelled to enable the market garden to be extended. The following year the whole interior was redecorated: "The more cheery colour scheme not only improved the appearance of the buildings but also had a psychological effect in brightening the general atmosphere." In 1949 furniture and items of equipment were transferred to Malone from the prison at Londonderry which ceased to be in general use from that year.[59]

In 1952 Woburn House at Millisle, County Down, was accepted by the Northern Ireland government in lieu of £18,250 estate duty,[60] and it was decided, not without some local opposition,[61] to open the premises as a borstal. Woburn was ready in 1956 and the same year the use of Malone for borstal purposes was officially discontinued.[62] The building there was employed exclusively as a Protestant male training school, a role it had fulfilled before and which it continued to fulfill until the school was in turn transferred to Rathgael, near Bangor, County Down, in 1968.[63] The Malone building itself has since been demolished.

The reasons for the move have already been explained. The choice could not have been better. Woburn is a large mansion in its own grounds, overlooking the coast of north Down: on a good day the coast of Scotland is clearly visible. Even before 1956 the view will have

[59] *The Roots of Rathgael*, p. 21,
[60] *H. C. Debates (N.I.)*, Vol. 39, cols. 1291–92, 10 May 1955: G. B. Hanna, the then Minister for Home Affairs.
[61] Below, chapter 8.
[62] Malone and Whiteabbey Training Schools Act (N.I.) 1956, s. 4.
[63] As envisaged in the Malone and Whiteabbey Training Schools Act (N.I.) 1968.

become known to the boys at Malone: for a few years selected boys formed a work party which travelled daily to Woburn to help effect structural alterations there. In the first year of residence, the boys were kept busy laying out the grounds and establishing, in temporary accommodation, vocational training courses in woodwork and building construction. A building programme was early drawn up and, with the passage of years, new buildings have made their appearance. In 1966, new vocational training workshops and two new classrooms were ready for use. Two years later a large new block was completed. It comprised residential accommodation for staff and two dormitories and a lounge cum recreation room for the boys. This block was intended for use as a hostel for boys reaching special grade "so as to assist them to further prove themselves suitable for release under supervision." A new gymnasium was finished in 1970. The following year saw the completion of improvements to the bricklaying shop, with the installation of an oil-fired heating system.

In 1963 a closed boys' borstal opened in Armagh Prison where a girls' borstal had previously been located,[64] thus increasing the borstal institutions in Northern Ireland to two. Although overcrowding at Woburn impelled the authorities to do this, there was another consideration: the undesirability of being restricted to one open borstal institution for all comers. A closed establishment from which boys could soon transfer to open conditions was a sensible enough arrangement; its existence meant that there was henceforth some alternative institution to prison to which the troublemaker at Woburn could be retransferred.

So long as Armagh has been available, borstal recalls have been sent there. (The plan, under the Treatment of Offenders Act (N.I.) 1968, is to send these recalls to the young offenders centre instead).

In the years since 1969, civil unrest in Northern Ireland has seriously interfered with the use of Armagh as a closed borstal. For a number of months in both 1969 and 1970, pressure on accommodation for adult offenders forced the closure of the borstal section at Armagh and the transfer of all boys to Woburn. The closure became more permanent in 1971. "All boys," said the *Home Office Services Report* for that year, "whether suitable or not for open conditions, were accommodated at Woburn House." This development and the political and other circumstances which underlay it can scarcely have been welcome to the staff at the latter institution. The *Report* for 1971 continued: "The general unrest in the province made itself felt in the Borstal and the need for a closed institution was very apparent." The borstal at Armagh has been

---

[64] Chapter 6.

in operation again since August 1972. It is planned to shut it finally when a new closed unit comes into operation at Woburn.

At Armagh, conditions have been somewhat cramped, but since the average length of stay was reasonably short, this did not represent too serious a defect. Matters were improved in 1968, when a prefabricated recreation building came into use.

Accommodation crises have occurred at regular intervals. The first took place soon after the Malone institution opened, when, not surprisingly, the judges in Northern Ireland began to impose more borstal sentences. One subsequent crisis at Malone was overcome, in 1931, by the opening of a new wing. At Woburn, the pattern has been repeated to some extent. An emergency in 1962 forced the temporary conversion of offices into dormitories and contributed to the decision to open the second borstal at Armagh the following year. The use of the Armagh premises for adult prisoners in 1969, and again between 1970 and 1972, naturally accentuated the accommodation problems at Woburn.

Régime

Substantial modifications in the old Prison Board rules of 1909 were introduced soon after the opening of the Malone borstal, as is clear from the details given by Edward Fahy in 1941.[65] At that time there were four grades. For the first three months the new arrival was kept in grade one; here the sole privilege was one visit a month. The next four months were spent in grade two, which entitled the boy to one visit and one parcel every fourteen days. Grade three followed after another four months, where the only change was that one letter was allowed in addition to the parcel and the visit. The privileges remained the same in grade three B (the probation class) which lasted for another four months. At the end of fifteen months, if he had made satisfactory progress, the boy entered grade four, or, as it was called, the 'blue stage' since the boys in it wore blue shorts, as opposed to grey. Boys in this grade were entitled to one visit, parcel and letter every week.

Other changes had been made too. In the early years at Malone, privileges such as attendance at the summer camp and membership of the scout group were confined to boys in the blue stage, as the philosophy of the 1909 rules required. By 1931, however, this restriction seems to have been removed. A system of privileges nonetheless remained firmly entrenched, as is obvious from differences, recorded in Fahy's account of 1941, in the daily evening routine for the various categories.

---

[65] Edward Fahy, "Borstal in Ireland", *Hermathena*, LVIII (1941), at 75–78. The details in this paragraph and the two following are based on Fahy's account.

After 8.30 p.m., those less than six months in the borstal had to retire to their rooms. Those who had been there more than six months, but less than fifteen, could remain in association until 9.00 p.m., playing badminton, billiards and table tennis. Those who had been in for fifteen months or more had the recreational facilities to themselves until 9.50 p.m. and were also allowed to smoke.[66]

Fahy has left a complete picture of the full daily routine at the time of his visit. Up to 8.30 p.m. it was as follows:

7.30 a.m.	Rise, wash, clean and tidy.
	Breakfast.
9.30 a.m.	Inspection. Work.
12.55 p.m.	Wash, parade, dinner.
1.55 p.m.	Work.
4.55 p.m.	Dismiss.
	Tea.
	Wash, change footwear for gym or evening shoes.
5.55 p.m.	Hall.
6.00 p.m.	News on the wireless.
	School (swimming, gymnastics, first aid).
8.00 p.m.	Supper, prayers.

As an alternative to ordinary school-work, boys could attend the handicrafts class (basket-making, leatherwork and painting). On Saturday, work stopped at 12.30 p.m. and the rest of the day was set aside for parents' visits, soccer, cricket and swimming. On Sundays there were church parades in the morning and religious instruction classes in the afternoon.

The first mention of a division of boys into houses comes in 1949. At that time a house cup was being awarded on points gained for work, conduct and games. This division into houses has continued at Woburn.

By 1961 the system had changed little. True, the names of the various grades had been varied: they were now called 'entrant', and 'general I, II, and III'. A boy usually remained three months in each, his privileges and his earnings increasing as he won promotion. If, after twelve months, a boy was promoted to special grade, he enjoyed exceptional privileges. He became eligible for appointment as group leader or prefect, could work free of supervision in the grounds and could be granted day parole leave once a month to visit his home or friends. A further privilege, established later, and confined to boys in general III and special grades, was that of extended Christmas parole.

---

[66] Smoking was introduced for long-term prisoners in Northern Ireland in 1936.

The reviewing body, established under the Prison Rules, met once a month. Its functions were threefold. It interviewed new arrivals. It scrutinised the progress of others, with a view to their promotion through the various grades, giving particular attention to boys who had served twelve months and who were therefore eligible for special grade. Following the adoption of a new rule in 1957,[67] the reviewing body also interviewed every boy who had been reduced in grade, telling him that both his conduct and his work would be carefully watched.

The borstal system in Northern Ireland has been further refined as a result of three recent developments: the introduction of employment on parole, the opening of a second borstal, and the enactment of the Treatment of Offenders Act (N.I.) 1968.

The inauguration of schemes of daytime employment on parole was envisaged in a prison rule of 1954;[68] a start was made in 1959 and the present scheme dates from 1964 when special II grade was introduced. Boys promoted to this grade enjoy the same privileges as boys in the former special grade (now termed special I); in addition, they are eligible both for employment outside the institution and for parole leave which can extend overnight. Boys qualify six months before the estimated date of release but not every boy is promoted. Provisional proposals for employment must accompany each report from the reviewing body recommending promotion and each case is decided by the executive. Promoted boys are treated as being on parole while they are outside the borstal. In particular, they must travel to their place of work by the shortest route and undertake neither to associate with persons of bad character, to enter public houses, nor to drink alcohol. The employer pays the borstal for the boy's services at the rate applicable to an ordinary civilian employee. The sum received is net of income tax and insurance contributions, and is distributed in the following manner:

(i) £1 per week to the boy;
(ii) £1 per week placed to the credit of the boy's personal cash account and given to him on discharge;
(iii) a sum to cover travelling and luncheon expenses;
(iv) the remainder to the credit of appropriations in aid.

A boy is permitted to work overtime subject to the veto of the borstal medical officer. One half of overtime earnings goes to the boy's personal cash account and the other half is credited to appropriations in aid.[69]

---

[67] Prison (Amendment) Rules (N.I.) 1957, rule 8.
[68] Prison Rules (N.I.) 1954, rule 178(2).
[69] Ministry of Home Affairs circular no. 4/65: "Borstal Inmates' Training—Employment on Parole Scheme".

Since the present civil unrest started in Northern Ireland in 1969, few boys have gone to employment on parole.

The opening of the borstal at Armagh altered the arrangements for the reception of all new committals. These were sent to Armagh and not, as formerly, to Woburn. From Armagh, boys who were thought to be suitable for an open institution were sent to Woburn after approximately three months. Three additional categories of boys were kept separate from the new committals at Armagh: those not sent on to Woburn at the end of three months, retransfers from Woburn, and those recalled from release on supervision. These arrangements did not, of course, apply during the closure of Armagh in 1969 and in 1970 to 1972.

The provisions relating to borstal contained in the Act of 1968 came into force in 1969. The Act, as we have seen,[70] not only narrows the category of offenders in the sixteen to twenty-one age group who can be committed but also reduces the minimum and maximum periods of detention, the former from nine months to six and the latter from three years to two.[71] Some telescoping of promotion arrangements has occurred but has not been very significant.

The authorities at the Northern borstals have had available to them a variety of disciplinary punishments. In the early years, the governor at Malone had the power to order (i) close confinement in an ordinary cell, (ii) reduction in diet, and (iii) loss of stage or privilege. After 1930 he was also empowered to cane but could only do this on the authority of the visiting committee.

The power to cane was introduced by Act of Parliament, the Criminal Law and Prevention of Crime (Amendment) Act (N.I.) 1930, following a recommendation from the visiting committee.[72] The measure split the parliamentarians into two camps. The proponents of the change presumably agreed with the anonymous compiler of the *Home Office Services Report* for 1930 who wrote that knowledge of the existence of the power would act "as a deterrent to unruly behaviour and have a salutary effect." Sir Dawson Bates, the Minister of Home Affairs, went further and pointed out that the power to cane existed in Britain and there was no reason why Northern Ireland practice should be different.[73] Roger Hood is authority for concluding that here Sir Dawson was either mistaken or misleading, for he shows that the infliction of corporal punishment in English borstals was stopped in 1921, following public concern over conditions at the Portland borstal.[74] (The power has

[70] Above, p. 29.
[71] 1968 Act, s. 11(1).
[72] *H. C. Debates (N.I.)*, Vol. 12, col. 293, 20 March 1930: Sir Dawson Bates.
[73] *H. C. Debates (N.I.)*, Vol. 12, col. 292.
[74] Hood, *Borstal Re-Assessed*, p. 33.

never been exercised in the South).[75] Sir Dawson expressed the view that the new power would not be much used; his own son, after all, had told him, following a visit to the institution at Malone, that he had no fear of going to school if it was as good as Malone.[76] The precise reason for the visiting committee's recommendation is hard to establish but it may be linked with an incident to which Sir Dawson himself drew attention when a boy on his way to church had thrown a stone through a plate-glass window, for no apparent reason.

Unionist MPs gave wholehearted support to the proposal. Two or three licks of the cane or a punch on the nose, one of them said, was a more apt punishment than a starvation diet or transfer to prison.[77] Another declared that he would not send his son to a school which did not inflict corporal punishment.[78] Other MPs were less enthusiastic. The Labour MP Mr Beattie declared his opposition. He had seen men lashed to a wagon wheel and flogged for trivial offences in South Africa. His party was progressive, and corporal punishment was reactionary. It was ridiculous, he added, that the visiting committee, which was responsible to no one, should report that the borstal was perfect and yet that the cane was required for boys who broke windows.[79] Cahir Healy also objected.[80] Provision of corporal punishment in the borstal would destroy the progressive vision; it was a backward step. After recalling that a little over a hundred years before, a Fermanagh man had been hanged for stealing a goat belonging to the Bishop of Clogher, he quoted from a speech of Isabel's in *Measure for Measure*:[81]

> . . . the poor beetle, that we tread upon,
> In corporal sufferance finds a pang as great
> As when a giant dies.

Despite these objections, the bill had no difficulty in securing a second reading and passed into law.

Rules made under the Act regulated the conduct of any canings. These could only be administered by an approved cane; strokes were not to exceed twelve and could only be administered on the hand or posterior (in the latter event, no clothing was to be removed). A caning could only be ordered by the visiting committee. It had to be carried out at the one time, as soon as possible, and in strict privacy. The medical

[75] Below, chapter 8.
[76] H. C. Debates (N.I.), Vol. 12, cols. 292–94.
[77] Col. 299: Mr Grant.
[78] Col. 304: Captain Chichester-Clark.
[79] Cols. 299–301.
[80] Cols. 295–96.
[81] Act 3, scene 1, lines 80–82.

officer had to certify that the recipient was fit, the governor or his deputy had to be present and a record had to be kept.[82] The Treatment of Offenders Act (N.I.) 1968 has abolished the judicial sentence of corporal punishment[83] but this leaves unaffected the right of the borstal authorities to avail of the cane.

The matter of borstal discipline receives considerable attention in the 1954 Prison Rules. Rule 174 treats of offences against discipline: idleness, carelessness and negligence; abuse of privilege; non-conformity to parole conditions; irreverent behaviour during divine service or prayers; disrespect towards officers and visitors; repeated and groundless complaints; false and malicious allegations against an officer; indecency in language, act or gesture.[84] The rule enables the governor to deal with these in any one of the following ways:

(i) administration of a caution;

(ii) removal from activities other than work;

(iii) award of extra work (not to exceed two hours a day and not to last longer than twenty-eight days);

(iv) forfeiture of right to additional letters and visits;

(v) stoppage of gratuity or earnings and withdrawal of spending facilities for a period not exceeding fourteen days;

(vi) reduction in grade, delay (not exceeding two months) in promotion to higher grade; and

(vii) confinement in a room for three days.

In 1957, punishment (vi) was altered to read "such reduction in grade as may be appropriate."[85]

Rule 175 is concerned with more serious forms of misconduct: an offence under the Prison Act (N.I.) 1953 (escape, smuggling goods in, and so on); mutiny or incitement to mutiny; assault on an officer; gross personal violence to officers or other prisoners; a serious or repeated offence against discipline in respect of which the powers conferred by Rule 174 are thought inadequate. If a boy is accused of any of these, the governor is required to carry out an investigation. If the offence is proven, he may then report to the Ministry of Home Affairs (now the Northern Ireland Office); such a report is mandatory in the case of Prison Act offences. The executive, in the exercise of its disciplinary powers, can punish offenders in much the same way as the governor may under Rule 174. It can order

---

[82] Corporal Punishment in Borstal Institutions Regulations (N.I.) 1930.
[83] S. 22.
[84] Prison Rules (N.I.) 1954, rule 30(2).
[85] Prison (Amendment) Rules (N.I.) 1957, rule 6.

(i) administration of a caution;
(ii) removal from activities other than work;
(iii) extra work (not to exceed two hours a day and not to last longer than twenty-eight days);
(iv) forfeiture of right to additional letters and visits;
(v) stoppage of gratuity or earnings and withdrawal of spending facilities for a period not exceeding *twenty-eight* days (*fourteen* days under Rule 174);
(vi) reduction in grade, delay, not exceeding *three* months (*two* months under Rule 174), in promotion to higher grade; and
(vii) confinement in a room for *fourteen* days (*three* days under Rule 174).

In 1957, punishment (vi) was altered to read "such reduction in grade as may be appropriate."[86] Rule 175 also enables the executive (now the Northern Ireland Office) to delegate its powers to the visiting committee—which it invariably does—and provides that the committee, in addition to, or in lieu of, punishments (i) to (vi), may order the administration of a caning. If the committee does so, the safeguards first introduced in 1930 apply.[87] This power to order a caning is still commonly availed of: there were twenty-nine in 1971.

Dietary punishment is now forbidden: the last year in which it seems to have been employed was 1946 (on six occasions). Punishment drill was a common punitive measure between 1946 and 1950 but was then practically abandoned. Close confinement was regularly employed until 1945 (twenty-six occasions that year) but after that was in frequent use only in 1961. It is specifically mentioned in the Prison Rules of 1954, as is stoppage of earnings, a more common form of punishment today.

A power of last resort is that of transfer to another penal institution. Transfer to prison is now made possible by a section in the Prison Act (N.I.) 1953.[88] Before the Minister (now the Secretary of State) can act, the visiting committee must report that a boy is incorrigible and a bad influence on others. There is no detailed case law, as there is in the South,[89] on the form such a report must take. The powers of the executive are confined to commuting the residue of the period of borstal detention to a term of imprisonment. One purpose of the Treatment of Offenders Act 1968 is to discourage the use of imprisonment for offenders under 21; nonetheless, the transfer power contained in the 1953 Prison Act is expressly preserved.[90] An alternative, and less drastic,

---

[86] Prison (Amendment) Rules (N.I.) 1957, rule 7.
[87] Prison Act (N.I.) 1953, s. 14(1)(e), (2)(c).
[88] S. 17(2). The power was originally conferred by s. 7 of the 1908 Act.
[89] Below, chapter 5.
[90] 1968 Act, s. 1(4).

solution, introduced on the opening of the borstal at Armagh, was the transfer there of any troublesome boys at Woburn.[91] Once the young offenders centre envisaged by the 1968 Act is operating, a further possibility will be transfer to it.[92] This institution is designed to cope with an assortment of problem offenders: borstal recalls will have to be sent there, as will all boys who commit offences whilst on release under supervision.[93]

In 1938 the Lynn Committee contemplated the use of a further weapon— the transfer of "difficult cases to England"—advocating this where special treatment was required.[94] This recommendation is of unusual interest because, in general, the committee opposed the notion of transfer to England, admitting frankly that maintenance costs there might be higher. Ever since Northern Ireland's first borstal was opened in 1926, the transfer power (at that time contained in section 9 of the 1908 Act) appears never to have been exercised for disciplinary purposes.[95] Following a confused legislative history, which is of more relevance to the Northern Ireland girls' borstal,[96] the transfer power was revived by fresh legislative enactment in 1961.[97] This new power was not conceived as a disciplinary measure. It exists to enable a boy sentenced in Northern Ireland, whose family has moved to Britain, to be sent to some borstal nearer home; the transfer as such depends on the prior application of the boy himself.

It should be noted that there is also power to transfer a borstal boy under 18 to a training school.

Work

It may be recalled that, in 1923, when the Moles Committee reported in favour of setting up a borstal in Northern Ireland, it recognised that, from the standpoint of vocational training, there was one grave disadvantage: numbers in a local institution were never likely to be high, so that variety in training must be restricted because of the costs.[98] When Parliament first discussed the question, Sir Dawson Bates conceded that financial considerations would inhibit capital expenditure on training facilities; facilities would be provided to enable boys to learn baking, carpentry and farming but he could promise no more.[99] Members

[91] *Home Office Services Report 1963*, p. 16.
[92] 1968 Act, s. 7(4).
[93] 1968 Act, s. 13(1), (6).
[94] *Lynn Report*, p. 167.
[95] In the period 1921–26, it was used merely to enable Northern Ireland boys to serve borstal sentences somewhere.
[96] Below, chapter 6.
[97] Criminal Justice Act 1961, s. 26 (Westminster legislation).
[98] *Moles Report*, p. 26.
[99] *H. C. Debates* (N.I.), Vol. 8, col. 788, 7 April 1927.

of Parliament well appreciated the difficulties in an institution which planned to cope with only thirty-seven boys in its first year of operation. Nevertheless, Mr Beattie was not stopped from offering advice, and made it clear that he was against teaching the old trades and in favour of inculcating the new:

> You could make them electricians for instance. You should endeavour to get away from the old category of trades such as cobbling and tailoring. I am not speaking disrespectfully of those trades. We are compelled by law to wear clothes, we have to get clothes made, and if we went out without clothes the law would deal with us, although the law would not provide the means of procuring them.[100]

In the early years, the lack of money was to restrict the range of 'training' available, but the light in which training was viewed was probably as great an obstacle to innovations of the kind which Mr Beattie had advocated. Trade training, the 1928 *Report* considered, was too short to enable the boys to become experts:

> The most that can be attained in this direction at the school is that each lad will acquire and preserve the habit of work, and will have an opportunity of starting life equipped in some measure with a useful groundwork to form the basis of an honest career.

Evidently, the emphasis was more on instilling a work-habit than on imparting instruction in a trade that would be of immediate value to the discharged boy.

In Malone's first year the 'industries' included tailoring, bootmaking and repairing, carpet-beating, carpentry, farmwork and the reconstruction and maintenance of buildings. Cookery was being taught by a voluntary worker in 1929, and in the two succeeding years plumbing and bricklaying were added to the list. Land reclamation was completed in 1933 and additional land leased in 1936; this enabled a larger number of inmates to be employed in farming, clearly of greater scope than the "dairy work and general garden work" of 1929.[101] The 1933 *Report* defended the requirement that all boys had to spend time in the tailor's shop, and pointed out that, as soon as possible, every endeavour was made

---

[100] *H. C. Debates* (N.I.), Vol. 8, col. 787.
[101] The grounds at Malone had been used for training in farmwork in the days when the institution served solely as a Protestant male reformatory. For conditions then, see the annual *Reports of the Inspector of Reformatory and Industrial Schools in Ireland* and the report of an application, made by the Malone trustees in 1916, for the fixing of a fair rent in respect of contiguous agricultural land: *Deacon v. Bristow* 50 I.L.T.R. 42.

to allocate boys to the industry to which they were best suited. In 1934 the so-called 'carpet-beating industry' was brought to an untimely end, following the destruction by fire of the hut in which it was carried on. No tears were shed: the industry, it was admitted, had not afforded any useful training for the boys; in fact it had been a positive hazard to their health. In its place, a mechanics shop was established and the boys were instructed in the elements of motor mechanics.

Fahy describes the arrangements regarding training in 1941.[102] Boys were first entered in shoemaking, tailoring or carpentry. If they proved unskilful in these crafts, they were transferred to the farm or to the general working party. On the farm there was ample opportunity for ploughing, cultivating, and for tending cattle and horses. The tasks of the general working party were to level the land, make drains, do excavating work for new buildings and make concrete. During the war and until 1947, parties of boys were organised to assist farmers in flax-pulling and general farmwork. In 1950 work on the Malone farm was helped by the purchase of a tractor. From 1947 until 1955 the economic aspect of the work undertaken was emphasised by the annual publication of details of the profits made from the sale of farm produce and items made in the tailoring and shoemaking workshops. From 1953 until 1956 senior boys were attached to the working party that travelled daily to Woburn to help in making structural alterations pending the transfer there of the borstal.

At Woburn the emphasis was more immediately on vocational training, reflecting the philosophy of the new Prison Rules that "the work of all prisoners shall, if possible, be productive, and the trades and industries taught and carried on shall, if practicable, be such as may fit the prisoner to earn his livelihood on release."[103] The tailoring and shoemaking previously carried on at Malone were superseded by carpentry and miscellaneous maintenance work. Two years later, in 1958, a course in welding was introduced and arrangements were made for the introduction of courses in other forms of engineering. By 1961 the new pattern of training was established. In the first few weeks all new boys were given the task of keeping the premises and the grounds in order. After that, those who were thought likely to benefit from the vocational courses (woodwork, carpentry, building construction, welding and light engineering, horticulture, painting and decorating)[104] were assigned to them. Special workshops were available, fitted out with modern equipment. All other boys were employed in providing various domestic

---

[102] Fahy, "Borstal in Ireland", 75–76.
[103] Prison Rules (N.I.) 1954, rule 46.
[104] Horticulture, painting and decorating were added in 1969.

services, sawing and chopping wood, clearing construction sites, and working with the trade staff on new buildings and on keeping existing buildings in good repair.

The *Report* for 1969 mentions individual successes attributable to the programme of vocational training: seven trainees in bricklaying were so well thought of that they were given basic kits of tools on release into apprenticeship; one trainee who had shown distinction in welding won a vacancy in a welding course at a government training centre. The *Report* for 1971 points out that the trunking for an oil-fired heating system in the bricklaying shop was made and installed by the boys in the engineering class.

Facilities at Armagh were necessarily more limited. As one might expect, there was a general working party responsible for maintenance and decoration; there was also a class in tailoring.[105]

Education

The *Report* for 1927 mentions educational training but it is difficult to determine what this amounted to, either then or in the immediately succeeding years. By 1933 educational classes were apparently compulsory for all boys and in 1935 the *Report* says that the "ordinary education classes (including singing)" were supplemented that year by classes given by voluntary teachers.

In 1947 and 1951 the *Reports* make special reference to the needs of the educationally backward and it is in this area that change has subsequently been most marked. In 1961, if not earlier, boys entering Woburn were required to sit an educational test on their arrival and tuition was arranged for those found to need it. Special staff were essential. In 1960 a part-time extern teacher was appointed to help with the educationally backward. In 1963 a full-time tutor-organiser was appointed, responsible for both prisons and borstals. In 1965, despite some concern about the cost,[106] two part-time tutors were hired for the Woburn and Armagh borstals and Woburn secured another part-time tutor in 1966.

Detailed tables setting out the educational ability of fresh committals, which first appear in the *Report* for 1963, make sorry reading. The implications are considered in the *Report* for 1968 which claims that there had been a progressive increase in the proportion of boys who displayed below average intellectual ability or educational attainment. Extra effort was needed to remedy this state of affairs and the *Report* urged the appointment of a full-time teacher. The results of an interim solution had been encouraging.

---

[105] On the occasion of a visit by the author, the boys were making clothes for the baby recently born to a woman detained in the adjacent women's prison.
[106] *H. C. Debates* (N.I.), Vol. 62, col. 1082, 16 February 1966: Mr Scott.

The introduction of programmed learning techniques has improved the ability in English expression and reading within the most severely retarded groups. It had been achieved by using the reading laboratory method developed by Science Research Associates. This produces results through the interest and enthusiasm stimulated by personal achievement.

In 1969, 176 trainees attended formal educational classes each week-day night between 6 and 8 p.m. In the same year, ninety-eight boys were categorised as severely retarded and these attended special classes during normal hours.

The library at Woburn was restocked in 1965 on the recommendation of the part-time tutor, and in subsequent years the local authorities for both Down and Armagh cooperated in stocking the libraries at the two institutions. A regulation 'quiet hour' was introduced at Woburn in 1965 for the benefit of boys not required to attend the evening educational classes. A policy of encouraging intellectual pursuits also led to the introduction of facilities for tuition by post and of the showing of a wide range of educational films. In 1966 Woburn became a recognised centre for holding GCE examinations and arrangements for taking these examinations were also made at Armagh.

Recreation

A feature of borstal life from 1927 to 1952 was the annual summer camp. [107] The *Report* for 1929 provides the following account of that year's camp:

> The annual summer camp opened in July 1929, at Ballydown, Islandmagee, in which 56 inmates participated. The conduct of the boys was excellent, and the privilege of attending this annual camp has been found to be not only beneficial to the general health of the inmates, but has proved of great value in improving their morale. The boys are thrown to a large extent upon their own resources, and, moreover, it has a most wholesome effect on the general discipline, inasmuch as on this occasion no inmates were allowed the privilege of attending camp who had not a satisfactory record during the year. Various forms of recreation were indulged in daily, and altogether a most pleasant time was spent and much appreciated by the inmates.

The original intention was to let only boys in the higher grade attend

[107] Camps were started in England in 1922: Hood, *Borstal Re-Assessed*, p. 115.

but soon nearly all boys were allowed to go. In 1929 and 1930 only boys in the blue grade qualified but, by 1931, all boys did, with the exception of those who had attempted to abscond. This more liberal policy entailed the risk that boys would succumb to the temptation (ever-present in the conditions at the camps) to escape. Indeed, down through the years several boys did get away, but the policy itself was not reversed and does not appear even to have been questioned. From 1927 to 1932 the camp was held at Islandmagee, from 1934 to 1938 at Mid Island, Greyabbey, and after 1938 across Strangford Lough at Gore's Island. The last annual camp was in 1952 but the borstal's move to Woburn in 1956 was some compensation in view of Woburn's situation on the coast.

Private citizens organised excursions for the inmates during the early years at Malone. In 1932 and 1933, a lady interested in the wellbeing of the institution took the boys on picnics to the seaside at Ballywalter. Discharges were delayed in 1932 because of widespread unemployment and the consequential difficulty of securing jobs, and the accompanying expression of gratitude in the *Report* for that year is especially fulsome:

> The Governor is satisfied that an outing of this sort is not only a matter of enjoyment, but also gives the staff an opportunity of seeing a side of the boys' characters which may not be so evident inside the school grounds.

Until the end of World War II, the Malone institution could boast of a flourishing scout troop, recognised officially in 1930 as the 72nd Belfast. Again, the original intention, as in the case of the annual camp, was to make participation a privilege, but this was abandoned in 1931 since "the troop proved so great an attraction", and by 1934 two-thirds of the inmate population were actively involved. Since 1965 the borstal at Woburn has been operating the Duke of Edinburgh's award scheme and several boys have managed to complete the so-called 'silver stage'. Boys participating in the scheme are the only obvious descendants of the scouts of the former 72nd troop.

Sporting activities have been a dominant feature of borstal life from the establishment of the Northern Ireland borstal to the present day. This interest in sport has been cultivated by succeeding generations of borstal officers[108] but it is unlikely that the boys themselves will have needed encouragement. It is in the nature of things that a group of reasonably

---

[108] For observations on the function of sport in borstal institutions in promoting job-satisfaction among borstal staff, see A. E. Bottoms and F. H. McClintock, *Criminals Coming of Age* (London: Heinemann, 1973), pp. 127–28.

tough young adult males should enjoy sport and games;[109] their interest in them has not unexpectedly outlived the annual camp, the Ballywalter picnic and the scout troop.

Swimming facilities have always been available.[110] As long ago as 1904 a swimming pool was constructed for the institution at Malone, and after the borstal itself was set up on the same site, the pool was to be fully exploited. Every boy at the borstal was given the opportunity to learn to swim, to be taught life-saving and even to compete in swimming galas. There is as yet no pool at Woburn though one is planned. However, swimming from the beach takes place in summer when the weather is fine, the tide is right and there are no crowds on the beach. A small boat, built by the boys themselves, is used for lifeguard duties.

Soccer teams were fielded early in the institution's history. In 1930 a team ended up fourth in the Northern Amateur League Table and during the same season several boys were selected to play in representative matches. In 1932 a team from the borstal reached the semi-final of the Irish Junior Shield. Thirty years later, in 1961, home and away fixtures were still being played regularly. The following year, however, the soccer team had to be withdrawn from the Northern Ireland Amateur League "as a steady balanced team to compete with the standard of opposition in the League could not be maintained." Friendly matches were substituted and these, together with inter-house fixtures, were said to have "provided keen and healthy competition."

Pre-eminent among the other sports catered for has been boxing. In 1932 the borstal was affiliated to the Ulster Amateur Boxing Association and in the same year an annual boxing fixture was arranged with the boys of Campbell College, a public school. A boy from the institution won the Northern Ireland junior featherweight championship in 1948, and boxing tournaments were being held as frequently as once a fortnight in 1950. In 1961 boys from the borstal were permitted to box in places as far afield as Belfast, Lisburn, Newtownards and Kircubbin.

Cricket was popular in the nineteen thirties, as was badminton in the war years. In 1964 boys competed in local league table tennis and darts. Gymnastics and athletics have also been encouraged. The present gym at Woburn was opened in 1970 and among the equipment is some made by the boys themselves; in 1962 a trampolene was made in Woburn's own workshops. The *Reports* occasionally refer to the annual sports day, a feature of the year at both Malone and Woburn. Despite the bad

---

[109] Stratta in *The Education of Borstal Boys* offers, at p. 106, some data on the proportion of boys she surveyed who counted sport and other 'active' pursuits among their leisure activities prior to committal.

[110] For a modern assessment of the value of swimming facilities for inmates of penal institutions, see Report of the Advisory Council on the Penal System, *The Régime for Long-term Prisoners in Conditions of Maximum Security* (London: H.M.S.O., 1968), p. 47.

weather at the Malone sports of 1929, "the various events", so that year's *Report* records, "were contested by the lads with the utmost enthusiasm and in a spirit of keen friendly rivalry, the gymnasium class giving a most interesting and efficient display." "The keen interest" and "competitive spirit" displayed at the Woburn sports of 1963 is likewise commended in a brief reference in the *Report* for that year.

A range of less strenuous recreational pursuits has always been on offer. An unusual option during the years at Malone was folk-dancing. After its introduction in 1933, it was soon reported that it had been "taken up with enthusiasm by the boys and . . . has in no small degree helped to keep the boys in a happy and contented frame of mind." The remarkable benefits of folk-dancing were not, however, available to all and sundry: a boy had to show keenness at his tasks in the institution. Folk-dancing flourished during the war years when displays were given regularly, and in 1947 a team of dancers appeared at a four-day military tattoo held at the Balmoral Showgrounds in Belfast under the auspices of the British Legion. The boys concerned later went on tour to Portrush, Newcastle and Lurgan. These boys' counterparts in 1964 might well have been envious: a 'treat' that year was to serve as 'arena boys' at horseshows at Carrowdore, Newtownards and Balmoral.

During the war years, there was a weekly dance at Malone, the music being provided by a band composed principally of borstal boys.[111] The success of the band, as of many of the other recreational activities, owed much to the voluntary outside workers. Soon after the Malone borstal was opened, they were on hand to give instruction in drawing and singing. The singing classes led to the formation of an institution choir which it was hoped to enter for the choral competition at the Belfast *feis* in 1932. Students from Queen's University were among the first of these outside workers. Also prominent was a group of women who formed themselves into a committee and who began instruction in handicrafts in 1932. The handicrafts class was extended soon after it started and at the end of 1932 the results of the boys' work were exhibited at a small sale of work. Rugs and basket and barbola work were on display, as were leather, fretwork and woodwork products. Recruitment for the handicrafts class was restricted in much the same way as recruitment to the folk-dancing circle. Instruction in all these various hobbies was officially welcomed on the grounds that it improved the boys' education and helped brighten their outlook. The classes, of course, also enabled the boys to come into contact with outsiders who had no preconceptions about them.[112]

[111] Who was danced with is not mentioned, but I have subsequently learnt that parties of girls were brought to Malone.
[112] See *The Régime for Long-term Prisoners in Conditions of Maximum Security*, p. 46.

In the war years the wife of the governor at Malone organised quizzes and whist-drives: the boys were split into teams of twelve and prizes went to the winners.[113] Generally, however, the entertainment at Malone and Woburn—plays, concerts, lectures, debates, film shows and even wrestling bouts—has been provided by outsiders. During the war, the boys at Malone were admitted free once a month to a local cinema. The entertainment committee of Toc H was showing films at Malone on a regular basis in 1947, and film shows have continued at Woburn despite the installation of television in 1961. A debating society was holding meetings at Woburn in 1962. It discussed topics selected by the boys themselves and was affiliated to a similar society at Queen's University, members from which participated in the debates.

Discharge

Release procedure has twice been altered. Before 1953 sentences were indeterminate: two to three years followed by a year's liability to recall. Release could be effected under licence prior to expiry of sentence but the offender remained liable to recall for a year beyond the termination of his sentence, irrespective of when he was released. Under the Act of 1953, all sentences were indeterminate within a three-year period but, whenever a boy was released, his supervision, and thus his liability to recall, ended exactly three years after the date on which he received his sentence. The 1968 Act has changed the procedure yet again. Under it, all sentences are indeterminate within a two-year period. Supervision, and hence liability to recall, continue for twelve months from the date of release.[114]

Before 1953, release on licence usually occurred at the end of two years. Release was sanctioned by the executive following the recommendation of the visiting committee. In the early years, this committee also constituted the Borstal Association and was thus enabled in a dual capacity to maintain contact with each boy; in 1928, for example, the committee was inquiring into each boy's capabilities, character and home background and pronouncing on the suitability of the job to which it was proposed to send him on discharge.[115] Under the second schedule to the Prison Act (N.I.) 1953, it was provided that release (under supervision) had to occur not later than three years from the date of sentence and never earlier than nine months from that date, save in exceptional circumstances. In fact, release usually took place between eighteen and twenty-four months after the date of sentence. Rule 179 of the Prison Rules stipulated

[113] Fahy, "Borstal in Ireland", 77.
[114] 1968 Act, s. 11(2).
[115] *Home Office Services Report 1928*, p. 18.

that release could not occur earlier than two years from the date of sentence unless the boy had previously enjoyed "special treatment", i.e. had been promoted to the top grade. A new rule introduced in 1957 also provided that a reduction in grade was not of itself to affect the period of detention.[116] The changes in the minimum and maximum length of sentence, introduced by the 1968 Act, have had their inevitable effect. The new position, following amendments to the second schedule in the 1953 Prison Act, is that release cannot take place later than two years or earlier than six months from the date of sentence.[117] Since 1953, the recommendation for release has been made in the first instance by the reviewing body to the visiting committee,[118] and the latter, in turn, have reported to the executive.

Rule 179 of the Prison Rules stipulates that no borstal prisoner is to be released until the executive is satisfied "that suitable arrangements for his settlement after release have been made." During World War II, the armed forces facilitated 'settlement': no less than 103 boys joined up on discharge, four of whom were to be killed in action.[119] In peacetime the problem has been intensified by the comparatively high level of unemployment. In 1932, for instance, the general unemployment delayed release and produced a longer average period of detention. The *Report* for 1932 insisted that this longer period was not to be interpreted as adversely reflecting on the borstal system. It was not

> . . . attributable in any way to misconduct on the part of the inmates, or to any necessity for detaining them for a longer period owing to the lack of success in their training, but rather to the state of the labour market. It has become increasingly difficult, owing to the prevailing unemployment, to find suitable work for the inmates at the termination of two years of their sentence. Accordingly, the Visiting Committee consider that it would not be in the inmates' own interest to discharge them on licence without first ascertaining that there was a definite chance of immediate employment. It is obvious that temptation to resort to their old mode of life, and perhaps to undesirable associations, is far more likely to be the lot of lads who, through no fault of their own, have no option but to remain in their homes with nothing to engage their attention, or to wander the streets or countryside in search of employment.

In recent years the priority given to finding a job for a discharged

[116] Prison (Amendment) Rules (N.I.) 1957, rule 9.
[117] 1968 Act, s. 11(1).
[118] The committee is appointed under the Prison Act (N.I.) 1953, s. 11.
[119] *Home Office Services Report 1939–46*, p. 19.

inmate has reduced the chances of these difficulties artificially delaying the time of release. Of course, none exist in the case of boys benefiting from the scheme of employment on parole.

A boy is usually discharged into civilian employment. However, there have been discharges to mental hospitals and, during World War II, there were instances of transfer to the military authorities and of deportation over the Border. At the present time, some difficulty is caused by the offender who, whilst actually undergoing his sentence, is prosecuted for another offence and is liable to receive a second sentence. One such situation is dealt with by the second schedule to the Prison Act (N.I.) 1953 which provides, where it applies, that the first sentence is to cease to have effect. The rule applies to a second sentence of borstal detention, in the limited cases where this is permitted,[120] and will also apply to a subsequent sentence of detention in a young offenders centre. Another problem is that of the offender who on a previous occasion received a suspended sentence and who then commits a second offence for which he is sent to borstal. Does such an offender, on release from borstal, have to serve the suspended sentence? Administrative practice and, since 1968, legislation, have provided that the intermediate imposition of a borstal sentence cancels the effect of the suspended sentence.[121]

After-care

On 22 March 1927, Sir Dawson Bates announced his intention to form a Borstal Association for the new institution, and said that he would be glad to have the services of any interested MP.[122] A year later, on 27 February 1928, the constitution of the Borstal Association was approved by the Governor of Northern Ireland, as required under the Criminal Justice Administration Act 1914.[123]

The Association's main concern was with the after-care of boys discharged on licence. It appointed a welfare officer and through both him and its own members "endeavoured to secure jobs and give support and assistance in the struggle against relapsing into vicious courses." Recognition of the Association under section 7 of the 1914 Act meant that it could secure a contribution from public funds. In 1928 the Association received £250 from that source, representing a grant of £1 for every £1 raised by private subscription, and this sum was devoted to the salary of the Association's welfare officer, the fund for discharged boys and the

---

[120] 1968 Act, s. 10(2).
[121] For the position prior to 1968, see Nial Osborough, "The Suspended Sentence in Northern Ireland", *The Irish Jurist* (*new series*), II (1967), 30 at 38; for that since 1968, see the 1968 Act, s. 18(4) and compare England's Criminal Justice Act 1967, s. 39.
[122] *H. C. Debates* (N.I.), Vol. 8, col. 238.
[123] *Home Office Services Report 1927*, p. 19.

fund to defray initial expenditure. In 1929 the grant totalled £102 and in the next year had risen to £120. In 1932 a decrease in receipts led the Association to express the hope that its activities would not be hampered for lack of support. There was a broadcast appeal for funds in 1935 and three years later the limit of the Exchequer contribution to the funds of the Association was stated to be £150.[124]

The Association still exists, but its functions have become relatively minor, a casualty (like the concept of a part-time probation service) of dissatisfaction with unregulated voluntary effort. At the present time, any funds which the Association has are devoted to such things as Christmas festivities and prizes for sports day. Discharge grants are still paid through the Association but this is little more than a book-keeping transaction.

In the early years, the main burden of after-care fell on the Association's welfare officer. In 1932 he was issuing quarterly reports on the circumstances of each boy discharged, either on licence or under supervision. A discharge to the armed forces during World War II or later caused no problem, but one to civilian employment always created difficulty. The complaint was often made that few employers appreciated the function of the Borstal Association. In other years, even if employers were aware of the Association's purpose, jobs were not always easy to obtain or, in an area of continuing unemployment, easy to hold on to.

In 1948 the first full-time welfare officer was appointed. Two years later he was complaining that it was hard to obtain employment because the usual number of discharges had trebled, but, by 1952, personal canvassing had resulted in all boys being found jobs. In 1951, the officer complained of the difficulty of finding lodgings for discharged boys, and in 1955 of the special problem of finding jobs for them in country areas. In 1954 the importance of after-care was stressed by the adoption of a rule which required staff in all penal institutions to consider the question of after-care from the very moment inmates began to serve their sentence.[125] Possibly a more dramatic change, so far as borstal after-care was concerned, was the transfer of responsibility to the probation service. Power to effect this arrangement was implicit in section 41 of the Prison Act (N.I.) 1953.[126]

The task was thus handed over to the probation service from a housemaster notionally responsible to the increasingly remote Borstal Association. This step had first been recommended in 1938 when it was also suggested that local juvenile welfare committees might likewise

---

[124] *Lynn Report*, p. 167.
[125] Prison Rules (N.I.) 1954, rule 103.
[126] See, too, the 1968 Act, s. 27.

assist.[127] In recent years the after-care load has been shared between full-time officers of the probation service and a part-time officer who is a former member of the staff of the Malone Training School. The division of case loads was mainly one of convenience but the feeling that boys should be supervised by someone of their own religious denomination was also taken into account, and the arrangement enabled this to be done.

[127] *Lynn Report*, p. 167. Some juvenile welfare committees were established in England, but few survived the war: Hood, *Borstal Re-Assessed*, p. 175.

CHAPTER IV

Borstal in the South 1922-1956

I happened to meet with some reports from a Governor of the Richmond Bridewell addressed to the magistrates of the Head Police Office during the time when that prison was under their exclusive control and supervision. In one of these documents the writer states the building to be in good repair, and perfectly adapted for the safe custody of its inmates, and that every ward was in a clean and wholesome condition. He proceeds to describe the good effects produced by the use he made of a barber, who, for riotous and disorderly conduct, had been committed for two months with hard labour. He had not put the delinquent to stone-breaking or oakum-picking but employed him in shaving and haircutting of the other prisoners, the effect of which was to improve their appearance, and to impart cleanly tendencies. He then expresses his regret that the barber's term of imprisonment had elapsed, and that the prisoners had become less cleanly-looking from remaining unshaven and uncropt. He terminates the report by earnestly and most respectfully suggesting to 'their worships' to avail themselves of the first opportunity that may offer for committing another barber for the longest term in their power.

F. T. Porter, a police magistrate in early Victorian Dublin, in his *Gleanings and Reminiscences* (2nd ed. Dublin, 1875).

Any account of the institutional treatment of young adult offenders in the Irish Republic must recognise the significance of the year 1956. Up till then, provision was made for a true borstal system and an institution existed which was administered on borstal lines. This system remained faithful to the primary task of providing training for selected young adult offenders in the age-group 16 to 21. The authorities admitted the system's defects and in the nineteen forties were to set about eliminating some of them.

Early in the history of the Free State, there was talk of dispensing with the borstal system, but it was not until the nineteen fifties that abandonment was seriously contemplated when judicial reluctance to impose borstal sentences forced the issue. Annual committals became insufficient to ensure the survival of an institution ostensibly devoted to borstal training and in 1956 the borstal system as such began to be phased out.

Alternative accommodation somewhere in the Republic had to be found for the detention of young adult male offenders. This was made available in Dublin in premises which were given the same name that the borstal at Clonmel had held since 1948. The 'new' St Patrick's Institution still serves this same need. Here, a 'home' and a 'training' of sorts are provided for young men aged 16 to 21. Since 1968, selected inmates have been eligible for transfer to the open institution at Shanganagh Castle, County Dublin, and since 1973, alternatively, to a second open institution, Loughan House, County Cavan.

Law

Reform of the court structure of the Free State in 1924 had little impact on the arrangements for committal to borstal. The Central Criminal Court and the Circuit Court assumed the powers of the former assize and county courts (quarter sessions) and the district courts took over the responsibilities of the former courts of summary jurisdiction.[1] The conditions that had to be met before a borstal sentence could be imposed remained those which had been set out in the Acts of 1908 and 1914.

However, there were changes to do with the right of appeal. The establishment of a Court of Criminal Appeal[2] enabled appeals to be brought from borstal sentences passed by the Central Criminal Court in *every* case, and by the Circuit Court in *any* case where sentence had followed conviction before it. Otherwise, there was no such right, as the Court of Criminal Appeal itself confirmed in *Caffrey*[3] in 1937. Caffrey had been convicted by a district court and then, under the

---

[1] Courts of Justice Act 1924.
[2] Courts of Justice Act 1924, s. 8.
[3] Court of Criminal Appeal, 8 December 1937; Robert L. Sandes, *Criminal Practice, Procedure and Evidence in Eire*, 2nd ed. (London: Sweet & Maxwell, 1939), p. 169. S. 10(5) of the 1908 Act provided for an appeal in such circumstances in England.

procedure laid down in the 1914 Act, had been forwarded for sentence to the Circuit Court. No appeal lay from the Circuit Court sentence. A series of more recent cases was also to highlight the absence of a right of appeal where the Circuit Court exercised a similar derivative criminal jurisdiction.[4]

The new district courts were professionally manned, unlike the previous courts of summary jurisdiction, but restrictions on sentencing powers were nonetheless maintained. The continuance of these restrictions was censured and critics drew attention to the inevitable and unwholesome delay between district court conviction and Circuit Court sentence. There was opposition, also, to the reluctance of the authorities to avail of a provision in the 1914 Act[5] which enabled a person forwarded to the superior court for sentence to be detained in the interim in borstal rather than prison. "The policy of the law," Edward Fahy wrote in 1941,[6]

> which admittedly and rightly aims at keeping youthful offenders *out* of prison, save in the very last resort, has been utterly defeated by a practice for which, owing to the existence today of a professional magistracy, there is no longer any justification. It is clearly wrong that a boy who has been convicted summarily must first get maybe several months of prison, with its accompanying stigma and possibly evil associations, before the commencement of his Borstal sentence, whereas a boy who has been convicted on indictment of a much more serious offence is sent direct to the institution.

As a remedy, Fahy himself proposed the adoption of one of three policies: (i) permitting the district court to sentence directly to borstal; (ii) using the authority in the 1914 Act to transfer the potential borstal detainee to borstal itself pending sentence; (iii) establishing remand institutions.

Nothing was done and until 1960 the position appears to have remained, as before, that district courts could not sentence to borstal. Some uncertainty in the matter, now solely a historical curiosity, is introduced by the words of section 24 of the Criminal Justice Act 1951. This section, in order, as it was put, "to remove doubt", conferred power on the

---

[4] e.g., *The People (A.G.) v. Tyrrell* [1970] I.R. 294, noted, *The Irish Jurist (new series)*, V (1970), 89. All the cases involved defendants who, having signed pleas of guilty before the district court and been forwarded for sentence to the Circuit Court (Criminal Procedure Act 1967, s. 13), had then discovered that they had no right of appeal against whatever sentence the Circuit Court had imposed. The defect in the law was cured by the Criminal Procedure (Amendment) Act 1973, s. 1.

[5] 1914 Act, s. 10(3).

[6] Fahy, "Borstal in Ireland", at 73.

Circuit Court to entertain appeals against various orders made by the district court, including that of a borstal sentence. The provision undoubtedly envisaged the passing of borstal sentences by the district court; whether it is capable of being interpreted as conferring a broad sentencing power is more difficult to determine. It has not been unknown for Irish courts to impose sentences for which there has been no clear legal authority—suspended sentences awarded at all levels, including that of the district or magistrates' court,[7] are one example and special custodial arrangements for young female offenders in the absence of borstal facilities[8] are another—but section 24 probably does not represent some belated authorisation of a sentencing practice which had become commonplace. The section may merely have been designed to ensure a right of appeal in the sole instance where the 1908 Act did authorise the lower court to sentence directly to borstal, that is, on conviction for the offence of a breach of reformatory school rules.[9] Certainly, no official source suggests that before 1960 the district justice ever exercised a wider sentencing jurisdiction.

Between 1924 and 1956 sentencing matters were considered by the Court of Criminal Appeal on four known occasions. In *Doyle* (1930),[10] the accused had been convicted of uttering counterfeit coins and was sentenced to three years in borstal. The Court was not convinced that this was the proper sentence and offered to substitute a short term of imprisonment in view of the age and unusual abilities of the accused. It says something for the manner in which the Court, as then constituted, carried out its task, for its members then left it to Doyle to choose. He opted to stay in borstal.

In *Page* (1931),[11] the accused, aged 16, had been convicted of carnal knowledge of a girl under 13 for which he had been given five years penal servitude. The Court again thought that the sentence was wrong and considered substituting a period of borstal detention. It was then told that the authorities at the borstal would be reluctant to receive Page because of the nature of his crime. The Court finally decided to reduce the original sentence to one of three years penal servitude and ordered Page to be included in the special régime for juvenile adults at Mountjoy Prison.

---

[7] *R.* v. *Wightman* [1950] N.I. 124; *Irish Law Times and Solicitors' Journal*, LIX(1925), 16; Nial Osborough, "The Suspended Sentence in Northern Ireland", *The Irish Jurist* (*new series*), II (1967), 30.

[8] *Cussen Report*, pp. 47–49; *Kennedy Report*, p. 39; below, chapter 6.

[9] 1908 Act, s. 2.

[10] Court of Criminal Appeal, 30 April 1930; Sandes, *Criminal Practice, Procedure and Evidence in Eire*, p. 177.

[11] Court of Criminal Appeal, 16 March 1931; Sandes, op. cit., pp. 169 and 177. Sandes describes Page as a "sexual pervert", but there is no evidence of this in the court records.

In *Carolan* (1943),[12] the dispute turned on what, for purposes of the 1908 Act, amounted to proof of criminal tendencies. The accused had been convicted of breaking and entering. He had one previous conviction, in 1938, for house-breaking and stealing two packets of cigarettes. On that occasion, he had been discharged under the terms of the Probation of Offenders Act 1907, although he was made to pay compensation. Carolan was a casual labourer with a poor education. The Court of Criminal Appeal set aside the borstal sentence and substituted twelve-months suspended imprisonment. The report before the Court was no grounds for holding that Carolan had criminal tendencies and it was not enough that the trial judge held the view that it would be to Carolan's advantage for him to be sent to borstal.[13]

McMahon, Whelan and others (1949)[14] was the converse of *Carolan*. In this case, six young men were all sent to borstal for two years by the Circuit Court judge. The official report on Whelan indicated that he was 'suitable for borstal' even though he had no previous convictions; the report on McMahon was ambiguous and no reports on the others were presented. In the Court of Criminal Appeal it was sought to quash the sentences because of their severity. It was also claimed that a trial judge could only send to borstal where there existed an official suitability report which recommended such a course of action. The Court disagreed. Provided, Maguire C.J. declared, that the trial judge had sufficient evidence before him, he was entitled to form his own judgment as to whether an offender suffered from criminal tendencies and thus qualified for borstal; the furnishing of a report was not an essential prerequisite for the imposition of a borstal sentence. All the sentences were affirmed.

The attitude of the Court of Criminal Appeal in this last case anticipated a subsequent development in Irish constitutional law which emphasises the primacy of the judge in the sentencing function.[15]

Accommodation

For most of the time between 1922 and 1956 the borstal institution was located at Clonmel in the same buildings which were first designated for this purpose in 1906. From mid-1922 to 1924, and again from 1940 to 1947, premises elsewhere were used.

Administrative responsibility for the penal institutions in the twenty-six counties was handed over to the provisional government early in 1922. Shortly afterwards, the outbreak of the Civil War forced the new borstal administrators to adopt a succession of makeshift arrangements.

---

[12] [1943] Ir. Jur. Rep. 49.
[13] Compare the Northern Ireland case of *R. v. Hayes*: above, chapter 3.
[14] *Irish Law Times and Solicitors' Journal*, LXXXIII (1949), 170.
[15] See, in particular, *Deaton* v. *A.G.* [1963] I.R. 170 and *The State* (O.) v. *O'Brien* [1973] I.R. 50.

In the summer of 1922 the premises at Clonmel were needed by the National Army, so the borstal was moved to the workhouse at Clogheen. The Clogheen building was selected hurriedly but it happened to be a reasonable choice. At any rate, Kevin O'Higgins, the Minister for Home Affairs, said so in the Dáil in October: "The place is in perfect repair, is lighted throughout with electricity and is provided with an independent water supply and up-to-date sanitary accommodation. There is all the necessary accommodation for inmates, officers, workshops and gymnasium."[16] No definitive assessment was ever made, for the following month, November, the premises were burnt down by incendiaries. The *Prisons Board Report* for 1922-23 tells what happened next:

> This arson necessitated the inmates being removed first to Cahir and then to Clonmel where they were housed until their transfer to Kilkenny, at which place a portion of the Union buildings had been acquired for them as a temporary measure.

Official records say little on this extraordinary tale of the fugitive borstal. However, the relevant *Appropriation Accounts* do show an increase in travelling expenses for borstal staff, as well as a saving on the rent of two small fields at Clonmel.[17] Of greater interest, perhaps, is the high number of escapes disclosed in the year's *Prisons Board Report*.

The borstal remained at Kilkenny until 1924. The usual 'industries' were established but the arrangements were unsatisfactory and did not impress the members of the Moles Committee from Northern Ireland who visited Kilkenny in 1923.[18] Nor did members of that committee view with favour conditions at the permanent base in Clonmel.

They were not the first to be critical. Before 1922 the Prisons Board itself had on several occasions attacked the restricted space and the unsuitable buildings; indeed, in 1920, it had drafted plans for a number of improvements. The political events in the years which followed lessened the prospects for the implementation of any of these schemes but the Board itself did not abandon hope, as is clear from its plea in 1923 for the purchase of a large farm "where boys could be taught every operation in farm work and in which they could get completely rid of slum ideas and the happy-go-lucky idleness of street life." However, the return to Clonmel in 1924 brought no obvious improvements. In 1927, the last year of its existence, the Board again drew attention to "the drawbacks of Clonmel, both from

---

[16] *Dáil Debates*, Vol. 1, col. 1639, 18 October 1922.
[17] *Appropriation Accounts 1922-23*, p. 36.
[18] *Moles Report*, p. 25; above, chapter 3. Further details in the rest of this chapter, unless otherwise indicated, are taken from the annual *Prisons Board Reports* or, after 1928, from the annual *Prison Reports*.

the point of view of location and facilities for the employment of boys on outdoor work." Clonmel is a little more than 100 miles from Dublin and such early criticism of the location is worth noting. No official response is recorded.

On the abolition of the Prisons Board in 1928, direct responsibility for prison and borstal administration was transferred to the Department of Justice. Any separate identity for the Prisons Board in the last months of its existence is hard to establish but, in defence of the Board and its functions, it is only necessary to glance at the ten or so years which followed. With the exception of the year 1934, whatever actually took place, a silence envelops borstal administration. Indeed, as regards physical conditions, on which the official prison report is not usually slow to provide details, the only recorded development is again for 1934: the installation that year of electric light. The Irish Prisons Board had never been so reticent.

In November 1940 the premises at Clonmel were commandeered for a second time by the military. The borstal moved on this occasion to Cork Prison where it stayed until 1947. Fahy, who knew the institutions at both Clonmel and Cork, had difficulty in understanding "exactly how either of these buildings came to be chosen as a place wherein youthful minds and characters could get a new outlook and a new bent." On balance, however, he found the premises at Cork to be slightly superior even if they were only intended to be used temporarily.[19] The building was not all stone, it did not have four-and-a-half feet wide cells or a high wall; in addition, it boasted a four-and-a-half acre garden. On the other hand, arrangements for recreation were poor. A small yard at the back of the building was used for football. "In this yard," Fahy wrote, "reminiscent of the days when stonebreaking was a form of hard labour, the visitor may still see the stone cubicles formerly used by the prisoners. That it is totally unsuitable for any proper recreation is self-evident." At a later date, both outdoor and indoor recreational facilities at Cork were to be substantially improved.[20]

Transferring the borstal to Cork had the unexpected dividend of awakening politicians' interest in the borstal. At intervals between 1940 and 1946 there was a series of exchanges in the Dáil. In October 1940 questions put by deputy James Dillon forced the government of the day to admit that better borstal premises were needed. It was a Pyrrhic victory. Dillon was bluntly told that the provision of a fresh building or the adaptation of an existing one would be an expensive business[21] and he failed in his efforts to get funds for a new building on an allocation

[19] Fahy, "Borstal in Ireland", p. 80.
[20] Below, chapter 8.
[21] Dáil Debates, Vol. 81, col. 160, 16 October 1940.

under the Employment Schemes Vote.[22] The following year Dillon urged the setting up of an inquiry into "what masquerades as a borstal system here."[23] The request for the inquiry was turned down, but Dillon's criticisms and the personal concern of the Minister for Justice, Gerald Boland, were to lead to the adoption of several improvements in the régime at Cork.

A change in location was also promised. In March 1942 the government announced that it was looking for alternative premises nearer Dublin,[24] but by July nowhere suitable had been found. The setback did not augur well. That same month the government declared that it was still hopeful that fresh accommodation might be found even if it proved necessary to look further afield;[25] in any event—and the qualification is important—nothing could be done until the end of the war. Hopes were again raised and a final stage appeared to have been reached at last when, in November 1944, Boland told the Dáil that a site had been provisionally selected near Dublin.[26]

There was to be no development at any new site. In October 1946 Boland announced another change of plan. The borstal was, after all, simply to be transferred back to Clonmel. Any new building, he tritely observed, could not be ready at once. The decision to use the premises at Cork exclusively for short-term prisoners left Boland with no alternative. He did not disguise the fact that the decision to return to Clonmel was not an ideal solution but added that conditions at Clonmel were superior to those at Cork: Clonmel had large rooms for use as workshops, classes and refectories and enjoyed better recreational facilities, both indoor and outdoor.[27] Fahy's conclusion, it may be recalled, was the exact opposite. Boland also had a plan, it transpired later,[28] to purchase a farm as an adjunct to the institution at Clonmel, even if it was some distance away. In the Dáil Dillon bitterly attacked Boland's announcement, reminding the minister that he had himself referred to Clonmel as a "dirty, damp, antediluvian prison." Dillon's principal objection was to the size of the cells at Clonmel. His description of them is telling. The return to Clonmel would entail, he declared, that "the boys will be sleeping in cells described as turf cellars at Portlaoighaise."[29]

The deterioration of the condition of the Clonmel premises delayed the return there until January 1947, something which enabled a complete

---

[22] *Dáil Debates*, Vol. 81, col. 351, 6 November 1940.
[23] *Dáil Debates*, Vol. 84, cols. 2513–14, 17 September 1941.
[24] *Dáil Debates*, Vol. 85, col. 2070, 4 March 1942.
[25] *Dáil Debates*, Vol. 88, cols. 287–89, 9 July 1942.
[26] *Dáil Debates*, Vol. 95, col. 1210, 30 November 1944.
[27] *Dáil Debates*, Vol. 103, col. 75, 23 October 1946; cols. 892–96, 14 November 1946.
[28] *Dáil Debates*, Vol. 183, col. 598, 29 June 1960: Mr Loughman.
[29] *Dáil Debates*, Vol. 103, cols. 75–76, 23 October 1946.

renovation to take place. It was at this time that many of the objectionable features of the former prison were removed. Old buildings and walls disappeared. The authorities also dispensed with the iron bars on windows and the iron gates with their heavy locks. Outside, stone flags were replaced by coloured cement and the main square was broken up and divided into grass lawns intersected by gravel paths. Flower beds were planted and the garden, which had fallen into neglect during the occupation by the military, was reclaimed and tilled.

In subsequent years the authorities pressed on with other improvements. One change effected in 1948 was of some psychological interest: an open-barred gate was installed at the entrance. For the first time it was possible for the grounds of the institution to be viewed from outside. Other recorded developments are the minutiae of year-by-year progress. In 1948 several buildings were replastered and coated with pebble-dash; there were renovations, too, in the dormitory wing, where cubicles had replaced the cells. The next year saw the installation of shower baths and dressing cubicles and the building and furnishing of a new reception hall, and in 1950 the old store room was converted into a reading room and new sinks and a range were fitted in the kitchen. In 1951 two new buildings, a fuel store and a greenhouse, were put up and work began on the repair and renovation of the chapel.

In 1948 the premises at Clonmel were formally redesignated 'St Patrick's Institution'.

Régime

A strict grading system had been introduced at Clonmel by the Prisons Board regulations of 1909. This continued after 1922 and indeed the regulations themselves were not finally revoked until 1960. Though the rules remained the same, the manner in which they were applied could vary, and the contrast between 1941 and 1948 was considerable.

The system introduced in 1909 had divided boys into three grades: 'ordinary' (for all boys on entry), 'special' (to mark satisfactory progress after six months) and 'penal' (to mark unsatisfactory progress). Promotion within the system was earned by industry, good behaviour and attention to instruction. In addition, marks were awarded (according to an approved scale) for industry and good conduct, and these entitled the boys to a gratuity. Good conduct badges could also be earned by boys in the special grade and each badge entitled its recipient to an extra gratuity. This system survived unchanged after 1922.

The severe régime did not appear to have been appreciably altered by 1941, to judge from Fahy's account of that date.[30] Boys in penal

---

[30] Fahy, "Borstal in Ireland", 79-85.

grade were denied visits, letters and the right to earn gratuities. Boys in ordinary (who wore distinguishing brown shorts) were permitted both to write and receive a letter once every six weeks and to receive, with the same frequency, one visit lasting twenty minutes. Boys in special could write and receive one letter per week and were allowed to receive every week one visit lasting thirty minutes. "These privileges", Fahy wrote, "are practically the only reliefs of a monotonous and deadly existence." The *Prisons Report* for 1934 differs on one detail: it refers to visits and letters being allowed once a week (and also adds that small parcels of fruit and cake were permitted at Christmas and Easter). It would be difficult to disagree with Fahy's conclusion that the atmosphere was no different from that in prison.

Fahy bases his conclusion in part on these details of the daily routine:

6.30 a.m.	Rise, make bed, clean and tidy cell.
7.00	Wash.
7.15	Ordinary grade boys: Sokol drill. Special grade boys: Fatigues.
7.50	Breakfast.
8.30	Return to cells (locked).
9.30	Cells unlocked. Work in workshops, garden and school.
12.20 p.m.	Dinner in association.
1.00	Return to cells (locked).
2.00	Cells unlocked. Work as in the morning.
4.30	Supper.
5.00	Return to cells (locked).
5.30	Cells unlocked. Prayers. Drill.
6.30	Ordinary grade locked in for the night. Special grade recreation period.
7.30	Special grade locked in for the night. Final light meal in cells.
8.30	Lights out.

There was respite from this routine on Saturday afternoons. Sundays, too, were different. Boys were roused at 7.00 a.m., were locked in after supper at 4.30 p.m. and given their last light meal in their cells at 6.30. Lights out was an hour earlier, at 7.30.

At Cork, a number of changes were to be introduced, the most critical of which, occurring in 1942, was to make tolerable the later return to Clonmel and its small cells. This was the practice of unlocking cell doors between 7 a.m. and 10 p.m. to enable boys to remain in association at work, at exercise and in recreation throughout the entire day.[31] Of equal significance, following an outspoken Labour Party report,[32] was the revision of prison regulations governing visits and letters and a change in the rules on early lock-up on Sundays and holy days and on the time of lights out.[33]

The daily routine of 1948 was proof of the far-reaching effect of these reforms:[34]

7.00 a.m.	Inmates rise, wash, shave, etc.
7.20 to 8.20	Physical training (Sokol drill).
8.20	Breakfast.
8.45 to 9.30	Inmates clean and prepare cubicles and dormitories.
9.30 to 12.30 p.m.	Work and secular instruction.
12.30 to 2.00	Dinner and recreation.
2.00 to 4.30	Work.
4.30	Tea.
5.00 to 5.15	Inmates go to chapel for recital of rosary.
5.15 to 9.45	Recreation with supper at 8.30 p.m.
9.45	Inmates retire to cubicles and prepare for bed.
10.00	Lights out.

On Sundays, mass was celebrated at 8.45 a.m. and boys were allowed to remain in bed for an hour longer. Recreation and games took the place of work and secular instruction. Thursday had become the weekly half-day and boys stopped work at 12.30 p.m.

The promotion system, and the privileges associated with it, still remained. All boys could now participate in recreation but extra privileges had been introduced for every boy who had successfully completed his first six months. These included the rights to go on a cycle run on Sunday afternoons or a long walk on the weekly half-day, to be taken to one of the local cinemas in the afternoons by a member of the Borstal Association,[35] and to receive a monthly food parcel.[36] Another innovation was the creation of positions of trust within the institution. One boy was placed in charge of the main gate, to which he held the key, another looked after the library and chapel, and a third helped the store-keeper and was allowed into town on messages.[37]

[31] Dáil Debates, Vol. 88, cols. 1292–93, 15 October 1942.
[32] Prisons and Prisoners in Ireland: Report on Certain Aspects of Prison Conditions in Port-laoighise Convict Prison (Dublin: for the Labour Party, 1946).
[33] The Labour Party Report had drawn special attention to the time spent in cells over the Whitsun weekend by certain prisoners at Portlaoise.
[34] Clonmel Notes, p. 20.
[35] ibid., p. 15.
[36] p. 9.
[37] p. 13.

There were further changes later in 1948. In October, smoking was allowed; it had first been granted over a year before at the prison in Portlaoise.[38] In December, the daily routine was altered once again when the working day was made to correspond more closely to that followed by people in the country at large. One result was that compulsory physical training was switched to the evening.

In the ensuing years the nature of the régime was perceptibly affected by the admixture of an increasing number of boys who were prison transfers and not usually subject to lengthy detention.

The régime was supported throughout by a variety of punishments. Muffs and irons existed at Clonmel at least until as late as 1940, but were rarely employed. There was provision too for confinement and dietary punishment, but, after the return to Clonmel in 1947, the main, if not the exclusive, form of punishment was the loss of remission of sentence or loss of privilege. The loss of the privilege of smoking was thought to be a particularly powerful deterrent. In the last resort, power existed to transfer to prison any boy who fell into the blanket category of 'incorrigible'.

In 1948 the visiting committee went to unusual lengths to point out that corporal punishment was not, and never had been, allowed,[39] and added, by way of afterthought, a short comment on the general approach to discipline at the time:

> The Borstal boy has a full and busy day and regulations governing his behaviour are chiefly related to the maintenance of good order and discipline. The discipline, therefore, cannot be said to be rigid or harsh, rather is it the discipline of a well-ordered and busy life.[40]

Work

In penal institutions committed to rehabilitation, two separate approaches have influenced the choice of employment for inmates. Under the first, the employment is seen as 'regenerative', capable of contributing to the reform of the offender within the institution; under the second, as 'vocational', enabling the institution to impart to the offender skills which he can make use of in a job after he leaves.[41] In Ireland, economic circumstances were to prevent the adoption of a programme of either regenerative or vocational training.

---

[38] The Labour Party *Report* again appears to have paved the way.
[39] The different position in Northern Ireland should be noted (above, chapter 3) and see below, chapter 8.
[40] *Clonmel Notes*, p. 16.
[41] For further discussion, see A. E. Bottoms and F. H. McClintock, *Criminals Coming of Age* (London: Heinemann, 1973), pp. 111 ff.

Both kinds were considered by the Prisons Board between 1923 and 1928 in a debate which it launched on the merits of farm, as opposed to industrial, training.[42] The best results could be achieved, the Board wrote in 1923–24, if a large agricultural farm were attached to the borstal. An identical view was expressed in the *Report* for 1926–27. Twenty-two out of the thirty-seven committals that year had been "homeless strays". "For this class of friendless and homeless castaways," the Board wrote, "there was no other proper effective means of influencing them to become useful citizens than by continuing the discipline of the institution with employment on skilful farm work."[43] The merits of industrial training, on the other hand, were extolled in the *Report* for 1924–25, in a visionary passage where the Board discussed the minimum requirements of a policy which involved continuation of the borstal system.

Economic circumstances made the debate peculiarly sterile. No funds were ever made available for the purchase of a farm where regenerative or vocational agricultural employment could be provided. Nor was money supplied for the acquisition of "all the plant and accessories appertaining to a modern industrial workshop" demanded by the suggested programme of vocational training of 1924–25. The decision can be defended, perhaps, for the possibility of re-employment in a skilled job, given the state of the labour market, was soon seen to be remote.

The Prisons Board's ideals were not attained, and the familiar borstal 'industries' of bootmaking and tailoring continued to monopolise the work programme. The Board itself had accepted this alternative, but far from willingly. In its *Report* for 1926–27 it records that no less than thirty-two of that year's thirty-seven committals had come from Dublin, and continues:

> With the present condition of the labour market, we are not sanguine that such instruction as we are able to impart at Clonmel in trades, such as bootmaking and tailoring, will be very helpful in enabling the boys to find employment on their return to Dublin on discharge and neither are we satisfied that training in these trades is the best possible method for effecting an improvement in their moral well-being and outlook.

The Department of Justice, directly responsible for the borstal after 1928, would not have viewed the situation differently.

---

[42] Official thinking in the years before 1922 should be compared: above, chapter 2.
[43] Agricultural training was reckoned to be the key to success at other penal institutions within the Free State. See the views of James Fitzgerald Kenney, Minister for Justice, on training at Portlaoise Prison, given in an interview in 1927: Denis Gwynn, *The Irish Free State 1922–27* (London: Macmillan, 1928), p. 175.

There is no critical assessment of the quality of trade instruction at the borstal in the nineteen thirties, comparable to that which exists for reformatory and industrial schools in Appendix H to the *Cussen Report* of 1936.[44] Anyone wishing to draw a favourable conclusion can point to the confident tones in which training in tailoring and shoemaking is referred to in the general account of the borstal system presented in the 1934 *Prisons Report* and also to the same *Report*'s mention of the recent introduction of training in gardening. The sceptic, on the other hand, can point to the continued lack of a farm and a proper industrial workshop, to the absence of any instructor in tailoring between March 1929 and July 1930, and to the fact that in 1934 trade training appears to have been optional.

He may, if he so chooses, also place an unfavourable interpretation on other extant information: that the uniforms and boots produced were earmarked for the staffs at various penal institutions; that, because of the gardening instruction, the institution produced enough vegetables and nearly enough potatoes to satisfy its own needs; and that the boys were doing cooking, cleaning and laundry-work. None of this amounts to proof that choice of employment had ceased to be determined by the regenerative or vocational approach to borstal work but was determined, instead, by economic stringency. The impression nonetheless persists that the institution felt obliged to emphasise the extent to which it was economically self-supporting. In short, trade training may not have been any less conscientiously viewed but there is a strong hint that further improvements could not have been carried out because of financial constraints.

Changes took place during the years at Cork. General labouring was introduced, a step necessitated by the decision to use borstal labour on the demolition of a wing of Cork Prison and, later, on the restoration and renovation of the premises at Clonmel. Boys were taught carpentry and plumbing as well as general repairs, and were released to help in the harvest, a departure which had as a precedent the actions of Major Dobbin in 1917 and 1918.[45] Temporary day releases during the harvest period also occurred after the return to Clonmel, as in 1951.

The vocational approach dominated the choice of borstal work on the return to Clonmel. Tailoring had been temporarily successful at Cork but was now dropped and replaced by carpentry "as it was considered that training in cabinet-making and general wood-working would prove more useful . . . to inmates on discharge." In addition, the range of industries now embraced shoemaking, gardening and general labouring; all are comprehensively described both in the reports for the remaining

[44] *Cussen Report*, pp. 70-80; see also pp. 29-32 of the same *Report*.
[45] Above, chapter 2.

years and in a pamphlet entitled *The Borstal Institution at Clonmel* which was published by the visiting committee in 1948.[46]

In the carpentry course the boys made tables, chairs, stools, forms, lockers, wardrobes, presses, office desks, cabinets and picture frames. A voluntary evening class in fretwork and modelling was connected with the course. In 1950 classes were started in elementary geometry and mechanical drawing but results were stated to be discouraging because of both the shortness of the period of detention and the boys' low educational standards. Three years later the same factors were singled out to explain why it was difficult to bring the average boy in the carpentry course to a standard higher than that of a first-year apprentice, and why only a few boys had reached a standard which could be regarded as satisfactory. In these circumstances, it is remarkable that in 1954 a second carpentry course (in furniture-making) was introduced, to which boys were transferred when they demonstrated ability in general carpentry.

In the shoemaking group, boys made boots, shoes and slippers by hand, and were also taught repair work. After 1948 they had the assistance of a power-driven boot-finishing machine.

The gardening group grew flowers and vegetables; admission to the group was often reserved for country boys who had no desire or aptitude for other trades. As far as was practicable, each boy was placed in charge of a particular section of the gardens or grounds and this section or plot became his personal responsibility.

General labouring covered instruction in carpentry, plumbing, plastering and painting. Once a boy proved his proficiency, he was allowed to work on his own.

By 1948 a practice was established that on reception each boy was given a choice of trade where he spent a probationary month. If, at the end, a favourable report was received from his instructor, he was permitted to continue in the trade. A different procedure was followed in the case of juvenile adults transferred from prison. As far as possible, all non-instructive tasks in the institution were allocated to these boys, but even this rule of thumb had to be abandoned in the crisis which overtook Clonmel and its training programme in the nineteen fifties. In 1953 the low numbers at the institution forced a cessation of all training courses, and every boy, whether prison transfer or borstal detainee, was employed on general maintenance. Some improvement occurred the next year but it was optimistic to restart the shoemaking course and launch the second carpentry course, for, towards the end of 1955, the basic carpentry course had to be stopped and, although a few boys were kept at shoemaking, most were transferred once again to general maintenance.

---

[46] *Clonmel Notes*, pp. 11-13.

Education

The educational attainments of boys committed to the borstal were well below average. In 1927 the Prisons Board reported that two of the committals in the previous year were illiterate and could not even distinguish the letters of the alphabet. The complaint was to be repeated in succeeding years.

School instruction was provided as a remedy, but in the earlier years, as, indeed, before 1922,[47] the annual reports, are silent on what was being taught. Of course, training of an educational kind was provided as an adjunct to trade instruction, and the brighter boy would have gleaned something from the books in the library and from the lectures of visiting speakers. The problem of the illiterate boy remained; access to library books was of little value to him.

On the return of the borstal to Clonmel in 1947, school instruction was again provided both for the twenty borstal detainees proper and the sixty-six transferred juvenile adults.[48] Twenty, in all, were reckoned to be completely illiterate. The matter of educational deficiency is first referred to at length in 1950. "The very low educational standard of practically all inmates", that year's *Report* relates,

> continues to be a matter for comment. Their secular education is very much under the average of youths of their age and their religious and moral education is deplorably low. It is unusual to find an inmate on committal who has reached even Third Standard level in Reading, Writing, Arithmetic, Catechism or Christian Doctrine and any knowledge of the other subjects of normal school programmes such as Irish, History, Geography, Composition, etc., is entirely absent.

The remedy lay in an altered programme of religious and secular education introduced during the year. Special instruction was given during the day to both the illiterate and those of a particularly low standard of education, and evening classes were started for all others.

Each inmate thus received continuous instruction throughout his sentence. Subjects taught included reading, writing, composition, simple grammar, arithmetic, history, geography, letter-writing, catechism and Christian doctrine. Elementary geometry and mechanical drawing were also taught.

Good results were immediately claimed, especially for the evening classes, and the authorities inferred that they were not faced with a

[47] Above, chapter 2.
[48] *Clonmel Notes*, p. 9.

problem of educating mental defectives. In the case of transferred juvenile adults, however, real educational progress was held to be "extremely difficult." One of the reasons for this was said to be the shortness of their detention, and in 1951 they were excluded from the educational programme.

In the crisis later in the nineteen fifties, educational classes were suspended for boys who were needed for general maintenance work, but a skeleton programme continued to be provided for the illiterate.

Recreation

The daily régime provided for compulsory physical training. The justification was that it effected improvement in the general condition of the boys, making "many who on committal were ill-nourished, under-developed and slovenly become smart, self-reliant and physically strong." Facilities for recreation were always provided and the development of these is what most marks the difference in the borstal institution between its early and later years. In retrospect, the development was inevitable, for the decision in 1942 to increase the length of time when boys could remain in association apart from work necessitated action to ensure that this long period was not, as it was put in 1948, "spent in aimless and listless killing of time." There were changes, too, in the official outlook on entitlement to recreation. At first, the old borstal rules appear to have been strictly observed and recreation in association remained a privilege. In later years, however, most forms of recreational activity became open to everybody.[49]

The precise form that recreation took is first indicated in 1934. Then, apparently, the only outdoor activity was football. In bad weather the boys could play draughts and quoits, read periodicals "of a good class", or listen to the gramophone or wireless. There were occasional concerts and also the library, which in 1937 was supplemented by 400 "interesting and useful books."

Fahy was depressed by the prevailing atmosphere of monotony on his visit to the borstal at Cork in 1941. The yard in which football was played was too small and the local community had not made adjacent playing fields available. His criticisms, and growing interest in the institution on the part of the people of Cork, produced certain improvements. Playing fields and an open-air swimming pool were in turn placed at the disposal of the borstal.[50] Tours on bicycles were organised by members of the Borstal Association,[51] as were walks in the environs of Cork and to places of interest in the city itself. The Association also

---

[49] There was a similar development in Northern Ireland: above, chapter 3.
[50] Below, chapter 8.
[51] *Dáil Debates*, Vol. 88, cols. 1292–93, 15 October 1942.

donated a table tennis set, took parties to places of entertainment, and promoted a series of lectures. In 1944 another series of lectures was given by the Presentation Christian Brothers. The library continued to be stocked with books on travel and history, fiction, weekly newspapers and, "fcr the less clever", pictorial journals. The cinema programmes that began to be shown in the recreation halls were open to everyone.

On the return to Clonmel, the authorities rented a small field for football, adjacent to the institution, and a committee of the boys started to organise games.[52] By 1948, however, the ground was thought to be not large enough and the attempt to organise tournaments was reckoned a failure.

Fortunately, the situation was alleviated the following year when local clubs allowed teams from the institution to participate in the local football league. The same year the local GAA authorities started admitting the boys free to watch games played at the Gaelic grounds in Clonmel and later on granted them permission to use these grounds on the Thursday half-holiday. In 1950 the institution acquired a new soccer pitch and games were played with local teams. A few boys began to be selected to play for Clonmel teams in competitions held in the town and elsewhere in Munster, and both the Clonmel Association Football Club and the local rugby club, like the GAA authorities before, granted free admission to sports fixtures arranged under their auspices.

Handball was played in a ball-alley constructed in 1947. Tournaments were held and prizes again given by the Borstal Association. There was provision too for athletics and basketball, but all other outdoor activity was a privilege of those who had earned promotion after a minimum of six-months detention.[53]

The boxing club was a success and was viewed with some pride. It was started in 1947 by Mr J. Healy of Clonmel, an ex-Irish champion and international representative, who offered his services voluntarily.[54] Tournaments were arranged with local boxing clubs and Army teams. The visiting committee noted a general improvement in the character and demeanour of the boys who were members, describing their performance in some of these early tournaments as showing "considerable zest and not a little skill." The club was affiliated to the Irish Amateur Boxing Association and arrangements were made to enable members to participate in fixtures held in Munster towns. Visits were also paid by other clubs, including, in 1950, the St Mary's and Army clubs. 1952 was a memorable season, when members of the club won three county championships and a Munster title. In 1948 two boys, shortly after their

---

[52] *Clonmel Notes*, p. 15.
[53] ibid.
[54] *Clonmel Notes*, p. 14.

release, participated in the National Junior Championships in Dublin. In 1954 the visiting committee reported, with satisfaction, that a former member of the club had since reached international standard. In view of these achievements, it must have been a disappointment when in the next year members were warned that, because of the low numbers in the institution, the club might have to disband, and even more so in 1956, when, before the transfer to Dublin, disbandment formally took place.

Games in the general recreation hall at Clonmel included table tennis, draughts, chess, and ring-boards. Hobbies were encouraged, as was reading. There was a radio; concerts and entertainments were given from time to time by local artistes; and the acquisition of a small cinema projector in 1948 enabled films to be screened.

Summer camps for inmates never appear to have been organised. In this respect, borstal boys in the North were more fortunate as, indeed, were boys in industrial and reformatory schools in the South. In 1935 boys from the reformatory at Glencree were taken to Gormanston, and the French Sisters of Charity regularly took their charges at the Drogheda junior industrial school to Termonfeckin.[55]

Discharge

The maximum length of a borstal sentence remained fixed at three years but release on licence was always possible after six months. A board, composed of officers of the borstal, examined each case. If it was satisfied that the boy's conduct, industry, and attention to instruction during his period of detention indicated that he could safely be discharged, the board referred the matter to the visiting committee. It, in turn, reported to the Minister for Justice.

The mechanics of discharge are described in *Clonmel Notes*, the pamphlet published in 1948. Near the date of his discharge, each inmate was interviewed by the governor and chaplain, with whom he discussed his plans for the future. On the actual day of discharge, he was provided with a complete outfit—a civilian suit, shoes, socks, underwear, shirts, collars, and so on—was handed any gratuity earned by him whilst in the institution, and, was given a free travel voucher to his place of destination.

In earlier years, release on licence was only recommended if suitable employment was immediately available. In many instances, this was not forthcoming and, to avoid hardship, a change of policy was introduced in the nineteen forties. As a result, boys began to be sent home on licence even though no jobs had been found for them. The position in 1956 was not untypical: twenty boys were released on licence, but only two

[55] *Cussen Report*, p. 23.

had jobs awaiting them. The claim was later to be made that many of the jobs were fictitious and that such offers were extended in the expectation that they would help accelerate the moment of discharge.[56]

There is no available information on either the average length of sentence served before release or on the proportion of inmates who served full sentences. In 1948, cases where discharge took place after six months, were said to be "frequent." Discharge was speeded up for a few offenders by the general Holy Year amnesty of 1949. Offenders, including borstal boys, who had less than one month of their sentences to serve on 1 January 1950, were given remission of half of the rest of their sentence.

After-care

The 1908 Act had envisaged after-care as an integral part of the borstal system and, to promote it, a Borstal Association, enjoying official support, had been founded at Clonmel.[57] On this society the main burden of the work fell, as much after 1922 as before. It managed to function during the period from 1922 to 1924 when the borstal was temporarily sited at Kilkenny but its work appears to have been interrupted on the return to Clonmel in 1924. The *Appropriation Accounts* show no grant to the society between 1924 and 1929.

By 1930 the Association was again firmly established, and its members were fulfilling four distinct functions: (i) disbursing to boys on discharge gratuities earned by them in borstal; (ii) providing special assistance grants in certain cases; (iii) undertaking supervision after discharge; and (iv) finding employment for boys on discharge. In later years, the Association (renamed the St Patrick's Welfare Association in 1952) shared some of these tasks with other bodies. Responsibility for the disbursement of sources of revenue to boys on discharge—the gratuities (varying in 1934 between £2 and £4 10s.) and the special assistance grants (to cover clothing, tool kits and travel vouchers)—appears, in some instances at least, to have been effectively transferred to the officers of the institution itself. Finding jobs was always the major problem and the Association must have welcomed the increasingly active role both of the institution's chaplains and, more especially, after 1948, of the Guild of St Philip.

This Guild was established by the Society of St Vincent de Paul to specifically attend to the re-employment needs of inmates of all Irish penal establishments. It appointed a paid director, opened an office in Dublin and received a government grant, at first £1,000 per annum. The Guild took an immediate interest in the institution at Clonmel

---

[56] *Dáil Debates*, Vol. 183, col. 598, 29 June 1960: Mr Loughman.
[57] Above, chapter 2.

and worked in conjunction with the Association, which by 1948 was largely recruited from the ranks of the same Society.[58]

The sole legal responsibility of the Association was to supervise boys on discharge. This responsibility attached where there was discharge on licence prior to expiry of the sentence and in all cases for one year after expiry. In practice, the power to recall a boy from supervision— itself a possible indication of the *quality* of supervision—appears to have been rarely exercised. No explanation is forthcoming. Indeed, information on this facet of borstal administration is sparse, a deficiency all the more regrettable in view of the detailed account to be found in the *Cussen Report*[59] of the supervision of boys and girls from industrial and reformatory schools.

The supervision exercised by the Association could, however, attract some attention. The picture disclosed by the case of Patrick Hagan in 1931 may be untypical, but the circumstances are certainly of interest. Hagan, who was from County Monaghan, had been sent to borstal for sacrilege. After release, he was subsequently reported to be employed for four shillings a week on a farm in County Tipperary, ostensibly under the auspices of the Borstal Association. A Dáil deputy then requested in the House that he be returned to his parents in Monaghan where, it was claimed, he might earn thirty-six shillings a week. The Minister for Justice, James Fitzgerald Kenney, replied at length. The boy had been discharged into the employment of the Tipperary farmer at a rate of five shillings a week; had then, without the approval of the Association, taken up work with another farmer and finally returned of his own accord to the first farmer, to work at the lower rate. No offer of employment at the rate of thirty-six shillings a week had been received. In view of the circumstances, the Association was not in favour of the boy returning to Monaghan; the boy himself did not wish to go back home and, even if the clergy supported the boy's return in order to supplement the income of the family, the father of which was disabled, the responsibility rested exclusively with the Association and the future welfare of the boy was the prime consideration.[60]

Securing employment for boys on discharge was the principal challenge. "When an inmate", the 1950 *Report* said,

who has indulged in criminal pursuits for a number of years before being received into St Patrick's goes out again into the world and

---

[58] *Clonmel Notes*, p. 17.

[59] *Cussen Report*, pp. 32–34.

[60] *Dáil Debates*, Vol. 40, cols. 2104–07, 26 November 1931. That it was often inadvisable to return a boy to his family environment was to be reiterated in 1960 by Mr Loughman, a former member of the Clonmel visiting committee: *Dáil Debates*, Vol. 183, cols. 598–99, 29 June 1960.

returns to his old environment and companions, with no hope of employment, it is too often only a question of time until he relapses into his former criminal pursuits. That a discharged inmate should obtain employment if he is to avoid crime is vital and cannot be too strongly stressed.

All agreed that, ideally, jobs should always be found, and this led to demands for a more vocational training, suggestions for new employment outlets, and regular requests for better cooperation from employers. Commitment to the ideal also produced experiments to establish boys in self-employment. Unfortunately, at every turn, the authorities met the problem of domestic unemployment.

In 1924–25 twenty-one boys were discharged but, because of the general trade depression, only two were successfully placed. Such disappointing results led the Prisons Board, in its *Report* for 1926–27, to support a clearly defined policy. It was easier, the Board said, to arrange discharge into farm work (a fact to be confirmed by the case of the Monaghan boy in 1931). It suggested that the emphasis during training should be on farm work, that courses in bootmaking and tailoring be abolished, and went on to propose the purchase of farm land. The traditional borstal industries, nonetheless, had some success. In 1944 the inclusion of tailoring in the training schedule at Cork was enthusiastically supported: many recently discharged boys had entered that trade and profited from it, "renovating and turning suits and overcoats." The enthusiasm, however, was short-lived; in 1947 tailoring instruction ended. Shoemaking had its quota of successes too. In the later nineteen forties it was common practice to set up boys as self-employed cobblers and provide them with Borstal Association gifts of leather and cobbler's kits. In some instances, it was claimed, the ventures prospered.[61]

Complete suspension awaited the training programme in the period after 1950 but, if the state of affairs described in 1948 still held true, its continuance would have made little difference. In a year when the visiting committee pleaded for greater cooperation from employers as "an effective mode of approach to the serious problem of the young delinquent",[62] the Department of Justice recorded that: "The finding of positions for the inmates on discharge is a difficult matter. They cannot secure employment in the skilled trades and the majority of them obtain positions as farm or builder's labourers." Constant, let alone better, vocational training could not have altered that.

If the labour market in Ireland was unfavourable, Britain's proximity,

---

[61] *Clonmel Notes*, p. 13.
[62] ibid., p. 19.

and the fact that access to its labour market was free, made re-employment of the Irish borstal boy a little easier. Of the 1947 and 1948 discharges, a few avoided the inevitable unskilled employment at home; some joined the R.A.F., one obtained a job as a tailor in Manchester and another found work in a slate quarry in the Isle of Man. The dual advantages of access to the British labour market were frankly spelt out in a comment in 1951 on the emigration of former boys of Clonmel:

> In the past five years over sixty discharged inmates have gone to jobs in England . . . only one of these was unsuccessful after release . . . this would seem to indicate that if, following a period of training in the Institution, a boy can be placed in employment away from his old environment and associates, the chance of his being a success is very high. The greatest cause of backsliding is a period of unemployment after release.

Access to the same labour market was naturally appreciated by the Northern Ireland authorities. However, the extent to which that market was availed of for jobs by borstal discharges from Northern Ireland is uncertain. Migration undoubtedly took place. Quoting from letters of discharges in May 1939, Mr Warnock, Parliamentary Secretary to the Northern Ireland Minister for Home Affairs, disclosed that one lad was working on a construction site on the Isle of Skye and earning £2 18s. a week, and a second was "going with the King to Canada on H.M.S. Glasgow." [63]

The end of a borstal system

Before 1922 the average number of annual committals to Clonmel was forty-eight. Following partition and an end to committals from Northern Ireland, this average fell dramatically. In 1922 the number was peculiarly low in view of the disturbed state of the country and the dislocation of the police and court systems, but an annual average of at least thirty was soon re-established. There was a reduction to twenty-six in 1925 and the Prisons Board contemplated the drastic step of a complete closure. Low committals and high overheads were major factors, but the Board was disturbed also by inadequate training facilities and poor employment prospects. "The case would be entirely different", wrote the Board, when recommending a closure,

> were there a great military establishment close by as at Borstal to absorb the boys on the expiry of their sentences; or sufficient industrial

---

[63] *H. C. Debates (N.I.)*, Vol. 22, cols. 1277–78, 3 May 1939.

life outside to afford them an opening with the equipment of skill in some trade or craft which they could acquire in an institution supplied with all the plant and accessories appertaining to a modern industrial workshop; or were they the young shoots of a well defined criminal class who lived in an atmosphere of crime, uninfluenced except in a haphazard way by moral and religious teachings.

The Board concluded that borstal inmates could be as satisfactorily accommodated in one of the ordinary prisons. Contamination by older prisoners was not an objection, for younger prisoners could always be kept isolated; the other objection—attachment of a prison stigma—was speculative.[64] Despite the force and authority behind the Board's proposal, no action was taken and the borstal system survived, for the moment.

A reduction in the number of committals, to eighteen in 1933 and to twelve in 1934, again caused consternation. The reaction of the Department of Justice was less dramatic than that of the Prisons Board in 1925. The Department pointed to an increase in young offenders sentenced to imprisonment, denying in consequence the existence of any reduction in crime, and urged the courts to take "great advantage . . . of the means afforded by the borstal system for the reformation of young offenders." It also emphasised that the imposition of a two- or three-year sentence did not necessarily entail detention for such a length of time and, in the *Prisons Report* for 1934, added, for good measure, an account of the then administration of the borstal system. The publicity appears to have had the desired effect and committals reached an annual average of over thirty between 1935 and 1938. This rise would not have taken place had not district justices in these years chosen to avail for the first time, to any appreciable extent, of their powers to forward offenders to the Circuit Court for sentence.

The annual average declines after 1938 and indeed only once again, in 1949, does the figure exceed thirty. In that year thirty-nine boys were committed to borstal, an achievement probably linked to the visit that year by members of the judiciary. The visiting committee who were in attendance will doubtlessly have given the visitors the identical message to that which appears in its report for the year:

. . . a normal term at St Patrick's[65] is more likely to improve a young lad at the outset of his career of mischief than is a series of short sentences in any ordinary prison where a juvenile must inevitably make undesirable contacts with habitual offenders.

[64] Below, chapter 8.
[65] The name which had been given the borstal in 1948.

By the late nineteen forties not enough borstal sentences were being passed. This explains the deferment of plans to open a fresh institution on the transfer of the borstal from Cork in 1947 and also accounts for the suggestion, made in 1948, that responsibility for the entire system should be handed over to the Oblate Fathers at Daingean, in County Offaly,[66] who already administered the boy's reformatory there.[67] Finally, it explains the decision to use the power to transfer juvenile adult prisoners to the borstal. In this way it was hoped that the population at the borstal could be kept at a level high enough to enable borstal inmates to receive proper training.

The extensive use of this power to transfer proved no solution to the problems at Clonmel, and the mixing of longer-term borstal detainees and shorter-term transferred prisoners invited trouble. "It is very difficult", the visiting committee reported in 1950,

> to run the Institution in a manner suitable for long term sentences without making the conditions possibly too easy for those who are only in the institution for a few months. Those serving a long sentence are liable to resent the presence of lads frequently committed for a similar offence, who need only stay for a few months before release.

Common training and educational courses were to be jeopardised by the shorter period of detention for transferred prisoners. The latter, it was claimed, also showed little interest in recreational pursuits such as boxing. The quality of general borstal training was thought to decline and was blamed for a poor success-rate.

The Department of Justice reacted by transferring to Clonmel only those offenders who had received a sentence of at least six months. While this helped the authorities at Clonmel, it gave rise, once again, to the question of the institution's viability. Numbers of borstal committals continued to be low and, from 1953, the number of transferred offenders fell too. For several months in 1953 and 1955, the population of the institution was so low that all trade training had to stop and every inmate, borstal detainee and transferred offender, had to be employed on general maintenance.

In June 1956 the Department of Justice was urged by a Dáil deputy to consider the cost to the Dublin parent of travelling to Clonmel.[68] Plainly, some radical solution could not be avoided, and in November it was decided that a single institution would accommodate the majority

---

[66] *Dáil Debates*, Vol. 111, col. 1772, 24 June 1948.

[67] If this plan had been implemented, there would have been an interesting parallel with developments at Malone in 1926.

[68] *Dáil Debates*, Vol. 158, col. 474, 19 June 1956.

of young offenders over 16 who received a custodial sentence. A new St Patrick's was opened, attached to Mountjoy Prison in Dublin, and the inmates of the Clonmel institution were transferred there. Thus, the town of Clonmel's fifty-year link with the Irish borstal system was brought to an end.

CHAPTER V

St Patrick's Institution 1956-1974

Borstal is not a boy's prison. To collect all prisoners under 21 and confine them in a corner of a large jail, and call the result a Borstal Institution is a sham and a pretence, a piece of administrative complacency defrauding a credulous public.

Sir Alexander Paterson, the English Prison Commissioner, in 1934.

Law

No legal changes took place immediately after the removal of St Patrick's to Dublin in 1956. Boys continued to arrive via the same avenues as before: judicial sentence or transfer from prison by the Minister for Justice.

Changes took effect from the enactment of the Criminal Justice Act in 1960. In the first place, the Act proscribed the term 'borstal'[1]: references to 'borstal' in existing legislation—the Acts of 1908 and 1914—were henceforth to be read as ones to 'St Patrick's Institution'. A second change was of greater practical significance. From 1956 on, the inmate population in Dublin, like that at Clonmel before, had been enlarged by the transfer of short-term prisoners of the same age group. These transfers formed the majority at St Patrick's and the 1960 Act sought to end the legal and administrative inconvenience of the arrangement: it envisaged that

---

[1] 1960 Act, s. 12.

youthful offenders who in the past were likely to be transferred to St Patrick's would in the future be sent there directly by the courts. The sentencing authority conferred by the Acts of 1908 and 1914 was expressly retained, but a new authority was added and this dispensed with any requirement of proof of criminal habits or tendencies, or association with persons of bad character.[2] One of the assumptions which underlay this second change was the belief that it was possible to make satisfactory arrangements for short-term and longer-term youthful offenders in a single institution. This supposition was queried during the Dáil debates on the Criminal Justice Bill in 1960, especially by Declan Costello,[3] but to no effect.

In law, the new sentence of detention in St Patrick's, for those in the 17 to 21 age-group,[4] is an alternative to other forms of custodial sentence; for those aged 16 to 17 the alternative is to a range of other sentences at the disposal of the judge. Section 13 (1) of the Act authorises the majority of committals:

> Where a person who is not less than seventeen nor more than twenty-one years of age is convicted of an offence for which he is liable to be sentenced to a term of penal servitude or imprisonment, he may, in lieu of being so sentenced, be sentenced to be detained in St Patrick's Institution for a period not exceeding the term for which he might have been sentenced to penal servitude or imprisonment, as the case may be.

The sub-section gave rise to two problems of interpretation.

The first was whether it authorised the district court to sentence directly to St Patricks. There had been a long campaign to extend the sentencing power of the court. In the nineteen forties Edward Fahy had supported such a move,[5] as had District Justice Reddin, who blamed the existing restriction on "an oversight by some Civil Servant amateur draughtsman."[6]

The matter was tested in 1963, in a habeas corpus application[7] prosecuted by one Dickensen.[8] His argument was twofold. He said, first, that since the district court continued to enjoy its limited power

---

[2] *The People* (*A.G.*) v. *Noonan* (1963) 97 I.L.T.R. 130; "Borstal and St Patrick's Institution", *Irish Law Times and Solicitors' Journal*, XCVII (1963), 11.

[3] *Dáil Debates*, Vol. 183, cols. 605–06, 29 June 1960.

[4] The Prisons Act 1970 makes provision for the lowering of the upper age limit to 19.

[5] Above, chapter 4.

[6] In a reply to an address by Sir Thomas Molony on "New Methods for Offenders" delivered in Dublin in 1940. See *Journal of the Statistical and Social Inquiry Society of Ireland*, XVI (1937–42) (93rd session), 49 at 60.

[7] For comment on habeas corpus applications, see below, chapter 11.

[8] *The State* (*Dickensen*) v. *Kelly* [1964] I.R. 73.

to forward an offender to the Circuit Court for sentence to St Patrick's, [9] the retention of the power was a nonsense if section 13 (1) of the 1960 Act meant that the district court could also sentence directly to the same institution. The second contention was somewhat lamer: the absence of any specific mention of the district court in the section. The President of the High Court, Mr Justice Davitt, rejected the submissions: [10]

> There is no ambiguity in section 13. If the legislature had intended that it should apply only to the Circuit Court or Central Criminal Court, the insertion of two words would have made that intention perfectly clear. It could have limited the application of the subsection to cases where the offender was convicted on *indictment*. Those words were not included. There is no reason for believing that this was due to an oversight; and the sub-section, according to the plain meaning of its terms, applies to persons summarily convicted in the District Court as well as to persons convicted on indictment in the Circuit or Central Criminal Court.

He continued: [11]

> There is, moreover, nothing really anomalous in preserving the District Court's jurisdiction under section 10 of the Act of 1914 coordinately with its new jurisdiction under section 13 of the Act of 1960. A District Justice might well consider that a youthful offender whom he could sentence only to 12 months' or perhaps only to six months' imprisonment or detention would benefit from a longer period of corrective training. In such circumstances he could send him forward to the Circuit Court which, if it thought proper to do so, could order his detention in St Patrick's Institution for one, two or three years. [12]

The legislative intention had certainly been that committals could continue in the same way as before. [13]

The second problem related to the length of sentence that might be imposed and was traceable to the ambiguity of the phrase "detention in St Patrick's Institution for a period not exceeding the term for which

---

[9] 1914 Act, s. 10.
[10] [1964] I.R. at 76.
[11] ibid.
[12] Murnaghan J. delivered a concurring opinion.
[13] *Dáil Debates*, Vol. 183, col. 563, 28 June 1960: Oscar Traynor, Minister for Justice. The Minister also envisaged that district courts would have the power to sentence direct to St Patrick's.

he might have been sentenced to penal servitude or imprisonment."
The phrase could have been interpreted to mean that the length of detention
was to be the same as the *maximum possible* period of penal servitude or
imprisonment. In *Boylan's* case,[14] the judiciary once again adopted
the more obvious interpretation: the Court of Criminal Appeal held that
what had been meant was that the length of detention was not to exceed
the length of the *likely* period of penal servitude or imprisonment properly
imposable under existing law. This last qualification is of some importance
in cases where the district court is enabled to try indictable offences
summarily, for here the maximum sentence cannot in any circumstances
exceed twelve months.[15]

The jurisdiction of the district court is, in addition, subject to constitutional restraint: article 38, section 5 requires every non-minor
criminal offence to be tried by a jury, and severity of punishment is one
indication that an offence falls into this class.[16] Sentences under twelve
months are not regarded as severe.[17] In *The State (Sheerin)* v.
Kennedy, [18] two applicants in certiorari and habeas corpus proceedings
had been convicted by a district justice of being in wilful breach of the
rules of a reformatory school and were sentenced to two years detention
in St Patrick's. The power to impose sentence in such a case was conferred by section 2 of the 1908 Act which the applicants argued was
unconstitutional. It enabled a two-year period of detention to be imposed,
and a sentence of such a length, according to precedent, indicated that
the offence attracting conviction was not minor in character. In
consequence, a right of trial by jury ought to have existed. The Supreme
Court agreed. For the constitutional purpose of identifying non-minor
criminal offences, detention in St Patrick's was, like imprisonment,
to be treated as a form of punishment;[19] section two of the 1908 Act
was therefore inconsistent with the Constitution and was not carried
over when the latter was adopted. "It can scarcely be contended", wrote
Walsh J. for the Court,

> that a sentence to a period of detention in St Patrick's Institution
> is not a punishment even if the punishment may produce more
> beneficial results by way of reform or rehabilitation in the offender

---

[14] *The People (A.G.)* v. *Boylan* [1963] I.R. 238.
[15] Criminal Justice Act 1951, s. 4; Criminal Procedure Act 1967, s. 13.
[16] *Melling* v. *O Mathghamhna* [1962] I.R. 1; *Conroy* v. *A.G.* [1965] I.R. 411.
[17] ibid.
[18] [1966] I.R. 379.
[19] In *The State (a 10-year old boy)* v. *District Justice McKay*, *The Irish Times*, 18 September
1974, Kenny J. is reported to have said the same of a period of detention in an industrial
school. The boy had been committed for five years and eight months.

than would an equal period in an ordinary prison. The deprivation of liberty is the real punishment.[20]

In *Dickensen's* case, Davitt P. confirmed the existence of two separate procedures by which offenders could be sentenced to St Patrick's: (i) that outlined by the 1908 and 1914 Acts, and (ii) that provided for in the 1960 Act. The distinction was earlier recognised in an Act of 1961 which provided that where a district court sentences directly under the 1960 Act and there is an appeal to the Circuit Court, the latter court is obliged, in the relevant case, to hear the appeal as an appeal against sentence only.[21] Nonetheless, in *Boylan's* case[22] the distinction was blurred by the Court of Criminal Appeal. The Court declared that even where a judge appeared to be exercising jurisdiction under the 1908 Act, i.e. had made inquiry into the offender's criminal tendencies, he enjoyed a discretion, imparted by the Act of 1960, over the length of sentence he might impose. It follows from this that an offender with a criminal record may earn less than the minimum sentence laid down under the 1908 Act even where the judge is satisfied as to his criminal tendencies. The decision thus marks a further departure from the old borstal system.

Two more legal changes were introduced by the Prisons Act 1970. Section 2 enabled the Minister for Justice to provide places other than prisons for the detention of offenders. This regulation henceforth regulated the status of an annexe in County Wicklow to which, since 1968, certain St Patrick's boys have been transferred; it also governs the status of a second extra institution opened in 1972. Section 6 of the 1970 Act also empowered the Minister to order a reduction in the maximum age of committal from 21 to 19. No such order has yet been made.

There are few cases on sentencing in the law reports. In *Buckley and Murphy* (1959),[23] the Court of Criminal Appeal was asked to set aside sentences of three-years borstal detention for offences of robbery with violence. Murphy had a previous conviction for housebreaking and Buckley had convictions for housebreaking, larceny, malicious damage and unlawful possession. Buckley had also been dealt with twice previously under the Probation of Offenders Act 1907. The Court saw no reason to interfere; if the sentences erred, it declared, it was on the side of leniency.

In *Deegan* (1962), [24] a twelve-months suspended sentence was substituted for two-years detention in St Patrick's. Deegan had been

[20] [1966] I.R. at 393.
[21] Courts (Supplemental Provisions) Act 1961, s. 50.
[22] *The People (A.G.)* v. *Boylan* [1963] I.R. 238.
[23] [1959] Ir. Jur. Rep. 65.
[24] Reported under *The People (A.G.)* v. *Boylan* [1963] I.R. 238, 245.

convicted of larceny. There were two previous convictions but, in the interval, he had had a clear record, got married and become a father.

A previous conviction was held not to be sufficient evidence of criminal tendencies in the cases of *Boylan and Wilson* (1962).[25] Both boys at the age of 17 had committed offences of office-breaking and larceny and were sentenced to two years in St Patrick's. The Court of Criminal Appeal substituted sentences of six-months. Neither boy, in the Court's view, and contrary to what the Circuit Court judge had maintained, possessed what amounted to criminal tendencies. Both boys were members of large families and had paid into the family budget a considerable portion of their weekly wages. Boylan had had a good school record and had been in well-paid, if not constant, employment. After their arrest, the boys had cooperated in the prompt recovery of the £127 they had stolen. At the age of 13, Boylan had been convicted of house-breaking and larceny and of stealing three comics. When Wilson was 15 he had been convicted of malicious damage. Both boys had been released under the Probation of Offenders Act.

A few of the boys committed to St Patrick's have been ordered to be detained there at pleasure following conviction for homicide.[26] There is no power to commit to the institution young adults in default on the payment of a fine, where this is an option to imprisonment, though it was proposed to change this in 1967.[27]

Sentences of detention in St Patrick's have been suspended or partially suspended. In a case in which a boy had pleaded guilty to the manslaughter of his sister, sentence was deferred for two years until the boy was 16. The judge, having then heard medical evidence that the boy's course of rehabilitation and education would take four years, sentenced him to six-years detention, with the qualification that, if having served four years, he had obeyed prison discipline, he would be brought before the court to have the remaining two years suspended.[28]

Accommodation

The *Kennedy Report* of 1970 described St Patrick's thus:[29]

> St Patrick's is an old style penitentiary building with rows of cells, iron gates and iron spiral staircases. Offenders, in the main, occupy single cells. These are small and gloomy and each one has a small barred window almost at ceiling level.

---

[25] [1963] I.R. 238.
[26] There is an example in *The State* (O.) v. *O'Brien* [1973] I.R. 50.
[27] Criminal Justice Bill 1967, s. 46.
[28] *The Irish Times*, 22 February 1972. This form of sentence is examined at length in *The State* (P. *Woods*) v. *A.G.* [1969] I.R. 385.
[29] *Kennedy Report*, p. 44.

Before 1956 the premises were part of the female prison at Mountjoy, and much reconstruction was necessary in the late nineteen fifties: alterations to the workshops, recreation rooms and dining hall, and the installation of adequate heating and lighting.[30] At the same time some of the institution's barred windows were removed, to produce, so the visiting committee thought, a certain improvement in the general physical appearance. In 1958 the classroom and library were renovated, tiles were laid over the stone floors in the cells, the administration block was reconstructed, and two new facilities were provided: an outside recreation shelter and an improved visiting room. Certain of these jobs appear to have been undertaken at the instigation of the visiting committee.

Much of the renovation carried out at St Patrick's has been done by the boys themselves. In 1959 the roof and the exterior facing of the two main buildings were overhauled; the boys who assisted, it was said, "took a particular pride in . . . such tasks as slating, glazing, painting, the renovation of stonework and were gratified at the pleasing appearance of their finished labours." The next two years saw the installation of showers, the repair of the Harry Clarke stained-glass window in the Catholic chapel,[31] and the conversion of the old stores building into a complex comprising recreation hall, school, visiting rooms and workshop. In 1962 yet another waiting room for visitors was opened, the dining room was extended, a modern toilet, urinal and wash-up unit was installed in the main hall, a new stairway linking the ground floor to the first floor in 'C' division was erected, an association cell provided, and new cycle and fuel sheds were built. In 1963 a kitchen in the female prison was incorporated into the institution and the following year structural alterations were carried out to improve security; also in 1964 the chapel was renovated and decorated and a new dome was fitted over the Circle. Among the work carried out in 1965 was the surfacing of the grounds with tarmacadam, and the erection of a garage for the car used in driving instruction. 1970 saw the installation of yet another new kitchen, and 1971 the conversion of part of the base of one wing into a new recreation hall and the replastering of all the cells. A more significant development was a new educational unit which came into use in 1972.

An expansion in accommodation in 1964 was not to prove sufficient. In both 1967 and 1968 the visiting committee drew attention to the deteriorating situation: the daily average population was approaching 200 and it was thought that conditions posed a threat generally. The inauguration of the open institution at Shanganagh in 1968 eased overcrowding, as did the addition of 25 cells from the adjoining female

[30] The detail here and throughout is provided, unless otherwise indicated, by references in the annual *Prison Reports*.
[31] It was presented in 1939: "The Young Lawbreakers", *The Irish Times*, 3 July 1967.

prison in 1969, but in the following year the visiting committee sounded a warning note once more:

> The daily average occupancy was 210 boys as against 194 during 1969. Many times the point of maximum accommodation was reached, and urgent consultations were needed to release some boys coming near to their date of discharge—in order to provide accommodation for the new entrants waiting at the gate. This atmosphere of crowded survival is not conducive to best returns from either the staff or the boys so badly in need of a period of planned corrective training.
>
> Although the outflow arrangements to Shanganagh provide a safety-valve, the acute congestion proved a continual strain on the staff, giving rise in turn to problems of discipline. This necessary emphasis on control did not leave much freedom or flexibility for any new programmes designed to aid character formation.

More remedies for overcrowding have since become available. Section 7 of the Prisons Act 1970 enables any excess population to be transferred straightaway to prison. The provision in section 6, enabling the maximum age of committal to be reduced,[32] could also alleviate the problem. A third development was the opening of a second open institution in County Cavan in 1972. It appears, indeed, that there are plans to establish a number of such institutions and, ultimately, to close St Patrick's.[33] In the *Prisons Report* for 1971 the visiting committee at Shanganagh, after comparing Shanganagh and St Patrick's, indicated the shape of things to come:

> It is no exaggeration . . . to say that, even allowing for the openness of Shanganagh, there is a tremendous disparity between the facilities in both places. The Committee would like to add its voice to the view, which it believes is held in the Department of Justice, that there should be five or six more open centres like Shanganagh Castle along with one institution of a security nature for the hard-core element among young offenders, in place of St Patrick's Institution.

Recreational facilities at St Patrick's remain defective. The lack of a proper gym and a swimming pool has been commented on by the visiting committee. "If boys", it wrote in 1969, "acquire an aptitude for sport and athletics during their stay at St Patrick's, this can be a great help

---

[32] From 21 to 19.
[33] *Prisons Report 1971*, pp. 21–22.

to keep them manly and straight as young adults." In 1970 the committee very much regretted that facilities were not available "to instruct the boys in swimming and life-saving techniques." A second drawback, in the eyes of the visiting committee, has been an absence of segregated accommodation. St Patrick's is separate from the male and female prisons[34] at Mountjoy, but within the institution itself special accommodation needs have barely been met; in fact, they exist only for remand prisoners. In 1963 the committee asked for more space "to segregate first-timers, sex offenders, psychopaths and incorrigibles and for better facilities for the grading and special treatment of mentally retarded boys." The same request, couched in different words, has been repeated in later years.

In the autumn of 1968 the first 'annexe' was opened at Shanganagh Castle, Shankill, County Dublin, which had been used previously as a Church of Ireland girls teacher training college.[35] The buildings are set in twenty-one acres of grounds, and in 1968 comprised a large house and a residential school built in the nineteen fifties. The initial plan was to provide for a daily average of fifty boys, most of them transfers from St Patrick's.

The first years were spent in reclaiming the grounds, clearing scrub and undergrowth, opening up areas for replanting, and preparing sites for building. Since then a large heated glasshouse has been constructed as well as a house for the governor. A recent addition is a complex embracing workshops and a gymnasium; the kitchen and stores area have been reconstructed as well. In physical terms, the contrast with St Patrick's was considerable. Naturally, life in a former gentleman's demesne was certain to vary from that in "an old style penitentiary":

> Over the entrance to the early 19th century Gothic mansion the arms of the first owner, Major General Cockburn, carries a motto not inappropriate to young delinquents, *Vigilans et Audax* . . . Inside, there are family portraits, finely-carved chimney-pieces and pillars, spacious well-proportioned rooms.[36]

In the spring of 1972, the second 'annexe' was opened at Loughan House in County Cavan. The 45-acre property, formerly a college which belonged to a religious order, is bounded to the north by Lough MacNean across which lies Northern Ireland.[37] Again, the contrast with St

[34] Peadar Cowan in *Dungeons Deep* (Dublin: for the author, 1960), pp. 26–27, was not satisfied that this separation was effective. Boys from St Patrick's, he wrote, went into the prison every day to cut timber, collect food from the kitchen and meet the dentist.
[35] *Hibernia Fortnightly Review*, 15–28 November 1968.
[36] Eileen O'Brien in her article, "No Bolts or Bars", *The Irish Times*, 3 March 1969.
[37] ". . . the surrounding countryside as a whole abounds in scenic amenities including lakes, rivers and mountains": *Prisons Report 1972*, p. 13.

Patrick's could not be more pronounced. Loughan House is two miles from the village of Blacklion and twenty-five from the town of Sligo.

Régime

Unlike those they replace,[38] the St Patrick's Regulations of 1960[39] are brief and general. Regulation 4 provides the 'philosophy' for the institution:

> An inmate shall, in so far as the length of his sentence permits, be given such training and instruction and be subjected to such disciplinary and moral influences as will conduce to his reformation and the prevention of crime.

Regulation 10 at the same time extends most of the Prison Rules 1947 to St Patrick's.[40]

Among the rules made applicable in this fashion are those dealing broadly with privileges. Regulation 7, however, does provide that extra visits are to be allowed and that a boy can write and receive more letters if the governor considers that these would promote his social rehabilitation. There is nothing specific in the regulations on gratuities and the right to earn them. In 1962 the level was raised from 6d a week to three shillings, with an extra 6d for the offender who was well-behaved and industrious. By 1970 the maximum level of earnings had been increased to seven shillings,[41] and it has since been raised again to 70 pence.

Regulation 5 states that inmates are to wear clothing provided pursuant to the directions of the Minister for Justice. Fresh instructions were given in 1972, as the visiting committee records in its report for that year:

> We record our appreciation of the cooperation received from the Department of Justice in accepting our submission to change the traditional 'uniform' worn by the boys over the years. The more acceptable and hardwearing jeans, together with a variation in the colour of shirts and pullovers, has had a good psychological response.

Regulation 9 reconstituted the visiting committee. The functions discharged by the committee are the same as for its predecessor: subject to rules made by the Minister, it may grant special privileges as a reward

---

[38] Above, chapter 2.
[39] S.I. No. 224 of 1960.
[40] Rules for the Government of Prisons 1947, S.R. & O. No. 320 of 1947.
[41] *Dáil Debates*, Vol. 247, col. 102, 26 May 1970: Desmond O'Malley, Minister for Justice.

for good conduct, because of ill-health or for other sufficient cause, award special punishments for breaches of discipline and hold inquiries on oath into charges alleging such breaches.

The appointment of welfare officers (the first was made in 1964) has meant changes—mostly in relation to after-care—but also on life inside St Patrick's. The officers are available to handle the boys' personal problems, including the management of any wages earned on employment release. They are also required to make an assessment of each boy and his background and this is taken into account when transfer to Shanganagh or to Loughan is being considered.

Information on these transfers is scanty. Boys sent to Shanganagh must be between 16 and 21,[42] and those to Loughan between 16 and 23.[43] The 1972 *Prisons Report* states that:

> The open centre at Shanganagh is designed to provide a suitable environment for boys who are not in need of the closer custodial situation which obtains in St Patrick's and who are deemed likely to respond to training in an open setting.

It can be assumed that the selection will principally be made from among first offenders or suitable offenders with longer sentences. It is debatable whether the selection procedure would be helped by a rule requiring the psychiatric assessment of every arrival at St Patrick's. On this issue, the Department of Justice and the Shanganagh visiting committee are plainly on opposite sides.[44]

Shanganagh boasts an "environment of relaxed discipline", described in the following language in the *Report* for 1968:

> Restrictions on offenders transferred to Shanganagh are not much more than apply at residential schools. Movement about the house and grounds is almost unlimited . . . Sleeping accommodation is in unlocked dormitory cubicles. The boys wear a casual outfit. Incoming or outgoing mail is not examined. There is no unreasonable limitation on visits and they are unsupervised.

Experimentation continued the following year when the authorities introduced a system of grading. Promotion, as in the traditional borstal system, depends on the boy receiving a sufficient number of marks for conduct and application. Boys in the special grade receive extra privileges such as home visits and exeats to attend football matches.

---

[42] Detention of Offenders (Shanganagh Castle) Regulations 1970, S.I. No. 313 of 1970, reg. 3.

[43] Detention of Offenders (Loughan House) Regulations 1973, S.I. No. 70 of 1973, reg. 3.

[44] *Prisons Report 1972*, pp. 11–12 and 25.

Individual attention is facilitated by a housemastering system, under which officers accept responsibility for groups of eight to ten boys.[45] All officers meet regularly to review progress and to plan and discuss activities. Several have attended seminars and lectures on human behaviour, and at the end of 1970 a series of fifteen staff group discussions was held in conjunction with the Department of Psychology at University College, Dublin, the topics dealt with including the personalities, attitudes, problems and treatment of young offenders.

The régime at Loughan House also differs appreciably from that at St Patrick's. This difference is signalled in the special regulations that govern the two open institutions. These rules extend many of the St Patrick's Regulations 1960[46] but state a separate progressive identity for both Shanganagh and Loughan. Regulation 4 in both the Shanganagh Regulations 1970 and the Loughan House Regulations 1973 includes the following:

(i)   Offenders shall, in so far as the period of their detention permits, be given such training and treatment as will encourage and assist them to lead law-abiding and self-supporting lives;

(ii) Any restriction imposed on offenders shall be kept to the minimum required for well-ordered community life;

(iii) In controlling offenders, officers shall seek to influence them by good example and leadership and to enlist their willing cooperation;

(iv) At all times the training and treatment of offenders shall be such as to encourage in them self-respect and a sense of personal responsibility.

The range of punishments at these open institutions is confined to a caution, forfeiture of gratuity, loss of remission and the restriction of visits, communications or outings.[47] A boy sent to either Shanganagh or Loughan may, of course, be sent back to St Patrick's or even transferred to prison.[48] Whether an absconder should automatically be returned to St Patrick's was questioned by the Shanganagh visiting committee in 1972 but the official position on the issue was not made clear. The committee had urged that the officers at Shanganagh and it itself should be given a discretion to decide.

---

[45] This is made possible by a high staff/offender ratio, 22 to 55 in 1970—*Dáil Debates,* Vol. 247, col. 192, 27 May 1970: Desmond O'Malley.

[46] Regs. 5, 6 and 8, together with the rules specified in reg. 10 (the Prison Rules 1947) "in so far as they are conducive to promoting the rehabilitation of offenders and are not inconsistent with these Regulations": Detention of Offenders (Shanganagh Castle) Regulations 1970, reg. 7; Detention of Offenders (Loughan House) Regulations 1973, reg. 7.

[47] Regs. 5 in the two sets of Regulations.

[48] The latter possibility is provided for in s. 5 of the Prisons Act 1970.

Punishments at St Patrick's include loss of remission, reduction of diet, forfeiture of part gratuity and forfeiture of the privileges of recreation and smoking. (The loss of the right to smoke may have been viewed more seriously since 1972 when, to the consternation of the visiting committee, the weekly ration of cigarettes was raised from 30 to 70).

A boy at St Patrick's can also be transferred to prison. In 1967, this last power was deemed ineffective by the St Patrick's visiting committee. Nonetheless, it is employed and is resented, to judge from the legal actions which have been launched to contest the validity of instances of the power's exercise. The relevant litigation is worth noticing, not least for the light it casts on the quality of the bureaucratic apparatus for handling transfers in this category.[49]

The power to transfer was set out in section 7 of the Act of 1908. The section, as amended, read:

> Where a person detained in [St Patricks Institution] is reported to the [Minister for Justice] by the visiting committee of such institution to be incorrigible, or to be exercising a bad influence on the other inmates of the institution, the [Minister] may commute the unexpired residue of the term of detention to such term of imprisonment, with or without hard labour, as the [Minister] may determine, but in no case exceeding such unexpired residue.

Three habeas corpus applications have queried the validity of the visiting committee reports to the Minister. In *Holden's* case,[50] Murnaghan J. rejected the argument that the particular document fell into the category of a mere "recommendation" rather than a "report". In *Dickensen's* case,[51] counsel was again unsuccessful in his objections, but Davitt P., in a passage with which Murnaghan J. agreed, expressly criticised the form of the report:

> In any such report . . . it should be clearly stated that the committee, as such, has considered the case of the detainee in question; and, as such, has come to the conclusion that he is incorrigible or that he is exercising a bad influence on the other inmates. The report should not leave itself open to the possible construction that the committee's proper functions in this respect may have been exercised, not by the committee itself, but by the chairman or someone acting on its behalf.[52]

---

[49] The following paragraphs are based on a note, "Disciplinary Transfers from St Patrick's Institution" appearing in *The Irish Jurist (new series)*, VI (1971), 325.
[50] *The State (Holden)* v. *Governor of Portlaoighise Prison* [1964] I.R. 80.
[51] *The State (Dickenson)* v. *Kelly* [1964] I.R. 73.
[52] At 77-78.

The matter was taken still further in *Brien's* case.[53] Here the visiting committee's report had contained the conclusion but none of the considerations on which it had been founded. For a unanimous Supreme Court, O Dálaigh C.J. wrote:

> It is not sufficient for the visiting committee merely to furnish its finding; it must also state its reasons so that the Minister may be put in a position properly to exercise his discretion under the section.[54]

Where the report states that a detainee is exercising a bad influence, the transfer order will be invalid if the Minister purports to act on the ground that the detainee is also incorrigible. The order scrutinised in *Brien's* case was invalidated on this basis. O Dálaigh C.J. anticipated the objection that the improper introduction into the transfer order of the second ground of incorrigibility was mere surplusage:

> The Minister has more to consider than the question of transfer; he has also to consider to what extent, if any, he shall commute the sentence. 'Incorrigibility' would weigh against a prisoner being given a reduction. Here incorrigibility was not reported by the visiting committee but the Minister purports to say he acted on their report to that effect, in addition to the report of bad influence. In doing so the Minister has failed to comply with his duty under the Act. He has introduced extraneous matter which is prejudicial to the prosecutor.[55]

The transfer order must also *ex facie* comply with the stipulation in section 7 that the transfer be legally brought about by the commutation of the sentence to one of imprisonment. The orders in the *Holden* and *Dickensen* cases did not so comply and consequently both were held invalid.

To be valid, a transfer order must, finally, be made at a time when the detainee is still in custody in St Patrick's. After Murnaghan J. handed down his decision in *Holden's* case, the Minister made a second order in respect of Dickensen. The Court found that this second order had been made at a time when Dickensen was not lodged in St Patrick's and thus declared it to be invalid. It is doubtful if the moral of this last ruling can have been fully learnt. At 7.30 a.m. on 18 August 1966, Brien was told to prepare for transfer to Portlaoise Prison. An hour and a half later his

[53] *The State (Brien)* v. *Kelly* [1970] I.R. 69.
[54] At 80.
[55] At 79.

journey started. The order purporting to transfer him was dated the same day. As we have seen, the Supreme Court invalidated Brien's transfer order on other grounds, but O Dálaigh C.J. intimated that if this had not been possible, Brien could have cross-examined the authorities with a view to showing that the Minister's order had not been made as early as 9 a.m.[56]

Section 7 of the 1908 Act also enabled the Minister to order that the substituted residue of imprisonment be served with or without hard labour. In *The State (Sheerin)* v. *Kennedy*, [57] even though the matter did not properly fall to be considered, the Supreme Court held that this enabling power was inconsistent with the Constitution: to order a term of imprisonment to be served with hard labour was to interfere in the administration of justice, a sphere reserved to the courts by article 34 of the Constitution.

Work

A number of 'industries' were established for the boys following the transfer to Dublin: tailoring and needlework and shoemaking and carpentry. Other boys were employed on maintenance and renovation work. By 1967 there were places for nearly 100 boys in the workshops and the number of instructors had risen to eight. The workshops housed tailoring, woodworking, shoemaking, car maintenance and mat-making. The car maintenance workshop originated in 1959 when a 'school' of motor car and light engineering had been set up with equipment partly donated by local firms. A programme of driving instruction was set up and some of the *Prison Reports* record the numbers of those who had passed their driving test. However, driving instruction has not been provided on a regular basis.[58] The workshop for mat-making was designed especially for boys serving short sentences. It was established in 1965 but on two subsequent occasions, 1968 and 1970, the visiting committee criticised some of the tasks that the boys were asked to perform. In 1970 the shoemaking workshop was closed down and upholstery was introduced instead. Contract work has not been easy to obtain but in 1969 an arrangement was concluded with a commercial firm for the assembly of electric lamps. More recently an instructional lathe and a miniature furnace have been installed in the engineering and metal workshops.

Daytime employment release, authorised by section 2 of the Criminal

---

[56] At 80.
[57] [1966] I.R. 379.
[58] See report of the St Patrick's visiting committee, *Prisons Report 1972*, p. 22.

Justice Act 1960,[59] was first introduced for St Patrick's in 1963. The visiting committee was enthusiastic: "Such opportunities for employment were appreciated not alone by the boys selected, but also by their fellow inmates. It may be described as an acceleration in the process of rehabilitation." The practice continues, and has since been introduced at both Shanganagh and Loughan. Most releases are on a day-to-day basis and are confined to a few boys nearing the end of their period of detention.

At the outset, trade training at Shanganagh was confined to woodwork (given with the help of a qualified teacher from the County Dublin Vocational Education Committee) but expansion is planned. The institution's 'open' character is thought to provide a bonus for training. The "lack of formal restriction", says the *Prisons Report* for 1968, "combines with the generally open character of the centre to foster a sense of self-control, which it is hoped will prove of lasting benefit to the boys on release." In 1972 Shanganagh started to grow tomatoes primarily to supply the prison service. The same year classes in woodwork and in motor engineering and maintenance were introduced at Loughan, a few months after the institution was established.

A practical difficulty is that proper trade training cannot be given to short-term offenders. If the time is not long enough to learn anything properly (and the average time spent in St Patrick's is four months), it is tilting at windmills to campaign for better instruction or different kinds of training, but it was certainly legitimate for the St Patrick's visiting committee to demand, as it did in both 1968 and 1969, the appointment of a trained psychologist to assess the educational or formative value of the entire workshop discipline. Now that a coordinator of work and training for prisons has been appointed,[60] presumably this entire matter will receive urgent attention.

Further problems falling within the bailiwick of the coordinator include what to do with the so-called 'unemployable' offender,[61] and where to find instructors for the summer months when the vocational schools are on holiday. Another was adverted to by an instructor at Shanganagh in a comment on the team spirit in his carpentry class:

> The boys are working well, working as a community helping one another, and there is no reason in the world why a union should not accept them except that they have not got the Group Certificate.

---

[59] Release for employment purposes is not, of course, the sole function of the temporary release power established by the legislation. Transfers to Shanganagh in the years 1968–70 were arranged under this power, as were those to Loughan in 1972–73.

[60] For the advertisement for the post, see *The Irish Times*, 7 August 1974.

[61] *Dáil Debates*, Vol. 247, col. 102, 26 May 1970: Desmond O'Malley. Mr O'Malley may not, of course, have had a St Patrick's problem particularly in mind.

A craft like this is not the best thing for them in this age of machines. An Chomhairle Oiliuna [The Industrial Training Authority] should set about training them in welding, soldering, light engineering, plumbing or sheet-metalwork so that they could get good semi-skilled jobs in industry. It would need recognition as a training centre and an arrangement between the training authority and the unions, and it could do a great deal of good.[62]

Education

The revised programme of classroom instruction, launched at Clonmel in 1950, was reintroduced at the new St Patrick's. The need for it was as pressing as before, for the standard of literacy remained low. One change was made: the programme was for all offenders irrespective of length of sentence. Although improvement has occurred in recent years, educational deficiency among St Patrick's boys continues at a level above the national average: in 1966 42 per cent. of boys were reckoned to be semi-illiterate and 3 per cent. illiterate, as against 25 per cent. and 3 per cent. respectively in 1969. A detailed survey was carried out between November 1966 and February 1967 by the Department of Psychology at University College, Dublin.[63] The research team studied a random sample of thirty-two boys aged 16 and 17 and found one mentally defective, ten border-line mentally defective, fourteen 'dull normal', and only seven average; the average reading ability was comparable to that of children in third or fourth grade in primary school. The findings confirmed earlier conclusions. In 1962, the visiting committee pointed out that as many as 60 per cent. of boys could read and write only imperfectly, and went on to express concern over "the non-enforcement of the School Attendance Act which allows boys of primary school age to neglect elementary education and drift into trouble with idle companions."[64]

It is unfair to expect St Patrick's to devise an effective remedy for this quandary: much of the harm has been done before committal and many boys receive short sentences. But clearly some effort to remedy the years of neglect has to be made if only to ensure that a boy obtains that extra educational foundation which gives him a chance to compete on something approaching equal terms with others outside the institution. The staff and visiting committee have consistently recognised this but the complaint was regularly heard that, even so, not enough was being

---

[62] Quoted in "No Bolts or Bars", *The Irish Times*, 3 March 1969.
[63] Anne Flynn, Nuala McDonald and E. F. O'Doherty, "A Survey of Boys in St Patrick's Institution: Project on Juvenile Delinquency", *The Irish Jurist* (*new series*), II (1967), 222.
[64] The UCD team found that 80 per cent. of its sample regularly 'mitched'.

done. In 1962 a member of the staff organised a special class for the most backward boys and in later years there were day and evening programmes of supplementary instruction drawn up in conjunction with Comhairle le leas Óige, a body which runs youth centres in Dublin. In 1968 instruction was given by philosophy students from Holy Cross College and trainee teachers from St Patrick's Training College. In 1970 a sister of St Joseph of Cluny, Mount Sackville, Dublin commenced daily instruction in general educational subjects, and the students and trainee teachers devoted themselves to individual tuition.

In 1966 chaplain and visiting committee cooperated to promote the first experimental group discussions. In the ensuing year, arrangements were more formal and twenty-four boys, all serving long sentences, were placed in two units for group discussion under women psychologists from the Eccles Street Adult Education Institute.[65] The visiting committee had been of the opinion that

> Many inmates are conscious of their need to develop an adult attitude to the problems of life, e.g. attitudes towards authority, work, trade unions, proper use of leisure, marriage, alcohol, thrift, smoking and general topics of civil interest . . . and the results of these discussions strengthened its conviction that there were deficiencies in the existing programme of corrective training.[66]

Appreciation of the need for individual care and counselling prompted the demand for the appointment of a specially qualified wholetime primary teacher and of an educational psychologist. Both proposals had won the support of the Interdepartmental Committee in 1963 and of the Kennedy Committee in 1970,[67] but time was to elapse before posts were created. The relative weakness of the educational programme led the visiting committee in 1968 to press once again for the appointment of a fully-trained teacher: "Teaching an ever-changing population of adolescent boys with many anti-social prejudices calls for great patience and a special skill born of experience." New arrangements were introduced to coincide with the opening of the recently built educational unit in St Patrick's, described in the *Prisons Report* for 1972:

> The new education unit, equipped with modern teaching aids, was opened in May. Teachers are provided by the Dublin Vocational Education Committee from Scoil Eanna in Cabra. The boys were psychologically assessed and suitable programmes of education to

[65] "The Young Lawbreakers", *The Irish Times*, 3 July 1967.
[66] On this entire aspect, see Erica Stratta, *The Education of Borstal Boys.*
[67] *Kennedy Report*, p. 44.

cater for individual needs were provided. The boys were classified into two main groups, one group undergoing a special course in literacy and numeracy and the other group following a general course in English, French, Geography, History, Mathematics, Drawing, Metalwork and Woodwork.

Expert advice on matters of educational psychology will now, presumably, be forthcoming from the recently appointed coordinator of education in the prison system.[68] Psychological testing as such is arranged through the vocational schools.[69]

Educational programmes were introduced at both Shanganagh and Loughan. One boy at Shanganagh managed to qualify for admission to university but this appears to have been exceptional since the majority of inmates have stood most in need of compensatory instruction in the 3 Rs and in general affairs "to overcome the more obvious results of neglected schooling." Both religious and vocational teachers have given instruction at Shanganagh. The vocational teachers also give much of the instruction in trade training in all three institutions.

Recreation

Outdoor sport continued to be encouraged when the institution moved to Dublin. Old buildings were demolished to make more space, the playing area was drained and relaid, and soccer and basketball were played. Soccer was the most popular sport. In 1959 a team played against selected boys' clubs and the students at Clonliffe College, "great favourites who always receive a very warm welcome." In 1960 a return visit by Clonliffe and one by Dalgan Park, Navan were hailed as "a welcome break in the monotony of institution life." In 1963 a team played Brugh Padraig[70] at Terenure and the "wonderful day ended with high tea and a film show at the Youth Centre." In 1969 the St Patrick's team was allowed out to play nine return matches. An all-weather tarmacadamed soccer pitch was available from 1972. Boxing has been predominant among indoor sports and in 1957 the new club became affiliated to the Irish Amateur Boxing Association. That year the visiting committee was at pains to justify the re-establishment of the boxing club:

Proper training in boxing skills under an experienced instructor can serve these boys well in this important period of the formation of their characters—it develops self-control and courage to face the

[68] For the advertisement for the post, see *The Irish Times*, 7 August 1974.
[69] *Prisons Report 1972*, p. 12.
[70] For an impression of this youth club, see "Kids of Brugh Padraig", *The Irish Times*, 27 May 1971.

battles of life, with an emphasis on self-defence as well as the instinct
to use their skill to help the under-dog and never with the arrogance
of the corner boy. In addition, the visits to and by outside clubs
provide a great up-lift for all the boys and provide a valuable link
with the outer world. Many boys later join these boxing clubs—
thus guaranteeing that their leisure time is well occupied. The officials
of these clubs strive hard to find satisfactory employment for the boys.

In 1962 two boys received permission to attend the National Stadium
and both won a Leinster Championship in his class and weight. There
have been tournaments with city clubs and boys have continued to
participate in club championships. In a championship organised by
Comhairle le leas Óige in 1968, boys from St Patrick's won three titles.

The visiting committee recommended the formation of a branch of
the army reserve in 1957:

> It would be a distinct advantage to have an FCA unit established at
> St Patrick's. The uniforms and equipment such as D/P rifles could
> be supplied by the Department of Defence. Knowing the calibre
> of the boys in our care, we strongly recommend this proposal to the
> Minister for his approval.

This idea, like the encouragement of boxing, was almost certainly
designed to facilitate placement on discharge. It was not implemented
nor is there any evidence to show what the reasons were. The Department
of Justice may have been opposed to the thought of St Patrick's boys
receiving instruction in weapons[71] but the real opposition may have
come from the Army. If the plan had been proceeded with, it would
have forced the Army to re-examine its rules on recruitment.

In 1959 the library was "overhauled, indexed and put in good
condition." Adventure stories and books on sport and travel were the
most popular but "well-illustrated encyclopaediae and books on
astronomy, space travel and modern scientific developments" were
also said to be much in demand. Radio, television, films, table tennis,
chess, draughts, cards and miscellaneous household games have provided
other forms of amusement. Regular annual diversions have included
the Christmas party and, appropriately, the concert on St Patrick's Day.

Lectures have been staple diet: in 1964 'The Tragedy of Berlin—The
Divided City' and, in 1966, 'Old Dublin'. In 1962 the Irish Red Cross
gave a course on first aid and seventeen boys passed the test. The talk

---

[71] For opposition to equivalent arrangements actually introduced in England, see
The Sunday Express, 4 December 1966 and *H. L. Debates* (5 series), Vol. 312, cols. 924–28,
17 November 1970.

given in 1964 by two members of Alcoholics Anonymous was said to have been listened to with special interest, "due to the fact that drinking to excess was a primary cause of the boys' delinquency." 'Looking for a job' has been another theme of talks. In 1960 a personnel officer with Lever Brothers spoke about the attributes which an employer sought from a potential employee; afterwards he was plied with questions from an audience anxious, it was said, to learn the technique of good behaviour during an interview. In 1964 an employer and a trade union official came to talk on what an employer expected from a loyal staff.

Comhairle le leas Óige recognised St Patrick's as an affiliated boys' club in 1964. Activities arranged during the evening recreational period subsequently included drama, singing and arts and crafts. In 1970 an instructor from the Comhairle gave instruction in physical training three mornings a week: this is in accordance with a provision in the St Patrick's Regulations.[72]

Outdoor recreation at Shanganagh has consisted of football, tennis, basketball, pitch and putt, and even mountain-climbing. There is swimming too at an open-air pool nearby. The indoor activity there has followed the pattern at St Patrick's. Prior to 1970, a member of St Mary's Novitiate of Christian Brothers taught classes. When the Novitiate closed, two sisters of St Joseph of Cluny stepped into the breach.[73] One innovation was a series of seminars on public speaking and general deportment held in 1969 under the auspices of Foras Éireann.

Vocational teachers from Kiltyclogher, County Leitrim assist generally at Loughan, but the range of recreational activities there, certainly in 1972, was more restricted:

> Outdoor recreation consists of gaelic football, soccer and basketball, and almost every Sunday a match is played with visiting teams from the surrounding locality. Indoor pastimes include television, billiards, snooker, table tennis and rings. Local musical groups also attend.

There is of course the lough to swim in.

Discharge

No immediate change took place in the procedure for discharge after the transfer to Dublin; borstal detainees were still entitled to discharge on licence after six months and juvenile adult prisoners to any remission available generally. Discharge itself was still unaccompanied by any

---

[72] St Patrick's Regulations 1960, reg. 6.
[73] It should be obvious by now how frequently the good offices of religious orders have been availed of.

immediate prospect of employment. In 1957 only 4 of the 19 borstal detainees and only 10 of the 223 juvenile adult prisoners had jobs to go to. A further 32 soon secured employment, many of them in England. Even allowing for incomplete information, the proportion is low. There has been improvement in recent years, but a majority of discharges still have no jobs to go to. It will be recalled that the rule followed at the borstal until the nineteen forties was that there could be no discharge on licence until a job had been found.

The introduction in the nineteen sixties of temporary day-time release has enabled boys to take up work prior to discharge but much is left to chance, even in the case of boys from Shanganagh, to judge from the *Prisons Report* for 1969:

> Pre-discharge leave was allowed to well-behaved youths serving long sentences where it appeared that they would use their short period of leave to make contact with employers or renew home ties and to accustom themselves gradually to normal life. So far the scheme has not been abused and in many instances the youths took the initiative in arranging for employment for themselves.

General conditions governing the temporary release of boys from all the institutions are the same.[74] They must undertake (i) to keep the peace and be of good behaviour; (ii) to be of sober habits; and (iii) not to communicate with, or publish or cause to be published, any matter by means of newspapers or any other publishing medium, or engage in public controversy.

Another development linked with the 1960 reforms further demonstrates the extent of the departure from the old borstal system. Release on licence has been abolished and all offenders, whether sentenced under the 1908 Act or under that of 1960, enjoy the same rights in regard to the remission, which any inmate sentenced for a period of detention in excess of one month is now eligible to earn by industry and good conduct. Remission does not exceed one-fourth of the entire sentence.[75]

After-care

In Dublin in 1956 members of the Guild of St Philip and of the St Patrick's Welfare Association, a praesidium of the Legion of Mary, pursued their

---

[74] For release from St Patrick's, see Prisoners (Temporary Release) Rules 1960, S.I. No. 167 of 1960; for release from the other institutions, see Temporary Release of Offenders (Shanganagh Castle) Rules 1970, S.I. No. 312 of 1970 and Temporary Release of Offenders (Loughan House) Rules 1973, S.I. No. 59 of 1973.

[75] St Patrick's Regulations 1960, reg. 8. The regulation is made applicable to Shanganagh and Loughan by the Detention of Offenders (Shanganagh Castle) Regulations 1970 and the Detention of Offenders (Loughan House) Regulations 1973 respectively.

interest in the welfare of discharged boys, but, as the visiting committee reported the following year, these voluntary organisations were restricted in what they could do:

> Every assistance should be given to these boys who have responded to training and have shown themselves as fitted and willing to take their place in society and accept the full responsibilities of young manhood. Much of the training received in one institution is nullified by the fact that so many boys leave St Patrick's without prospect of employment and with no home and no visible means of support. So far as the committee is aware, no charitable organisation exists as yet to help such boys promptly at their first point of contact with the outer world, when it is essential to have them in a position to earn a livelihood. The various Prison-Aid societies carry out excellent work in supplying footwear, clothing and transport expenses where required. No one of these groups, however, is in a position to find shelter or employment for necessitous cases on release.

The full-time chaplain had been appointed to help ease the problem of rehabilitation. By himself, however, he could achieve little on the two fronts where the visiting committee rightly recognised that advance was essential: the establishment of a hostel for homeless boys and the improvement of employment prospects.

Many St Patrick's boys have been made homeless or abandoned by their families. For these, a job has been of little permanent worth unless they had somewhere to live. The visiting committee first suggested the need for a hostel in 1957. Two years later it did so again. Many a boy, it said, had no home, no relatives "for safe anchorage", and no prospect of a job. In spite of the training he had received, and even with the best efforts of members of the after-care societies, he soon lost heart and grew embittered. For such boys a well-run hostel was essential, and it would also meet the needs of boys with jobs whose slender pay-packet did not allow them enough even for modest digs. A first step was taken in 1960 when the doors of the Catholic boy's home in Middle Abbey Street were thrown open to St Patrick's boys, but the arrangement cannot have been ideal, for two years later the visiting committee expressed the hope that a "more convenient and better equipped hostel" would soon be available. In 1963 a new hostel for homeless boys, Our Lady's in Eccles Street, was opened. More recently, accommodation has also been made available in non-denominational hostels for homeless boys run by the Los Angeles Society. None of these hostels has confined its intake to boys discharged from penal institutions. The arrangements thus differ from those in force at the hostel for ex-prisoners opened at Coolock in north County Dublin in 1970.[76]

There has been no shortage of ideas for improving employment prospects for discharges. Boxing was encouraged in part because officials of outside clubs made useful contacts and could be counted on to help find jobs for some boys. An attempt was made to breach the rule forbidding the employment in a state job of young men with a criminal record. Forcing the removal of the Army's similar rule may have been the aim of the forlorn attempt to establish an FCA unit. Better schooling and more practical industrial training ought also to improve employment prospects, and there is some evidence that they have. Soon after the opening in 1959 of a workshop in light engineering, one of the after-care societies observed that the workshop was responsible for "a noticeable improvement" in the outlook of boys recently discharged: "These boys show a keener desire to secure employment and to maintain and improve their position. They show more interest in their work and less tendency to drift from job to job."

However, other factors have to be taken into account. Educational neglect, impoverished intelligence, and the shortness of time spent in the institution, make it difficult to equip the individual boy with the skill he would need to hold down a job outside. In addition, there is trade union opposition to the recognition, for apprenticeship purposes, of experience gained inside a penal institution.[77] Finally, of course, there is unemployment. In a reference to it in 1958, the visiting committee dwells on an initiative which did not, however, bear fruit:

> It is tragic that the scourge of unemployment is ready to strike at these boys when they emerge to face the world again, full of hope and courage and with a new confidence, born of their achievements under training. We welcome the report that the Trade Unions, the Vocational Committee for the city of Dublin and the Youth Organisations are about to re-examine and tackle this problem which is a malignant growth in this age of much vaunted progress in other respects of social welfare.

The authorities at St Patrick's have invited representatives of management to give talks. Television coverage and organised visits for employers and trade unionists have helped demonstrate the needs of boys in the

---

[76] Mary O'Flynn, "Prison After-Care in the Irish Republic", *The Irish Jurist* (*new series*), VI (1971), 1.

[77] Contrast the success of the joint venture of the unions and the authorities in England at the Eastwood Park detention centre in Gloucestershire: *People in Prisons*, Cmnd. 4214, pp. 31–32.

institution. In 1959, in another publicity exercise, the chairman of the visiting committee sent the following circular letter to managers of industrial and commercial firms:

Dear ——,
St Patrick's is a Centre of Corrective Training for young men between the ages of 16 and 21.

The Institute operates under the direction of the Minister for Justice with the aid of a special staff experienced in the discipline and guidance of youth. The attentive care of a full time Chaplain is a vital link in the formation of the character of these boys.

Most of these young people find themselves in trouble, either from the root cause of unemployment, or the absence of a proper home environment. They quickly respond to the discipline of a well-ordered day, and develop latent skills under the patient eye of an understanding teacher. The programme includes woodwork, metal work and light engineering, boot repairing and shoemaking, tailoring, as well as a full programme of physical training, indoor and outdoor sports. This balanced programme fits a boy to adapt himself to a wide variety of employment later, and gives him a firm foundation in the discipline and habit of work.

Experience has shown that if a boy can be placed in useful employment a very real step has been taken towards his permanent rehabilitation as a useful member of society. By placing even one such boy in employment, your firm will have made a very real contribution towards the solution of one of today's urgent social problems.

We fully understand the disinclination to engage these boys, and particularly when others of unimpeachable character may be readily available.

Nevertheless, until this vicious circle is broken, it is hard to see how this vitally important and very real problem of rehabilitating juvenile offenders and reinstating them once more as useful and acceptable members of society is to be solved.

You can lend a real helping hand to the members of the Visiting Committee in this work. We know these boys' strong points and their weak points. We have many boys ready and eager to prove their mettle, if given a chance. You can help in this practical rehabilitation by offering an opening for employment to a suitable lad. We will not send for interview any boy unless he has proved himself to us over a very definite period.

For our past members we have a Boys' Club run by an After-Care Committee. The club is under the personal direction of the Rev Chaplain, and this acts as an added assurance to an employer who feels more secure to learn how a boy is occupied during his leisure time.

Perhaps at your convenience, you would write or 'phone No. 43744 to let us know if you are interested. This will enable us to keep in contact and advise you when a boy we can recommend is available.

We are anxious to increase the openings for employment of these boys at home, and we appeal for your support in this noble work for the real welfare of our youth.

The visiting committee did not expect a dramatic response, which would, indeed, have constituted an embarrassment,

. . . as it is our clear intention only to recommend boys who have been with us for a sufficiently long period of training and under observation, so as to enable us to feel as reasonably sure as one can ever be, in predicting such a variable as an adolescent boy. It is essentially a slow movement, one of education to convince personnel officers and entrepreneurs that it is unjust and unfair not to give these boys a fair chance to make good.

The actual response heartened the committee, the boys placed as a result of the appeal gave no cause for complaint, and the committee, in turn, was glad to be able to record their satisfactory performance. "In every case," the committee recorded, "the employer concerned was good enough to advise us that he was very pleased with the boy. One employer expressed his appreciation by presenting a magnificent Perpetual Cup for an Annual Tournament." By 1962, however, this enthusiasm appears to have subsided. Candidates for jobs, the committee observed, had to disclose their backgrounds, and not all potential employers were sympathetic.

The visiting committee was certain that there was a role for the voluntary worker. Indeed in 1963 the after-care committee associated with the Legion of Mary won special commendation. One member of it

. . . concentrated on personal interviews with firm managers. Such intensive policy yielded 21 new offers of employment within the past two months. This contagious enthusiasm has persuaded more employers to grant opportunities for our boys to prove their ability to make the grade, if only they receive a fair chance.

The visiting committee drew an obvious lesson, however: "A full-time trained welfare officer would give greater sense of purpose to this splendid group of voluntary workers." In the following year, the authorities turned to social scientists for some guidance:

> With the cooperation of Rev Dr Conor Ward of the Department of Sociology, University College Dublin, a preliminary Social Survey was carried out over a limited field of enquiry. The voluntary members of the After-Care Committee worked hard to break down the prejudice of employers towards St Patrick's boys. This pilot survey was an attempt to evaluate objectively the success or failure of these efforts.

In 1964 the first full-time welfare officer was appointed. From 1968 this officer was also responsible for the welfare of boys at Shanganagh but his workload was later reduced on the appointment of other welfare officers both for St Patrick's and Shanganagh. The 1964 appointment was predictably welcomed: it would ensure ". . . a firmer continuity in good advice and the encouragement to persevere in employment in spite of misunderstanding or personal difficulties." A major task of each welfare officer has indeed been in this field. He is responsible for securing jobs on release, arranging pay and conditions, and maintaining good relations with employers.

Further developments in after-care will place additional burdens on the welfare officer. In 1966 the St Patrick's visiting committee urged the establishment of a countrywide after-care service.[78] In the 1972 *Prisons Report*, its Shanganagh counterpart touched on the same theme:

> The establishment of a comprehensive After-Care Service would . . . need to combine the establishment of an adequate After-Care Fund administered by the Welfare Officer and the provision of suitable employment opportunities . . .

The Department of Justice replied to the committee's remarks earlier in the same year's *Report*. There were limits, the Department felt, to the burden that could be placed on the welfare officer:

> As regards the establishment of an After-Care Service it should be noted that the Welfare Service of the Department provides supervision and positive support for offenders while they are on conditional release following detention. After that time this continues to be provided voluntarily by the Welfare Service for those who request it.

---

[78] With the extension of the welfare service of the Department of Justice to all rural areas, mainly to handle probation work, this will come near realisation.

Once sentence termination date is reached there is no legal entitlement to supervise an offender and consequently the provision of after-care must be on a basis of voluntary acceptance.

The assistance of the part-time voluntary worker has continued to be encouraged. In 1966 the establishment of a second praesidium of the Legion of Mary made possible more intensive visiting, which was thought especially desirable when the home environment fell short of the ideal. Support of voluntary effort is reflected above all in the grant from public funds to the Guild of St Philip. The grant itself was increased from £1,000 to £1,200 per annum in 1965, little enough when it is recalled that the Guild's responsibilities embrace ex-prisoners as well.

Money to live on is a recurring problem for the discharged offender and obviously little can be provided from the funds of the Guild. Gratuities earned inside are one source of support but the discharged offender will be likely to have ready access to funds with any realistic purchasing power only if he has been on employment release and earning wages. Many discharged boys continue to join the ranks of the unemployed. Their particular plight is briefly mentioned in the 1971 *Report*. The waiting period for the payment of unemployment benefit was then under examination. If it were reduced, the boys' immediate financial difficulties could be removed.

CHAPTER VI

Custodial Provision for Young Women

*They say that if it could be done without these prejudices, it would be much
to the convenience and utility of the country if the house should be founded for
nuns, for there is no other house of nuns where knights and other free men in
those parts may have their daughters brought up or maintained, nor in three
counties adjoining.*
Calendar Justiciary Rolls Ireland 1295–1303, p. 155.

Borstal was planned primarily for young men. Soon after 1908, however,
when the sentence was placed on a statutory basis, the authorities in
Britain decided to extend the experiment to young women, and borstals
were opened for English girls at Aylesbury in 1909 and for Scottish
girls at Dumfries in 1911.[1] There has been a considerable expansion
of the British female borstal system since then, but the training provided
has not escaped criticism. A retired Lady Inspector of Prisons, Dr Mary
Gordon, wrote that a girl might pass through all the necessary grades
and yet her character be "no more affected than it might be by her taking
a course of comparative anatomy, or an examination in jig-saw puzzles".[2]

Ireland before partition

The suggestion that Ireland should introduce borstal for young women
was first made in 1915. Before then the Irish Prisons Board had introduced

---

[1] Ann D. Smith, *Women in Prison* (London: Stevens, 1962), pp. 256–57 and 159.
[2] Quoted, ibid., p. 257.

a modified system of borstal training for the young of both sexes who were detained under short sentences in various local prisons.[3] The enactment, in 1914, of legislation extending the power to impose borstal sentences led the Board to urge further action. "This new legislation", it wrote in its annual *Report*,

> will also raise the question of establishing a borstal institution for females in Ireland. Up to the present no such institution has been established in this country, as the number of females of the juvenile adult class convicted on indictment is so small. There are, however, many girls sentenced summarily from time to time for various minor offences to short terms of imprisonment, which are worse than useless from the reformatory point of view, who would be suitable for treatment. [4]

The Board added some statistics: "During the period of twelve months ended 30th April 1915, 164 female juvenile adult prisoners were received after summary conviction, many of whom had been more than once convicted and nearly all of whom appeared to be entering on a criminal career."

No action was taken. There was no support for the idea that longer sentences for young women would be the better solution and, as a result, the potential population for a female borstal remained small. In the circumstances, the financial argument against the provision of a separate institution was unanswerable.

Northern Ireland

For over twenty years no Northern Ireland girl was sentenced to borstal. The attitude of the courts was understandable, in the absence of a local girls' borstal. In 1923, the Moles Committee had briefly considered whether one should be provided, but had advised against, citing the same economic argument which had determined the Irish government's attitude in 1915 and later. But hostility to the very thought of placing girls in borstal had been forcibly expressed in evidence given to the committee, and this may have been a contributory factor.[5]

The Lynn Committee examined the matter afresh in 1938.[6] It was critical of the custodial arrangements then prevailing for girls within the borstal age group. The only institution available for women offenders, Armagh Prison, was inadequate in a number of respects. It was a small

[3] Below, chapter 7.
[4] *Prisons Board Report 1914–15*, p. xiii.
[5] *Moles Report*, pp. 26–27.
[6] *Lynn Report*, pp. 154–55.

local prison with little room for open-air exercise or recreation. Segregation was desirable but the size of the Armagh institution made this difficult. The committee expressed the unanimous conviction that imprisonment for the young woman offender was especially objectionable. Women, it said, suffered more than men from the degradation of prison life and from having to wear prison clothes. The committee continued:

> What is clearly needed is some institution in which special treatment and training would be provided for young women delinquents. The numbers under the age of 21 would not at present justify the setting up of a Borstal Institution for girls and probably the most practicable arrangement would be to send Northern Irish girls to the English Borstal Institution at Aylesbury. We feel very strongly that the few girls who get into trouble should not be deprived of the proper reformative treatment simply because there are not more of them.

It took six more years before a Northern Ireland court first passed a borstal sentence on a girl. There was still no local borstal, but in 1944 and the ensuing years the Minister of Home Affairs acted on the suggestion made by the Lynn Committee and sent Northern Ireland girls to a borstal in Britain. The administrative difficulties of this policy were never considerable: borstal sentences on girls were rare—one or two a year at most—and the frequency has remained constant. In transferring local girls to Britain, the Minister made use of the same legal power in the Act of 1908 which had enabled Sir Dawson Bates to transfer Northern Ireland boys to Feltham between 1921 and 1926.[7]

In 1954 the adoption of a different policy was necessitated by an unforeseen consequence of the enactment of the English Criminal Justice Act 1948. Among the legislation repealed by this measure was the whole of the 1908 Act, and that entailed the loss of the power permitting intra-United Kingdom transfers. The Northern Ireland Criminal Justice Act of 1953 did not repeal the relevant section for Northern Ireland but the view was formed that, for the validity of any transfer to borstal in another jurisdiction to be recognised, the practice would have to be valid according to the laws of both jurisdictions. That was no longer certain. The Northern Ireland government decided that it had no option but to set up its own female borstal.

This borstal was opened in 1954 in the old hospital grounds of Armagh women's prison. The hospital and part of the grounds were designated a borstal and the girls were kept segregated from the women prisoners. The building was adapted to provide initial sleeping accommodation for

---

[7] *Home Office Services Report 1954*, p. 17.

six and there was room for expansion if the courts decided to commit a greater number.[8]

The borstal was short-lived. In Parliament, as early as 1955, Miss Maconachie effectively drew attention to the psychological risks involved in operating an institution for as small a group as six.[9] At Armagh the numbers fell below even that low figure: in 1955, the daily average was 5, in 1960, 1.5. The statistics on punishment tell a depressing story. In 1955 four girls shared nine punishment drills and eleven losses of stage (there had been two cases of serious misconduct); in 1957 five girls shared twelve losses of stage.

In the end, the decision was taken to close the institution. The 1961 *Home Office Services Report* explained that the few committals meant that it was not practicable to provide adequate training facilities. These had not amounted to very much: in 1956 the *Report* mentioned institutional cooking, domestic cooking, household management, sewing and knitting. One hour's general education had also been provided. The smallness of numbers was the critical factor, as it was in the case of the English girls' open borstal at Moor Court in Staffordshire where a daily average of 17 forced its closure a mere two years after it had been opened.[10] And a similar fate awaited the detention centre for girls which was opened at the same location.[11]

The closure of the Armagh institution immediately raised the problem of what was to be done with girls subsequently sentenced to borstal. Legislation enacted at Westminster provided the answer: section 26 of the Criminal Justice Act 1961 enabled the Ministry of Home Affairs to transfer girls to Britain, and this is what has been done since. The borstal normally chosen is the Scottish one in Greenock. Greenock is easily reached by sea and air from Northern Ireland and the Scottish environment is thought to be not so different from that locally. Girls are still detained in the women's prison at Armagh until arrangements are concluded for their reception elsewhere.

So, girls are again required to cross the Irish Sea to serve their borstal sentences. Similar requirements for boys prior to 1926 were criticised in evidence to the Moles Committee[12] in 1923 and identical objections could doubtless be levelled today. First, however, it is right to inquire about the effect that the absence of a local borstal has on sentencing policy in the North. This matter is not explored by English and other authors

[8] ibid.; *H. C. Debates (N.I.)*, Vol. 38, cols. 2132–33, 18 May 1954: G. B. Hanna, Minister of Home Affairs.

[9] *H. C. Debates (N.I.)*, Vol. 39, col. 1142, 3 May 1955.

[10] Smith, *Women in Prison*, pp. 269–70.

[11] Interim Report of the Advisory Council on the Penal System, *Detention of Girls in a Detention Centre* (London: H.M.S.O., 1968).

[12] Above, chapter 3.

for an obvious reason: English and other jurisdictions have usually possessed the full range of institutions contemplated by their penal legislation. This is not so in Northern Ireland nor in the Irish Republic. Yet, any inquiry into the effect that the absence of a local female borstal has on sentencing, however worthwhile, might yield no satisfactory conclusion. In the circumstances, the sentencer may view a borstal sentence as especially severe and avoid imposing it if he can, choosing, instead, non-custodial sentences such as probation, fine or a suspended sentence. A short term of imprisonment is a further alternative, though it will clearly cease to be so when the Treatment of Offenders Act (N.I.) 1968 is fully effective. The sentencer then may reserve the borstal sentence for cases where he considers it desirable that the girl be sent out of Northern Ireland, away from the temptations and influences of her local environment. On the other hand, the sentencer may adopt a different approach. The question of sending a girl to borstal may be dealt with in exactly the same manner as that of sending a boy there. In short, the sentencer may be of the opinion that it is none of his business if the girl is later transferred to Scotland by the executive.

Plans have been drawn up for a new women's prison to replace Armagh.[13] These include provision for a young offenders centre for 16 to 21-year olds. In 1971, nineteen young women under 21 were committed to the prison at Armagh; two others received borstal sentences and were transferred to Scotland.[14] What effect the opening of the new centre will have on borstal sentences on young women in Northern Ireland remains to be seen.

Republic of Ireland

The Republic, like the North, had to face the problem of what to do with a potentially small female borstal population. Political independence, however, naturally prevented adoption of the solution now employed in the North. The alternative solution, the opening of a female institution, was consistently opposed. Such a proposal was first made in the Dáil in 1925 and was resisted then on predictable economic grounds by Kevin O'Higgins, the Minister for Justice.[15] On the occasion, O'Higgins went on to point out that girls of the relevant age received a form of borstal 'treatment' in prison; they were segregated from older offenders, taught light trades and given a certain amount of primary education.[16] The Cussen Commission examined the proposal again in 1936. It was obviously worried by the absence of suitable custodial facilities for certain

---

[13] *The Irish Times*, 1 March 1973, 19 November 1974.
[14] *Home Office Services Report 1971*, pp. 10 and 17.
[15] *Dáil Debates*, Vol. 11, col. 596, 30 April 1925.
[16] On modified borstal training generally, see below, chapter 7.

young women offenders, but found no evidence to warrant the establishment of an institution for girls along the lines of the boys' borstal then
at Clonmel.[17]

The decision would probably be the same today, even though the
number of females committed to prison has increased considerably.
Of 245 females committed in 1972, some seventy-eight were under 21.
The sentences were, for the most part, very short, as is shown by the
figures for the daily average populations at the two women's prisons:
16.5 at Mountjoy and 9.9 at Limerick.[18]

The lack of any female equivalent either of borstal or of the modern
St Patrick's has not caused consternation to Irish sentencers. The situation
is not unique. The Children Act 1908 sanctions committals to industrial
and reformatory schools. It also envisages the existence of separate de-
nominational schools,[19] but no non-Catholic ones exist today in the
Republic.[20] The same Act also contemplates the passing of a sentence
of committal to a place of detention for twenty-eight days,[21] but,
for a period after the summer of 1972, no such place was duly certified
in the Dublin metropolitan area.[22] Even where an appropriate institution
has existed, the sentencer has not always had the last word. The Children
Act 1908 empowers the industrial or reformatory school manager to
refuse to accept an offender[23] and this power is certainly exercised.[24]
In the case of borstal, the authorities could never refuse admission but
the protracted proceedings over one young sexual offender in the nineteen
thirties might indicate that at that time the authorities at Clonmel were
trying to establish a precedent.[25]

On a few occasions, the lack of corresponding female institutions
has attracted attention. In Limerick in 1970 a district justice sentenced
a girl for throwing a petrol bomb into a restaurant. She received two

---

[17] *Cussen Report*, pp. 47–49.

[18] *Prisons Report 1972*, pp. 6 and 30.

[19] Children Act 1908, s. 133(18), modifying, so far as Ireland is concerned, s. 66 of the
same Act.

[20] Informal residential arrangements involving the use of probation have been made in
the rare cases where a Protestant child or young person, otherwise qualifying for committal,
appears before the courts. The Meath industrial school, the last Protestant school in the
twenty-six county area, closed down before the Free State was established. See further
Cussen Report, p. 8.

[21] Children Act 1908, s. 106.

[22] Committal to prison, via a transfer power, on grounds of unruliness or depravity
of character (Children Act 1908, s. 102) was held invalid when it was shown that there was
no "place of detention" to which the juvenile could be sent in the first place: *The State
(Hanley)* v. *Governor of Mountjoy Prison*, High Court, 12 January 1973. The legislation also
envisages remand to a duly certified "place of detention": *The State (two 15-year old boys)*
v. *District Justice Kennedy*, *The Irish Times*, 30 November 1974; *The State (eight children)*
v. *Superintendent of Bridewell Garda Station*, *The Irish Times*, 24 and 25 January 1975.

[23] S. 62.

[24] *Kennedy Report*, p. 38.

[25] Above, chapter 4.

months imprisonment but it is plain that the district justice would have preferred to send her to some female counterpart of St Patrick's. The press report of the case indicates that the local garda (police) inspector was asked to telephone the Department of Justice in Dublin to ascertain if there was no alternative institution to which the girl could be sent.[26]

More celebrated is the affair of Hannah Carey who in 1965 was actually sentenced to three years detention in St Patrick's; her case is remarkable in that the judge who sentenced her was aware that St Patrick's only catered for male offenders.[27] At Killarney Circuit Court on 23 November 1965, Miss Carey, a wages clerk, pleaded guilty before Judge Ó Briain to the larceny of £951 from her employers. The judge postponed sentence. When the matter came up at Limerick Circuit Court on 2 December, the judge was adamant that a three-year sentence should be passed. There had not been, he said, any reasonable explanation, or indeed any explanation at all, as to the fate of £700 of the stolen money. The Attorney General, through counsel, indicated that if the judge's mind was made up, the only possible sentence was three-years penal servitude; St Patrick's catered for males only and, if the girl was ordered to be sent there, the authorities would be compelled to release her since no proper provision could be made there for her detention. Judge Ó Briain rejected counsel's submission. For the court to accept it, would "be to abandon the purpose of its existence, which is to ensure that every person coming before it, including the accused girl, shall receive the full measure of his or her legal rights, not one iota more and certainly not one jot less." Carey was accordingly sentenced to three-years detention in St Patrick's.

She was kept at St Patrick's for an hour before an order was made by the Minister for Justice to transfer her to the female section of Mountjoy. This order was patently unlawful.[28] Rather than release the girl, which might have seemed dubious practice, the authorities had recourse to the courts. On 8 December application was made in the High Court on behalf of the Attorney General for two orders against Judge Ó Briain, one of certiorari directing him to show why his order for detention should not be set aside, and one of mandamus directing him to sentence the girl in accordance with law. Counsel for the Attorney General submitted that the judge had exercised his sentencing discretion so unjudiciously and capriciously that it amounted to a refusal of jurisdiction

[26] *The Irish Times*, 21 December 1970. Did the district justice, his clerk or the inspecto not know?

[27] The episode had at least one precedent. In *The Old Munster Circuit* (London: Michael Joseph, 1939), at pp. 257–58, Maurice Healy tells of a woman, found guilty of civil contempt, who was committed to Mountjoy men's prison. This, however, appears to have been a genuine mistake.

[28] And was to be so conceded later. On the relevant case-law, see above, chapter 5.

On 18 December, in the interim, Hannah Carey was admitted to bail by the High Court.

On 25 January 1966, the Court of Criminal Appeal allowed an appeal by Carey against sentence. Counsel for the Attorney General announced that in the circumstances he did not propose to proceed further with his applications in the High Court. The Court of Criminal Appeal allowed the appeal on the grounds that the duration of the sentence of detention was excessive. Ó Dálaigh C.J. considered that Judge Ó Briain had not given sufficient weight to three factors: the extremely young age at which the girl was placed in a position of trust; her hitherto blameless character; and the fact that she was shortly to give birth to a child and would be faced with providing for its welfare and upbringing.

The Court substituted a sentence of four months imprisonment to date from December 1965 but suspended the rest of the sentence on the girl's undertaking to enter Seán Ross Abbey and remain there until the birth of her child and such reasonable time after as was customary. In all, Hannah Carey was in custody from 23 November until 18 December; she was in and out of court for two months.[29]

In the normal case,[30] it is sensible to suppose that the absence of a female equivalent of St Patrick's is accepted and that the judges merely think twice before imposing a sentence of imprisonment, making greater use, where they can, of non-custodial sanctions. Prison sentences on young women, however, are not uncommon and until an adequate study is undertaken, it is impossible to determine precisely what policy is being pursued.

Some such study may also throw light on the extent to which alternative informal residential arrangements are made. The Cussen Commission first dealt with this subject, at some length, in 1936. In the Commission's view, the practice of sending a girl to a home conducted by a religious order, provided that the girl consented to go there and the home agreed to accept her, was

> undesirable, for obvious reasons, chief among them being the absence of specific power enabling the judges and justices to commit to these homes. Further, the Courts have to rely on the generosity and

---

[29] *The People (A.G.)* v. *Carey*, *The Irish Times*, 3 December 1965 and 26 January 1966; *The State (A.G.)* v. *Judge O Briain*, *The Irish Times*, 9 December 1965.

[30] There has been at least one repetition of the *Carey* case. On 8 November 1974, two young girls pleading guilty at Limerick Circuit Court to offences of shop-breaking and larceny were both sentenced to six months in St Patrick's. The girls were not taken there in the absence of facilities to receive them, and the same day were released by the gardai. The Circuit Court judge purported to resentence both girls on 28 November but the orders made then were both successfully impugned in High Court proceedings in January 1975: *The State (two girls from Limerick)* v. *Limerick Circuit Court Judge*, *The Irish Times*, 23 January 1975.

cooperation of the religious orders conducting these institutions who accept such cases without payment.

The Commission proposed that the practice should be placed on a statutory basis: it recommended that the courts should be empowered to commit a girl to a "certified place" for a maximum of three years and that provision should be made for the transfer of any girl who proved refractory. Certified institutions would be remunerated but, since the girls were likely to be of commercial value, it was further recommended that a portion of the cash value of the work they did in the institution (laundry work and so on) should be paid to the post office savings bank or to a philanthropic society so that funds would be available for the girl on her discharge.[31]

In 1970 when the Kennedy Committee reported, homes and convents were being used in much the same way, especially in the case of girls charged with recurring sexual offences or found to be pregnant, whom the girls' reformatories were increasingly disinclined to accept.[32] The Kennedy Committee found that the basis for detention in such places might be lawful: a probation order, coupled with a residence requirement. But convents, it added, could be used for remand purposes by the courts and also for extra-judicial placement by parents, relatives, social workers, welfare officers, clergy or gardaí (where girls were thought to be in moral danger or uncontrollable).

The committee drew attention to the dangers in continuing the practice:

> This method of voluntary arrangement for placement can be criticised on a number of grounds. It is a haphazard system, its legal validity is doubtful and the girls admitted in this irregular way and not being aware of their rights, may remain for long periods and become, in the process, unfit for re-emergence into society. In the past many girls have been taken into these convents and remained there all their lives. A girl going into one of these institutions may find herself in the company of older, more experienced and more depraved women who are likely to have a corrupting influence on her. In most cases the nuns running these institutions have neither the training nor the resources to enable them to rehabilitate these girls and to deal with the problem.[33]

There are few references in the *Prisons Reports* to the needs of women prisoners, whatever their age, and the Commission on the Status of

---

[31] *Cussen Report*, pp. 47–49.
[32] *Kennedy Report*, p. 38.
[33] ibid., p. 39.

Women has nothing to say on the topic in its *Report* of 1972,[34] although it finds room to mention the problems facing prisoners' wives and the under-representation of women on prison visiting committees.[35] The commission's acknowledgement of the difficulties experienced outside by girls wishing to become craft apprentices[36] is a pointer to the obstacles likely to be encountered in any radical revision of the work programme in either of the two women's prisons. The opportunity to effect such a revision will certainly be provided on the opening of the new women's prison, planned for Kilbarrack, County Dublin.[37]

[34] Prl. 2760.
[35] At pp. 153 and 198 respectively.
[36] pp. 102–04.
[37] For a reference to this new prison, see *Dáil Debates*, Vol. 277, cols. 1012–13, 23 January 1975: Patrick Cooney, Minister for Justice.

CHAPTER VII

Other Custodial Régimes for Young Adult Offenders

The Rules require that provision should be made in every prison for the instruction of prisoners in reading, writing and arithmetic during such hours and to such extent as the General Prisons Board may deem expedient, provided such hours be not deducted from the hours prescribed for hard labour. Under this Rule the practice has been that the prisoners are taught separately in their cells, chiefly during the dinner hour, by schoolmasters or clerk warders, passing from cell to cell, and giving each prisoner about four or five minutes instruction. Sir John Lentaigne gives it as his opinion that the present system is utterly useless and very defective. We entirely concur with this opinion, and think that some system should be devised for the instruction in classes of such prisoners as from their age, length of sentence, and conduct are likely to receive benefit thereby. We cannot refrain from remarking that, in almost every prison we visited, we found the books in the prisoners' cells torn and scribbled over.
Reports of the Royal Commission on Prisons in Ireland (1884), p. 36.

Traditionally, borstal represented a special régime for young adult offenders within a particular institution. From the outset, attempts were made to put the borstal system to use in other institutions where such offenders happened to be detained.

Ireland before partition

The first moves were made in England in 1905 when the Prison Commissioners decided to extend the principles of the borstal system to all
offenders in the 16 to 21 age-group who were committed to prison.
This measure was officially introduced in the summer of the following
year,[1] and soon after similar action was taken in Ireland.[2]

One of the schemes was at Belfast Prison. There, in 1907, a modified
borstal régime was instituted for 176 males and 31 females who had
received sentences of under nine months. At Belfast, as elsewhere, the
scheme entailed the segregation of these short-term juvenile prisoners.
By 1910, Belfast, Cork and Mountjoy prisons were established as collecting
centres, and standing instructions required the provision there of schemes
for males of the requisite age who came within one of two categories:
(i) those committed to the particular prison with a sentence of over
one month, and (ii) those transferred there with a sentence of four months
or more. Governors at all other prisons were instructed to make their
own arrangements for short-term male prisoners. However, the policy
for short-term female prisoners had already changed, and governors
were not now required to launch similar schemes for them. On the
other hand, they were admonished to treat such girls as if they enjoyed
the privileges which were now made available to boys.[3] The difficulty
of introducing any satisfactory scheme for girls was well illustrated in
the following year: only four girls of the specified age received sentences
of four months or more.[4]

Doubts soon arose about the efficacy of these modified borstal schemes.
By 1913 the Prisons Board had lost confidence in the value of the schemes
in force at local prisons and was far from satisfied with the arrangements
which existed elsewhere. Instead, it came to support the attachment of
a modified borstal unit at Clonmel to which, it was envisaged, young
prisoners might be transferred. The plan was not implemented. In any
event, modified borstal training was to be a casualty of the dislocation
in the penal system produced by political events in the years after 1918.[5]

Northern Ireland

At the end of 1921 no modified borstal training was offered at Belfast
Prison and any reintroduction of it was unlikely. The new Ministry of
Home Affairs had other matters to think about. The short-term plans

---

[1] Hood, *Borstal Re-Assessed*, pp. 17–18.
[2] *Prisons Board Report 1907–08*, p. x.
[3] *Prisons Board Report 1910–11*, pp. vii–viii.
[4] *Prisons Board Report 1911–12*, p. viii.
[5] For the later history of the modified borstal system in England, see Hood, *Borstal Re-Assessed*, pp. 25–27.

for Belfast Prison emphasised total reorganisation: the transfer of women prisoners to Armagh and the conversion of part of the premises into a convict prison suitable for the detention of long-term offenders.[6]

The modified borstal system was not entirely ignored in this period of reconstruction and in 1923 the Moles Committee made specific reference to it. The committee suggested, as one way of reducing the cost of operating the proposed new borstal, that a modified borstal training unit should be attached to it to which young prisoners could be transferred.[7] This suggestion echoed the view expressed by the Prisons Board in 1913 and foreshadowed a somewhat similar plan in the South in the nineteen forties and fifties. Nevertheless, it was not acted on when the Northern borstal opened at Malone in 1926.

Yet a modified borstal system was eventually reintroduced at Belfast Prison. A parliamentary reply of October 1935 disclosed that such a system had been in force for some years. Details are scanty. Young prisoners who qualified were, it appears, kept in a special part of the prison and given better food. They were employed in the open air (on gardening and mailbag-making) and instructed in drill and gym. In the evenings they were given lessons in a school run by Toc H organisers.[8]

Arrangements were much the same in 1938. Under standing orders, young men committed to the other male prison, in Londonderry, were transferred to Belfast in almost all cases where the sentence was longer than a few weeks; the catchment area for Belfast was thus the whole of Northern Ireland.[9] Whatever the merits of this modified borstal system at Belfast, the objection could be made that it was undesirable to continue to include young prisoners in an institution which also served to accommodate adult convict prisoners.[10]

The opening of a young prisoners centre in Belfast Prison in 1963 represented one further effort at the establishment of a satisfactory custodial régime outside borstal. The centre was planned to cater for those aged 17 to 21 who had little or no experience of prison. Its object was to prevent a sequence of further committals for young offenders "of promising quality." Educational classes were provided as was instruction in handicrafts; youths sentenced for a sufficiently long time were taught a trade. The inmates of the centre dined communally, could watch television and listen to a radiogram; they also had access to a library. Yet, offenders were not necessarily committed to serve their sentence at the centre.

---

[6] Hitherto, Belfast Prison had been merely a local prison: *Prisons Report (N.I.) 1921–23,* p. 4.

[7] *Moles Report* p. 26.

[8] *Senate Debates* (N.I.), Vol. 17, col. 485, 29 October 1935: Viscount Charlemont, Minister of Education.

[9] *Lynn Report,* pp. 150–51.

[10] The Lynn Committee made the objection: ibid.

On committal, all young prisoners were located in what was called the young prisoners reception ward. Here the régime was more exacting and the privileges fewer. Regular reports were prepared on the progress of each individual and a boy was not transferred there until he had reached the accepted standard and appeared likely to benefit from training in the centre. Persons committing fresh offences after release who were again sentenced to imprisonment could not qualify for the centre, since it was felt that their presence would not have a good effect on the other young offenders.[11]

There was no dearth of candidates for the centre. In 1968, the average age of all those in prison in Northern Ireland was 19,[12] and in 1971, 712 of the 2,215 total male convicted prisoners were aged between 17 and 21.[13]

The introduction of internment in August 1971 meant that space was henceforth to be at a premium in all Northern Ireland's penal establishments. The programme at the centre suffered at once, as the year's *Home Office Services Report* records: "Formal education classes for young prisoners were held only during the period of January to August 1971 as the classrooms were required for use as dormitory accommodation due to the large inmate population." In June 1972 the centre effectively ceased to exist. However, educational classes have been provided at the two makeshift prisons where, subsequently, most young prisoners have been accommodated—The Maze and Magilligan.

Implementation of the Treatment of Offenders Act (N.I.) 1968 will entail the succession of yet another differentiated régime outside borstal for the same age-group. The Act provides for the prohibition of sentences of imprisonment on young offenders except where a sentence of three years is felt appropriate.[14] When this prohibition becomes law, it is unlikely that many young offenders will thereafter be sent to prison. The borstal system is retained by the Act[15] but important changes have been made. The minimum sentence has been reset at six months and the maximum at two years.[16] For those young offenders whom the court thinks ought to receive a sentence of more than two years (but not three), or a sentence of under six months, or whom for any reason (including a previous history of institutional life at borstal), ought not to be sentenced to borstal, the 1968 Act makes plans for an entirely

---

[11] *Home Office Services Report 1963*, p. 5.
[12] Address by Mr Hilditch, assistant governor at Belfast Prison, to the Tyrone juvenile court panel: *Belfast News-Letter*, 26 April 1968.
[13] *Home Office Services Report 1971*, p. 10.
[14] 1968 Act, s. 1.
[15] Above, chapter 3.
[16] 1968 Act, s. 11. This section was brought into force by the Treatment of Offenders Act (N.I.) 1968 (Commencement No. 2) Order 1969.

new institution, the young offenders centre.[17] The first such centre is scheduled to open in 1977.[18] It does not seem possible to retain at this centre the simple philosophy which has underlain the young prisoners centre at Belfast Prison. In 1968, William Craig, the then Minister of Home Affairs, indicated that the new centre would house two sections with differing régimes and that the centre's primary purpose would not be to provide instruction in a trade.[19] It appears probable that one of the sections will be developed along the lines of an English detention centre.

Republic of Ireland

In June 1923, the change in the political and social climate permitted the re-establishment of a modified borstal system at Mountjoy Prison in Dublin. The *Prisons Board Report* for that year describes its operation:

> A trained gymnast was selected to impart instruction in Swedish drill and before the termination of the year the boys showed a marked improvement in physique. Where the length of sentence permitted, instruction was given in some useful trade. Special school instruction was also given and good progress made, some of the boys who had been wholly illiterate on committal to prison being able to read and write on discharge.[20]

In subsequent years, certain juvenile prisoners at Mountjoy continued to be segregated but, in general, sentences were short (the three years conditional on inclusion in the 'juvenile prisoner class' imposed in one recorded case[21] was exceptional) and this made it difficult for any system of modified training to succeed. The 1936 *Report* provides further information on the routine at Mountjoy but the matter to which it relates is scarcely of central importance: the use of juvenile prisoners as guinea-pigs in an experiment which the Department of Justice hoped later to extend to the borstal detainees at Clonmel and to all prisoners under the age of 45. This was the Sokol system of physical culture, designed to improve the physical and mental condition of prisoners. The exercises were carried out "under the supervision of instructors of the Army School of Physical Culture kindly lent by the Minister for Defence."[22]

In the nineteen forties and fifties the practice became well-established

---

[17] 1968 Act, ss. 2 and 5.
[18] *The Irish Times*, 3 July and 19 November 1974.
[19] *H. C. Debates (N.I.)*, Vol. 70, col. 730, 3 July 1968 (during the debate on the second reading of the Treatment of Offenders Bill (N.I.)).
[20] *Prisons Board Report 1923–24*, p. x.
[21] *Page*, Court of Criminal Appeal, 16 March 1931; above, chapter 4.
[22] *Prisons Report 1936*, p. 7.

of transferring short-term juvenile prisoners to the borstal, later St Patrick's. One apparent casualty was the system of modified borstal training at Mountjoy. The abandonment of the borstal system itself in 1956 altered the picture yet again. For a while, it appeared possible that St Patrick's in Dublin would evolve into the institution to house all offenders falling into the particular age-group. But this was not to be, and the ordinary prisons still cope with large numbers of offenders under 21. In 1972 there were 704 of them.[23] The needs of this inmate group do not receive special attention in the *Prisons Reports* but, doubtless, many of those qualifying for the corrective training unit at Mountjoy, commenced in 1962,[24] have come from among it. The plight of remand prisoners under the age of 21 was briefly touched on by Peadar Cowan in his pamphlet *Dungeons Deep*;[25] he suggested, as a solution, greater use of the power to grant bail.[26]

In 1972, 649 other youthful offenders were sentenced to detention in St Patrick's Institution,[27] where they were all made subject to the same régime. Distinctions can be, and are, drawn: there may be 'promotion' to Shanganagh or Loughan. Similarly, in the North, there has been 'promotion' from Armagh to Woburn. In neither jurisdiction has a philosophy of differentiation thus disappeared, even though in the case of the Republic the traditional borstal has been superseded.[28]

---

[23] *Prisons Report 1972*, p. 6.
[24] For a description, see *Prisons Report 1964*, p. 14. The functioning of the unit was temporarily suspended in May 1972, following a serious riot at Mountjoy: *Prisons Report 1972*, p. 9.
[25] Peadar Cowan, *Dungeons Deep*, p. 7.
[26] If the maximum age for committal to St Patrick's is reduced to 19, which is provided for in the Prisons Act 1970, interest could begin to focus on the 19 to 21 age-group in the prisons.
[27] *Prisons Report 1972*, p. 39. There were also seventy-five transfers from prisons.
[28] Sites are being acquired for 'detention centres' for juveniles in both Dublin and Cork: *Dáil Debates*, Vol. 277, col. 1013, 23 January 1975: Patrick Cooney, Minister for Justice.

CHAPTER VIII

The Institutions and Society

The share of national resources given to the prison service and the probation and after-care service must, in a democracy, reflect in part the degree of public knowledge, public understanding and public support of their work . . . A society that believes in the worth of individual human beings can have the quality of its belief judged, at least in part, by the quality of its prison and probation services and of the resources made available to them.
People in Prison (British Government Command Paper, 1969).

It is worth inquiring into the attitude of people in Ireland towards those detained in Irish borstals and equivalent institutions, for, as Winston Churchill once remarked: "The mood and temper of the public in regard to the treatment of crime and criminals is one of the most unfailing tests of the civilisation of any country."[1]

Some indication of the public's attitude is furnished, first, by the state of relations between institution and local community. Custodial institutions are likely to arouse controversy even before they are officially established; merely to suggest that one be opened in a particular locality may provoke opposition. The fears of local residents have to be taken into account by the authorities, and this has been acknowledged even in a judicial context. In an important case in England, the House of Lords

---

[1] *H. C. Debates* (5 series), Vol. 19, col. 1354, 20 July 1910.

held that the Home Office would be answerable for damage inflicted by a group of borstal boys who had escaped the surveillance of their officers.[2]

One of the law lords, Lord Pearson, observed:

> The needs of the Borstal system, important as they no doubt are, should not be treated as so paramount and all-important as to require or justify complete absence of care for the safety of the neighbours and their property and complete immunity from any liability for anything that the neighbours may suffer.[3]

It is clear that the anxieties of local residents also represented a formidable obstacle in the nineteenth century, when governments sought to implement plans for opening various kinds of custodial institution. In the late eighteen forties, Dundrum, then outside Dublin, was chosen as the site for the Irish criminal lunatic asylum; the choice was unpopular, and local opposition was quelled only when a high wall was built to enclose the new institution.[4] Some years later, local hostility also delayed the opening of the first Irish reformatory school. Walter Crofton had earmarked a site on the Curragh but was forced to abandon this in favour of a second site at Lusk, in north County Dublin. In the end, Lusk was opened as a prison and the first school was set up in disused military barracks in the isolated hamlet of Glencree in County Wicklow.[5] Many similar incidents occurred elsewhere.[6]

Irish borstal institutions have generally been situated in or adjacent to cities and towns. The borstal at Clonmel was physically surrounded by the town; that at Malone lay within the south-west perimeter of Belfast. Two of the institutions in use today, St Patrick's and the second borstal in Northern Ireland, lie within the cities of Dublin and Armagh. There was apparently no objection to these locations,[7] nor to the sites chosen for the open institutions now at Shanganagh and Loughan, but the

---

[2] *Home Office* v. *Dorset Yacht Co.* [1970] A.C. 1004.

[3] [1970] A.C. 1056.

[4] "The greatest apprehensions were excited in the neighbourhood of the asylum— a populous and highly respectable district—by the residence in it of all that fancy could combine in maniacs and murderers": *Fifth General Report on the District, Criminal and Private Lunatic Asylums in Ireland 1851*, p. 13 (C. 1387), H.C. 1851, xxiv, 73.

[5] "At that time feeling was so strong against reformatories that nobody would allow a reformatory on the cultivated part of the country; and as Glencree was a wild barren mountain amidst bog and heath, Lord Powerscourt gave it to us": *Reports of the Royal Commission on Prisons in Ireland 1884*, Vol. II, *Minutes of Evidence*, p. 156 (C.4233-1), H.C. 1884-85, xxxviii, 418, per Sir John Lentaigne.

[6] There was recent controversy in Northern Ireland over the plan to open the Lisnevin training school and remand home at Newtownards, County Down. Local objections were overruled after a public inquiry (*Report of a Public Inquiry into the Proposal to acquire Kiltonga House, Newtownards, for the establishment of a training school and remand home* (Belfast: H.M.S.O., 1973)) and the school has since been opened.

[7] For English awareness of the likelihood of such objections, see Hood, *Borstal Re-Assessed*, p. 160.

proposal that Woburn House be opened as a borstal was opposed[8] and there were other teething problems there too.

In 1956, residents of the north Down village of Millisle realised, four years after the initial decision had been taken, that a borstal was to be opened in their midst. With the support of local clergymen, they launched a campaign against the imminent transfer from Malone and petitioned the government. In their petition, Millisle residents alluded specifically to the absence of a local police station and asked the government to consider an alternative plan to open Woburn House, not as a borstal, but as a home for spastic and other handicapped children or for convalescents. In Parliament on 1 May 1956, Terence O'Neill, then Minister of Home Affairs, replied for the government. He drew the members' attention to correspondence in the local press from two of the chaplains at Malone, who had written that the arrival of the borstal offered no grounds for alarm, that no net of criminals was about to descend on Millisle and that their work with the boys at Malone had been among their most rewarding experiences. O'Neill agreed with the chaplains and urged rejection of the petition.[9] Woburn opened as a borstal later in the year.

The individual citizen may have a personal grievance when the proximity of a custodial institution restricts his right to use his property as he wishes. In 1967 the former owner of Woburn, who retained property next to the borstal and close to the sea, applied for permission to develop it as a caravan and camping site and holiday centre. Permission was refused and the owner appealed against the decision. At the appeal he maintained, through counsel, that ordinary planning considerations ought to apply: the borstal was an 'unnatural' use of land, out of character with the rest of the neighbourhood, and it could not, and should not, stultify the 'natural' development of adjacent property. The local authority and the Ministry of Home Affairs together supported the refusal of permission. The lawyers, in presenting arguments on their behalf, may have overstated the case. Counsel for the Ministry imagined a situation where three hundred holiday-makers were 'just over the fence' and asked what effect this would have on ninety boys undergoing carefully selected training. To allow the appeal and approve the owner's plans, counsel maintained, might entail an end to the borstal's system of progressive trust. Counsel for the local authority envisaged some future instance of theft from a caravan. Suspicion, he said, would inexorably fall on the borstal. In short, a borstal and a caravan site were a contradiction:

---

[8] The plan to establish an open prison at Shelton Abbey near Arklow did, however, give rise to objections: *Evening Herald*, Dublin, 18 August 1972.

[9] *H. C. Debates (N.I.)*, Vol. 40, cols. 1005–07, 1 May 1956.

they could not exist so close together.[10] The Ministry of Development upheld these submissions and dismissed the appeal.[11]

Opposition to the borstal in Millisle soon subsided. Indeed, in 1959 residents purchased a sports cup for the institution. Boys of rebellious temperament at Woburn or elsewhere may possibly scorn the gift of a sports cup, but in the past there were other gifts and instances of community goodwill which undoubtedly were appreciated. Any list naturally risks being incomplete.[12] In 1914 the Pembroke Charities Fund, through the good offices of a Captain Nevile R. Wilkinson, gave Clonmel £100 with which they bought a cinema projector and musical instruments for the band. The same year the Borstal Association presented a gramophone. Predictably, books have been regularly presented to all the institutions by local authorities and such bodies as the Royal Dublin Society.[13] The support of individuals made possible the picnics, cinema trips and camps, so long a feature of life at Malone, and the entertainment outings, cycle tours and visits to the swimming pool at Cork.

The position at Cork is worth mentioning. When Edward Fahy first visited there, the authorities of University College, whose grounds bordered the borstal, had refused to release one of their playing fields for use by the boys. This decision was soon reversed but, before it was, the College's attitude earned Fahy's rebuke as "symptomatic of the indifference shown by the public generally to any proposal for the better treatment of boys under borstal detention."[14] When the College changed its stand, it made further amends by mounting film shows for the borstal boys. In return, the boys helped demolish a wing of the prison to facilitate university expansion.[15]

Sport has always played a large part in the life of the institutions and local communities have helped in a number of ways. Various organisations have released their grounds for use by the boys or allowed them free admission to sporting fixtures; teams from the institutions have been allowed to join local sports leagues, and outside teams have participated in events held within the institutions. Certain individuals, such as policemen, have assisted in a very practical fashion.[16] A succession of outsiders have also come to show films, perform plays, give lectures, concerts and record programmes, and even hold wrestling bouts. University

[10] County Down Spectator newspaper, Bangor, County Down, 11 July 1967.

[11] For a letter criticising the Ministry's decision, on the grounds that it ignored the interests of the caravan industry, see Belfast Telegraph, 6 November 1967.

[12] The list is based on information contained in the various official reports.

[13] It is appropriate to mention that neither Irish jurisdiction knows the equivalent of the Arthur Koestler prizes for work done by those in custody which displays talent in art, literature, music, vocational training and industry: see People in Prison Cmnd. 4214, 1969, p. 37.

[14] Fahy, "Borstal in Ireland", Hermathena, LVIII (1941), 85.

[15] Prisons Report 1946, p. 19.

[16] For example, in promoting boxing at Clonmel: Clonmel Notes, p. 14.

students and seminarians have held debates, and other volunteers have taught just about everything from reading and arithmetic to singing and handicrafts. The assistance of other members of the public in securing jobs for boys on release affords further proof of the scope for voluntary effort and of the impact which it can have.[17]

The single attempt to justify the promotion of local interest in the work and life of the institutions is to be found in the *Home Office Services Report* for 1928. "The mere fact", the *Report* observes,

> that the boys [at Malone] are thus afforded evidence in a very tangible form of the sympathetic interest taken by the public in their welfare, cannot but have a good effect. To boys at an impressionable age nothing is more important than the fostering of a sense of obligation to make good; and nothing is more likely to induce them voluntarily to apply themselves to do credit to their benefactors than such instances of voluntary kindness.[18]

Unfortunately, perhaps, the assumptions which underlie these observations are suspect. Human nature is not always amenable to blandishment: gratitude does not invariably follow the gift. Equally, however, there can be little doubt that a place exists for voluntary effort. Recent trends confirm that this is so, even if, in the spheres of education and after-care, the tasks to be performed have increasingly devolved on the professional.

The community's general attitude may also be tested by the provision of employment for boys on discharge, although the test is not completely reliable. There is the hard logic of the labour market: scarcity of labour must at any time facilitate the finding of employment, and a surplus produce the reverse effect. Another decisive factor is the number of personnel deputed to seek out jobs for borstal boys to go to on release. Economic conditions in Ireland have not made the task of finding jobs an easy one: endemic unemployment has always meant that many, even of the law-abiding young, have been forced to emigrate. The authorities at Woburn nonetheless have been able to claim in all recent years that every discharged boy has been found a job. The small numbers of boys at Woburn and the welfare staff available there scarcely make it fair to draw a comparison with St Patrick's where the position has not been satisfactory. Nowhere is re-employment assisted by the selective employment practices of state bodies, and at Woburn the severe circumscribing of employment on parole since 1969—due exclusively to the

[17] See further the Report of the Working Party on the Place of Voluntary Service in After-Care, *Residential Provision for Homeless Discharged Offenders* (London: H.M.S.O., 1966); Second Report of the Working Party, *The Place of Voluntary Service in After-Care* (London: H.M.S.O., 1967).

[18] p. 18.

civil unrest in Northern Ireland—speaks for itself. Political distractions, of course, hamper administration at every level.

Cooperation by certain employers in providing job opportunities for boys on parole deserves a special welcome; there are precedents for the day-release programmes at present in force North and South which they have made possible.

In the North during World War II and up to at least 1947, boys at Malone were released for flax-pulling and other agricultural work, and over the same period similar schemes were in force at both Cork and Clonmel. In fact, Clonmel pioneered such a scheme in 1917. However beneficial this kind of work was, and however much appreciated by the boys themselves as a change of routine, it is possible that there may have been some exploitation of cheap labour. The financial aspect to the World War I releases at Clonmel is well documented in the reports for the period but the same cannot be said of the World War II releases in either the North or the South: nowhere, it seems, is the ultimate destination of any monies received from the outside employer clearly indicated.[19] This compares unfavourably with the clear rules governing the disposition of wages earned by boys on daytime employment release today.[20]

In the provision of jobs for discharged boys, it is less easy to determine the attitude of organised labour. It is known, however, that the harvesting operations at Clonmel during World War I were brought to an end by 'labour troubles'.[21] In recent years, too, complaints have been voiced about the refusal of trade unions to recognise, for apprenticeship purposes, industrial training provided within custodial institutions for the young offender.

The community's goodwill can also be gauged by the response to appeals for financial support for the work of the after-care societies, but, unfortunately, the only extant information on this relates to Clonmel in the years before 1922. The officers of the first society founded there in 1906 fixed the subscription at five shillings.[22] The local press supported the society but, to the disappointment of the officers, the number who subscribed was very low. If the local support was poor, that in the cities from which most of the boys hailed was worse. In 1907 the society reported that 1,000 circulars had been distributed but that, outside the

---

[19] The history of concern over such matters may begin with Sir Samuel Romilly's success early in the nineteenth century in securing the withdrawal of the Spilsby Poor Bill, a bill promoted by local authorities in Lincolnshire. The bill had given the directors of work-houses the power to hire out inmates as labour, at 9d. per day, to anyone they considered suitable. See Patrick Medd, *Romilly* (London: Collins, 1968), p. 244.

[20] For the Northern Ireland rules, see above, chapter 3.

[21] Above, chapter 2.

[22] *The Nationalist* newspaper, Clonmel, 19 May 1906.

immediate vicinity of Clonmel, only £4 1s. had been received. It added, despairingly: "[If] it were not for the Government grants given upon the recommendation of a Gaol Committee, the Society would necessarily cease to exist."[23] Annoyance at the financial burden thrust on the people of Clonmel and County Tipperary helps explain the bitterness of the society's attack on Dublin and Belfast in its report for that year:

> The well-to-do people in either of these places do not seem to think that they have any obligations with regard to those poor boys whose offences are oftener [sic] than not the result of evil surroundings; and yet there can scarcely be conceived a higher form of charity than an attempt to bring back these lost sheep to the fold.[24]

The parsimony of the Irish contrasted strikingly with the generosity of the English. A few years earlier, an appeal for funds for the London Borstal Association produced "only a disappointing result",[25] but the philanthropic instinct of the English soon responded to the needs of borstal after-care, and today there is even a charity to provide travelling expenses for low-income relatives of boys in English borstals.[26] There is no equivalent fund in Ireland. In 1971, however, the Republic did set up a comparable scheme to facilitate visits by parents to children in reformatory and industrial schools.[27]

Unlike voluntary workers, employers, and founders of charities— who all assist in the realisation of the purposes for which the institutions exist—, the community at large can cause positive harm. For a start, it may thwart the attainment of the purposes of the institutions by distorting the uses to which these are put. Any custodial institution, it has long been understood, can be turned into a social magnet capable of attracting within its walls the victims of local unconcern and prejudice. In the nineteenth century, admissions to workhouses were arranged in dubious circumstances and today anxiety is frequently expressed over committals to mental hospitals. The 'screening process' for committal of a sane delinquent to a prison or borstal is reasonably intricate, and it appears inconceivable that a boy could be sent to borstal, or its equivalent, merely because there has been pressure from within the community temporarily

---

[23] *Prisons Board Report 1907–08*, p. x.
[24] ibid.
[25] Sir Evelyn Ruggles-Brise, *The English Prison System* (London: Macmillan, 1921), p. 92.
[26] A sum of £10,000 was left for this purpose: Hood, *Borstal Re-Assessed*, p. 117n.
[27] The scheme is part of a more general arrangement allowing free travel facilities for a limited number of visits by parents or guardians to children who will be in care for a considerable period. The scheme also covers visits to hospital as well as to special schools (reformatory schools) or residential homes (industrial schools). The arrangement has been costing approximately £1,000 per year.

to lock him away. Yet, Carolan's case in 1943 [28] suggests that something of this kind might have happened in the South; at least, it was not beyond the range of the fanciful. The Court of Criminal Appeal quashed the borstal sentence on Carolan on the grounds that his alleged criminal antecedents had not been properly established. The Court had heard from a senior garda officer that it was the view of the boy's employers that it would be best for him if he did not return to his own neighbourhood.

Post-discharge supervision itself provided a means by which the unpopular individual could be kept out of a community which had no desire to see his return, and official encouragement of emigration for young delinquents could achieve this same objective. But the decision in 1931 to keep a boy in supervised employment down in Tipperary and away from his home in Monaghan, where he had committed sacrilege, shows that a less drastic device (again quite lawful) was open to the authorities. In that one instance, so the authorities believed, it had been used to advantage. [29]

Communities stigmatise the offender. Communities also stigmatise the institution in which he is incarcerated. If an institution, for whatever reason, earns a bad reputation, the community will cease to be cooperative and understanding. Community and institution thus again react and interact on each other and Ireland is no different from elsewhere. What is a little unusual in the history of the Republic's penal system is the seriousness with which the supposed stigma of the term 'borstal' has been viewed: pressure was to build up for the term to be dropped and finally it was.

The stigma of incarceration is a recurring theme in the source material for the institutions in the South. The obloquy of prison, Fahy argued in 1941, would attach to boys remanded there in custody by the district court while awaiting to be sentenced to borstal by the Circuit Court. [30] The members of the Prisons Board might not have agreed. In 1925, when they suggested the closing of the borstal and the provision of alternative accommodation in prison, they were scornful of the suggestion that boys might be stigmatised because of this. [31] The idea that a stigma might be linked with the mere name of an institution was advanced in 1936 by the Cussen Commission in its *Report on Industrial and Reformatory Schools*. The commission did not favour the titles 'industrial school' or 'reformatory school' and urged the substitution of the terms 'National Boarding School' and 'National Approved School'. Indeed, the commission

[28] [1943] Ir. Jur. Rep. 49.
[29] Above, chapter 4.
[30] Fahy, "Borstal in Ireland", p. 73.
[31] *Prisons Board Report 1924–25*, p. ix. The passage reads: "A distinct institution might possibly save an inmate from the stigma which a term in prison is supposed to give but we are not impressed by the value of this."

went on to say that it was "very desirable that the titles National Boarding School and Approved School should be used for legislative or administrative purposes only and that each school should have its own individual name which should not include the classification title."[32] In due course, those responsible for the administration of the borstal system became impressed by this argument. In 1948 the institution at Clonmel was renamed St Patrick's and that name travelled with the borstal when it was transferred to Dublin in 1956. Subsequently, there was a campaign, firmly supported by the St Patrick's visiting committee, to remove the term borstal for all legal and administrative purposes. The campaign prospered, and with the passing of the Criminal Justice Act in 1960, the term was finally deleted from all legislation.

How seriously are arguments of this calibre to be taken? How well-founded were the convictions of the people who urged the change in name? Such questions are not easy to answer. Nor will it have been simple for the penal administrator to decide how to respond to them. The validity of the criticisms is impossible to test and some administrators may justifiably have considered that the change was for the sake of change alone and, as such, a pointless exercise. James Dillon, for one, certainly sounded a sceptical note in the course of his contribution to the Dáil debate on the Criminal Justice Bill 1960:

> Do not let the House reconcile itself to the fact that because we have changed the name of Borstal to St Patrick's, it is a suitable atmosphere into which to toss a miscellaneous group of troublesome youngsters for periods of one, two, three, six or twelve months.[33]

Unfavourable comments from informed sources pose a special threat. In the South, in recent years, the independent visiting committees have drawn attention to a number of matters found by them to be amiss. These have been remedied, if not always as swiftly as the committees might have preferred. The role of the committees, indeed, promises to become more important, for an amount of evidence now exists which suggests that those for St Patrick's and Shanganagh at least are increasingly prepared to advise on policy.

A recurring problem is allegations of irregular treatment inside the institutions. When these allegations are duly notified, the regulations provide for the holding of an inquiry by the appropriate visiting committee. The conclusions reached by the committees have rarely

---

[32] *Cussen Report*, pp. 19–20. In 1970 the Kennedy Committee recommended adoption of the term 'residential home' for industrial school, and 'special school' for reformatory school: *Kennedy Report*, pp. 16 and 41.

[33] *Dáil Debates*, Vol. 183, col. 584, 28 June 1960.

been critical of the prison authorities, if at all, but no sustained attacks on any individual committee have taken place, and the explanation for this may lie as much in public confidence in the committees' ability as in public indifference to their work. At the same time, those in detention have naturally not been well-placed to publicise their views.

Conditions in the institutions are of equal concern to members of the public and it would be surprising if every visitor had been content with what he had found. Edward Fahy plainly was not, but the publication of his critical account of borstal in the South appears to have been instrumental in producing certain administrative changes.[34]

Relations between critic and administrator have not always been unruffled. When the borstal was based at Cork, a visitor censured the régime;[35] similar criticisms continued to be made, and in 1948, by which time the borstal had returned to Clonmel, the visiting committee published the pamphlet, *The Borstal Institution at Clonmel*, which was designed to set the record straight. In an introduction to this publication,[36] the committee discussed two newspaper articles, one appearing in the United States, the other in Dublin:

> The American publication purported to describe the flogging of a boy in 'an Irish prison for boys sixteen to twenty-one', presumably the Borstal. The description was supposed to be supplied by an American visitor (not named), who claimed to have been present at the flogging—a claim which, in itself, makes the story incredible to any person of experience. The article was illustrated by a 'picture' of the actual flogging and by the reproduction, verbatim, of the words, supposed to have been used by persons present. The boy's offence (it was stated) was that he threw a potato at another boy.
>
> The Dublin publication referred to the Borstal as being located in Cork Prison and described the inmates as 'young boys'.
>
> The facts are:—
>
> (a) Corporal punishment has never been used in the Borstal. Incidentally, we understand from the Department of Justice that no such punishment has been inflicted in any prison, by way of discipline, for over twenty years, and that such punishment is expressly forbidden by the present Rules.[37]
>
> (b) The use of Cork Prison for Borstal purposes was merely a temporary measure necessitated by the military occupation of the Clonmel premises during the Emergency, and the Institution had

---

[34] Obituary in *The Irish Times*, 2 January 1971.
[35] *Prisons Report 1946*, p. 20.
[36] *Clonmel Notes*, p. 3.
[37] Prison Rules 1947, rule 72.

gone back to Clonmel for quite a long time before the article in question appeared.

(c) The description of the Borstal inmates as 'young boys' is very misleading. The average age, at the present moment, is 19.

The maintenance of good public relations requires that the administrator be prepared to go further than merely answer ill-founded criticism—essentially a defensive exercise. One option available is for government to engineer publicity favourable to itself, but, understandably, the intelligent layman will have reservations about so crude an operation. A second would be to invite the accredited journalist to portray 'the reality' of the custodial institution, leaving him 'a free hand'.[38] The risks are obvious but they have been taken. In the Republic, in the autumn of 1973, the Department of Justice organised extended tours to a number of institutions for members of the press. Ten years earlier, too, An Radhairc production team of priests shot a film on St Patrick's Institution which was later shown on Irish television.[39] Yet overall, official suspicion of the media persists and feeds on occasional instances of unbalanced or injudicious reporting.[40]

There has been little professional interest in the life and work of the various institutions. In recent years, social science and psychology students from University College Dublin have undertaken various research projects on St Patrick's: background of committals,[41] follow-up studies, and the reluctance of employers to offer jobs to discharged boys. In 1970, at Shanganagh, staff seminars on a range of problems associated with delinquency were held in conjunction with the Department of Psychology at University College.

Politicians ask questions. Among the matters raised in the Northern Ireland Parliament have been an accident which befell a workhouse boy with foster parents,[42] allegations of brutality against a captured absconder,[43] and of a failure to provide psychiatric help.[44] In addition

---

[38] For the vetting of a journalist by Sir Evelyn Ruggles-Brise, the English Prison Commissioner, see Rupert Cross, *Punishment, Prison and the Public* (London: Stevens, 1971), p. 40. Somewhat later, the Prison Commissioners refused permission to Tony Richardson, the film director, to go into a borstal to shoot scenes for a film based on Alan Sillitoe's *The Loneliness of the Long Distance Runner*: Sewell Stokes, "Filming a Borstal", *The Listener*, Vol. LXVIII, no. 1753, pp. 715-16, 1 November 1962, and the reply from the Prison Commissioners, *The Listener*, Vol. LXVIII, no. 1755, p. 819, 15 November 1962.

[39] A year earlier there had been criticism of St Patrick's on television. The criticism was then dealt with by members of the visiting committee who were given a right of reply.

[40] See remarks of Patrick Cooney, Minister for Justice, reported in *The Irish Times*, 15 February 1975, and see, generally, Report by Justice and the British Committee of the International Press Institute, *The Law and the Press* (London: Stevens, 1965), p. 21.

[41] Anne Flynn, Nuala McDonald, E. F. O'Doherty, "A Survey of Boys in St Patrick's Institution: Project on Juvenile Delinquency", *The Irish Jurist* (new series), II (1967), 222.

[42] *H. C. Debates* (N.I.), Vol. 15, col. 2032, 3 October 1933.

[43] *H. C. Debates* (N.I.), Vol. 38, col. 1228, 4 March 1954.

[44] *H. C. Debates* (N.I.), Vol. 64, col. 180, 9 June 1966.

to the exchanges in the early nineteen forties[45] over the future of the
entire borstal system and over the move to Dublin in 1956,[46] the Dáil
has debated subjects as diverse as the after-care arrangements for the
Monaghan boy convicted of sacrilege[47] and the absence from the dietary
of the modern St Patrick's of fish and chips.[48]

   The eminent have paid visits, though probably unaware of the fact
that, in so doing, they were performing one of the seven corporal works
of mercy.[49] Malone was seen by the Governor of Northern Ireland,
the Duke of Abercorn, in November 1929 and a day's holiday was
declared in consequence. Ministers of Home Affairs in the North and for
Justice in the South have also visited, as have members of the judiciary.
Considerable effort went into the organisation of a visit of a number
of judges to the Clonmel institution in 1949 without producing the
desired result: an increase in the level of committals. Changes in social
convention, rather than disappointment at the failure of that exercise,
may explain the absence of any mention of visits by the judges in more
recent reports. The references before 1922 to the frequent visits to
Clonmel by Sir Thomas Molony, the last Irish lord chief justice,[50]
are in marked contrast. These may have been designed to flatter Sir
Thomas but it is not impossible that, on the occasion of his visits, he
permitted himself to be canvassed on some pressing issue which demanded
a decision in Dublin Castle.

   Judges may not wish to fill such a role today, being content, like
others, to leave the superintendence of affairs and the inauguration of
changes to the staff of the institutions, civil servants, ministers in government and, conceivably, visiting committees—in short, to those whose
business it is thought to be.

---

[45] Above, chapter 4.
[46] *Dáil Debates*, Vol. 183, cols. 585 ff., 29 June 1960. For parliamentary questions
anticipating the closure of Clonmel, see *Dáil Debates*, Vol. 158, col. 5, 12 June 1956 and
col. 474, 19 June 1956.
[47] *Dáil Debates*, Vol. 40, cols. 2104–07, 26 November 1931; above, chapter 4.
[48] *Dáil Debates*, Vol. 247, col. 137, 26 May 1970: James Tunney.
[49] It would be interesting to know whether prison visitation as such is represented in
any extant example of church art in Ireland.
[50] *Prisons Board Report 1917–18*, p. ix; T. F. Molony, "The Prevention and Punishment
of Crime", *Journal of the Statistical and Social Inquiry Society of Ireland* (74–76 session), XIV
(1919–30), 1 at 12.

CHAPTER IX

Life within the Institutions

I

How hard is my fortune
And vain my repining;
The strong rope of fate
For this young neck is twining;
My strength is departed,
My cheeks sunk and sallow,
While I languish in chains
In the gaol of Clonmala.

II

No boy of the village
Was ever yet milder;
I'd play with a child
And my sport would be wilder;
I'd dance without tiring
From morning 'till even,
And the goal-ball I'd strike
To the light'ning of Heaven.

III

At my bed foot decaying
My hurl-bat is lying;
Through the boys of the village
My goal-ball is flying;
My horse 'mong the neighbours
Neglected may fallow;
While I pine in my chains
In the gaol of Clonmala.

IV

Next Sunday the patron
At home will be keeping,
And the young active hurlers
The field will be sweeping;
With the dance of fair maidens
The evening they'll hallow,
While this heart once so gay
Shall be cold in Clonmala.

Jeremiah Joseph Callanan (trans.) "The Convict of Clonmel".

There are no first-hand impressions of life inside an Irish borstal. Seán
Bourke mentions briefly the reformatory at Daingean[1] and Brendan
Behan's *Borstal Boy*[2] is, of course, concerned exclusively with borstal
in England.[3] The deficiency is regrettable. However embellished any
such account might be, the overall picture would be no more liable to
criticism than that conveyed by the official reports. These could scarcely
be counted on to deal adequately with, say, the effect of the institution
on individual boys or on their outlook during and after their period of
detention.

Similarly, there is no work of fiction which treats of life in any of the
Irish institutions, but a set of letters sent to Clonmel during the period
of World War I somehow manages to put flesh on the otherwise anonymous inmates of those years.[4] The letters may be found in a section
of the *Prisons Board Report 1917–18*[5] where, all claim to privacy set
aside, portions of them are reproduced for the light it is claimed they
shed on the characters of boys recently discharged into the army. At the
time, one boy had secured a commission, several had been distinguished
for brave conduct, and a number of others had been killed or wounded.
One boy, the *Report* records, had drowned while trying to save a "native"
soldier. Another had written to say that he was recovering from being
shot in the back by a Bulgarian sniper; he wondered how the institution
was getting on and hoped they were still showing "the pictures" in the
dining-room. A third had written, while waiting to be sent to France:

> I hope all the boys are playing the game and not giving you any
> trouble. Soldiering is a grand life. I hope it won't be long until I see
> some of the Borstals [sic]; tell them I was asking for them. Did any
> go into the Army since I left? Had you a good return out of the
> garden? It ought to be a nice place now.

There was this poignant letter, too, from a parent:

> Just a line to let you know my dear son is dead; he took influenza,
> contracted pneumonia, and I think it is my duty to let you know,

[1] Which he called, with some exaggeration, the "Irish Alcatraz": Seán Bourke, *The Springing of George Blake* (London: Cassell, 1970), p. 2. The institution at Daingean was replaced at the end of 1973 by a new special school at Oberstown in north County Dublin.
[2] Brendan Behan, *Borstal Boy* (London: Hutchinson, 1958).
[3] A German film of the nineteen thirties, Max Kummich's *A Life for Ireland*, purports to deal with an Irish boy in what appears to be an English borstal. The film shows the son of an Irish patriot being forced to undergo revolting—and minutely recorded—'initiation tests' at the hands of fellow inmates. See Richard Grunberger, *A Social History of the Third Reich* (London: Weidenfeld and Nicolson, 1971), p. 384.
[4] Much is learnt of recent inmates of Shanganagh from their written compositions, parts of which were reproduced in the article "No Bolts or Bars" in *The Irish Times*, 3 March 1969.
[5] pp. ix–xi.

two days before he died, he thought he was up in Clonmel, his thoughts were always with you.

Some of the boys at least remembered with gratitude their months at Clonmel.

Further letters received at Malone in 1930, and the success in the Republic in recent years of the officially sponsored reunions of St Patrick's boys, suggest that some boys at institutions besides Clonmel retain favourable impressions too. In 1968 the St Patrick's reunion took the form of a retreat at Ravenswell, Bray, but earlier reunions in 1963 and 1964 had been, ostensibly, more convivial affairs. In 1963 two parties were held, at Dún Laoghaire when almost 100 boys and their girlfriends were present, and at Rathmines, for over 200 boys and their partners, "meaning 400 teas". The visiting committee was enthusiastic about the innovation:

> A remarkable spirit of friendship is noticeable at these reunions. It is encouraging to hear so many boys enquire of the staff and speak with appreciation of what they had learned while in St Patrick's. The chaplain has a very busy time on these evenings, meeting and greeting friends, old and new, giving advice and hearing confessions.

In 1965 an annual party and four social functions were organised which, it was claimed, enabled as many as 200 ex-inmates to be reacquainted.

In the absence of personal reminiscences and sociological surveys,[6] the official reports remain the only authority for a portrait of daily life. They are not an ideal source but nonetheless do contain valuable information and cannot be ignored. The official reports deal exhaustively with the systems of grading, as does Fahy, and consequently the detail to hand is comprehensive. These grading arrangements very clearly evoke prevailing conditions and attitudes. So too do those for recreation, another area which is fully documented in the reports. Some of the details of life in borstal in Northern Ireland speak for themselves. At Malone in 1941 the governor's wife organised quizzes and whist drives every Friday evening. In 1947 the Malone folk-dancing team visited Portrush, Newcastle and Lurgan. At Woburn in the early nineteen sixties the boys debated such topics as divorce, trial marriage, mercy-killing and press censorship. At its 1964 sports, seven records were broken:

---

[6] Much valuable insight into relationships within an English borstal is provided in Bottoms and McClintock, *Criminals Coming of Age*, *passim*. In a discussion of 'inmate solidarity', the stereotypes of 'the daddy', 'the cheeser' and 'the Joe' are all considered (pp. 160ff.).

the 100 yards, the mile, putting the shot, throwing the javelin, the high jump, the long jump and the hop, step and jump.

Information in the official reports touching on other aspects of daily life—religion, discipline and staff—will now be examined.

Religion

In the life of the institutions, the place occupied by religion, and also the role of the chaplain, has varied considerably. In Clonmel in the early years chaplains of the three main religious denominations (Catholic, Church of Ireland and Presbyterian) played a reasonably active part. With the medical officer and other senior staff, they sat on the committees which handled marks, promotions and remissions of sentence. They also organised choir practice, and the Catholic chaplain gave lectures on temperance and offered his services to those wishing 'to take the pledge'.

In Northern Ireland, conversely, neither at Malone nor at Woburn have chaplains had a measurable impact on the daily routine. One reason for this may have been that there were no chapels within the precincts of the institutions: on Sundays boys have gone out on church parade, and priests, rectors and ministers have not come to the institution to hold religious services for those of their persuasion. Whatever the explanation, the Northern Ireland reports have little to say on the work of the chaplains.[7]

In the South since 1922 the position has been different yet again. At the outset, the institution at Clonmel, like the prisons but unlike the industrial and reformatory schools, was administered by the state; this arrangement was unaffected by the transfer of governmental authority in 1922. Nonetheless, partition meant an end to committals from Northern Ireland, and, in turn, the Southern institution became the receptacle for an exclusively Catholic delinquent population. Some 'Catholicisation' of the institution was foreseeable and was to occur, although it is difficult to chart all the stages in the process. Before the return to Clonmel after World War II, the process may not have been taken very far. For some years, there had been lectures from the Christian Brothers and visits from the Sisters of Mercy; the Catholic chaplain had always offered instruction in catechism but his only other recorded function was to help organise entertainment. Of course the state preferred some religion to none.[8] State funds were expended on improvements to the borstal chapel, and in Cork in 1944 disciplinary sanctions were enforced on a boy who went on hunger strike in protest against compulsory attendance at mass.[9]

[7] For an exception, see above, chapter 8.
[8] Cf. rules 47–53 of the Prison Rules 1947.
[9] See further, Peadar Cowan, *Dungeons Deep*, pp. 20–21.

In the late nineteen forties consideration was given to a plan to hand over responsibility for the operation of the Southern borstal to a religious order. The plan came to nothing, but, with such ideas being mooted, it is no surprise to learn that the atmosphere within the institution should have become both more religious and more Catholic. The visiting committee certainly sought to convey this impression in its 1948 pamphlet and the remodelling of the régime on the lines of a school, as opposed to that of a prison, probably helped too. Change had indeed taken place. In 1948, the institution (significantly just renamed St Patrick's) boasted one chaplain and three assistant chaplains; they all played a much larger part in the life of the institution and one of them always attended the interview at which the governor discussed future plans with a boy nearing discharge.

Extra provision was made to facilitate religious observance. Mass was celebrated each Sunday and holy day in the chapel, and this was followed in the evening by rosary, sermon and benediction. (There was a chapel choir which sang to the accompaniment of a harmonium played by one of the inmates.) Each weekday evening, the rosary was again recited. The blessed sacrament was reserved in the chapel and boys could always go there in their spare time. Confessions were heard on Saturdays and there was also an annual retreat. The visiting committee's pamphlet, from which these details are drawn, also mentions that on reception each boy was given a prayer book, rosary beads and the New Testament and was allowed to retain any religious books approved by the chaplain and any pious object.[10]

The move to Dublin in 1956 brought about further changes. A full-time Catholic chaplain was appointed, who, unlike any predecessor in Clonmel, was expected specifically to assist in training and rehabilitation. The priest immersed himself in the life of St Patrick's: he taught secular subjects in the 'school', kept boys in touch with their homes, sought employment for them on release, and even opened a club for former inmates. Until the appointment of the first welfare officer in 1964, he appears to have operated a one-man welfare service. He received many tributes for his work. In 1957, "the prevailing excellent atmosphere in the institution" was said to be due largely to his influence. In 1960, Oscar Traynor, the Minister for Justice, went so far as to suggest in the Dáil that the chaplain held the key to success:

Having regard to the preponderance of offenders serving short sentences, prolonged training in the accepted sense is impracticable for most inmates of St Patrick's and for them the Institution must

[10] *Clonmel Notes*, pp. 10–11.

remain primarily a place of detention. Yet even for these 'short-termers', a period spent in St Patrick's can contribute to their better-ment and this is because the spiritual training of the Catholic youths, who constitute virtually all the inmates, has been in the hands of a full-time chaplain since the Institution was transferred from Clonmel.[11]

The chaplain's responsibility was indeed heavy.

The pattern of religious observance appears to have altered little over the years. The first annual retreat at the new St Patrick's was held in 1957; in 1964 a second retreat was organised during Advent, to ensure "that many short-term inmates had the benefit of attending these spiritual exercises." Special lectures with a religious flavour were also introduced. In 1959,

> Mr Charlie McDonald, whose cure at Lourdes has been passed by the International Medical Bureau, held his audience spellbound with a graphic account of his illness and miraculous recovery. This was a most moving experience and provided much food for thought and discussion in the days that followed.

The next year, a Jesuit gave a talk on Matt Talbot.[12] The *Prisons Report* records that "as most of the boys were familiar with the setting of the story and the type of people involved, they listened with rapt attention and had many questions for the distinguished speaker."

Talks have been given regularly on the life of St John Bosco.[13] On St Patrick's Day in 1958 there was "a special blessing and distribution of the shamrock and a word to explain its real significance for Irishmen the world over." In 1961 colour slides and films of the Dublin Patrician Congress were shown. Three years later, following a special talk on the Ecumenical Council, a majority of the boys, on their own initiative, arranged for a spiritual bouquet of masses and prayers for its success and Pope Paul, in reply, sent his apostolic blessing to the boys and their parents.

---

[11] *Dáil Debates*, Vol. 183, cols. 556–57, 28 June 1960.
[12] The working-class Dublin ascetic who died in 1926.
[13] Born in Piedmont 1815 and died in Turin 1888. Donald Attwater in *The Penguin Dictionary of Saints* (Harmondsworth: Penguin Books, 1965) writes (p. 197): "St John Bosco, who once wrote that he did not remember ever having formally to punish a boy (and some of his protégés were what are now called 'juvenile delinquents'), was an outstanding figure in the efflorescence of heroic sanctity in North Italy in the nineteenth century. His work was beset by many difficulties, some of them gratuitously put in his way by both anti-clerical civil authorities and unsympathetic ecclesiastics: what he achieved is the index to his life and character."

Religious observance has been important at Shanganagh too. The chapel was the first major scheme to be completed and in the same year, 1970, a resident chaplain was appointed there. Attendance at daily mass averages 30 per cent. and two retreats are held each year.

Discipline

Breaks from routine merit special attention in any sketch of life in the institutions. A boy's routine may be interrupted to enable him to see the governor, doctor, dentist or a lawyer. Other interruptions stem from challenges to the fundamental principle of order on which life in an institution is made ultimately to depend: escapes, attempts at escape and other breaches of discipline. The information about them comes principally from the South.

The first crop of escapes dates from 1922 and 1923, a period of general civil unrest when the administration of the borstal system was especially difficult.[14] The frequent shifting of the borstal increased the risks of escape and it is no surprise that there was a large number of successful escapes from both Clogheen and Kilkenny.[15]

Not until the borstal moved to Cork in 1940 do the reports again mention escapes. At Cork, concession of the right to attend an outside football ground and swimming-pool proved too great a temptation for some; others were still prepared to attempt a harder means of escape from within the institution itself. When the borstal returned to Clonmel in 1947 the opportunities for escaping from there were greater than ever before: a more liberal daily routine, first introduced at Cork, tended to make escape easier, but another contributing factor was the decision deliberately to relax security, which in the years before 1940 had made escape from Clonmel particularly hazardous. The Northern Ireland authorities well appreciated the risks they ran when somewhat earlier they had made identical changes at Malone. Their counterparts in the South learnt the same hard lesson, for these changes at Clonmel were followed by a rash of attempts to escape, most of them unsuccessful. In recent years escapes and escape attempts have continued but, in general, they have passed unremarked in the official reports.[16]

Too much should not be read into the information in the reports on other breaches of discipline: it is unlikely that it will prove enlightening on the character of the institution itself. There is the apparent exception, of course: for instance, the incident of the boy at Cork who went on hunger-strike in 1944 in protest against compulsory attendance at mass.

[14] Above, chapter 4.
[15] *Prisons Board Report 1922–23*, p.v.
[16] Except as bald statistics in the official reports.

Other incidents possess their own interest, the best example perhaps being the affair of the boy with a history of mental trouble, who at St Patrick's in 1962—so the visiting committee found—was prevailed upon by other boys to level false charges against a member of the staff. Information on preventive measures, though scant, is interesting. At St Patrick's, in 1971, feeding arrangements were altered so that the boys would henceforth be enabled to take their meals in their cells. The visiting committee wrote:

> [The change] has also eliminated an area of potential trouble, where a small but unruly group were always on the look-out for an opportunity to start a mock-fight in a crowded dining hall.

Events outside the institutions may inspire mass breaches of discipline. This is the obvious explanation for what happened in 1972 when groups of boys, both North and South, in clear imitation of more adult prisoners in Ireland and England, staged roof-top sit-downs to draw attention to a variety of grievances.[17] (Not to be outdone, three boys at Armagh went on hunger-strike the following year to protest against being denied political prisoner status).[18] But unruliness is not always the result of outside influences. In the South in 1948, as the *Prisons Report* for that year discloses, 36 boys at Clonmel were punished on 128 occasions. The offences had occurred, it is declared, because:

> . . . inmates on committal are inclined to be unruly, undisciplined and resentful of authority. Abuse of officers and the use of filthy and obscene language is very common in the early period of sentences . . . With three exceptions all the offences for which punishment was awarded were committed in the early stages.

The threat to discipline from fresh arrivals has long been recognised but until recently nothing was done to counteract it. Indeed, the decision to establish a second Northern institution at Armagh as an induction centre represented the first attempt in Ireland, North or South, to forestall indiscipline. One of the considerations in setting up the centre was the necessity to reduce the number of escapes from the relatively 'open' institution at Woburn. In the South, though little has been done to cope with the problem of a 'mixing of streams', its existence has been admitted. The difficulty was first recognised at the time when short-term juvenile adult prisoners began to be sent to Clonmel to swell the numbers there and thus promote the institution's economic viability. The policy had

---

[17] *The Irish Times*, 15 May (Woburn); 16 August (St Patrick's); 11 September (Armagh).
[18] *The Irish Times*, 24 January 1973.

certain disadvantages, as the visiting committee was soon to point out. It complained about the lack of discipline among the transferees, a grievance which matched that of borstal detainees over discriminatory sentencing. The atmosphere at Clonmel appears to have grown increasingly unsettled and matters did not improve when, in the final years, proper borstal training was curtailed. The mixing of short- and long-term offenders continued when St Patrick's moved to Dublin; indeed, the facilitation of this appears to have influenced the move to the capital. In 1959, however, the new visiting committee expressed its view that the arrangement was far from ideal:

> These short term inmates tend to unsettle the general balance. As they come and go so soon, the penalty imposed ceases to be an effective deterrent, and they react with an assumed indifference to the consequences of the law. Their short sojourn gives little opportunity to a conscientious staff for exercising on them any formative influence.

The range of sanctions available to the authorities at the institution says much about the character of the place itself. On the question of sanctions, there has been a marked difference between Northern Ireland and the South. In the South, dietary punishment is still employed; in the North, this has ended, but, on the other hand, stoppage of earnings remains commonplace, whereas this is rare in the Republic. In the North corporal punishment continues to be available. Special legislation was enacted to enable it to be imposed[19] and the authorities have not refused to use it. In the South, on the other hand, corporal punishment is not available, and it may be remembered that in 1948 the visiting committee vigorously denied that it ever had been. The likeliest explanation for this difference is that the entire régime in the North has been consciously modelled on that within a public boarding school, for the general attitude to the use of corporal punishment has probably been similar in the two communities.

Complaints regarding food are predictable in any closed society of men, and dissatisfaction with the prescribed institution diet might be expected to lie at the back of certain breaches of discipline. Yet, if this has been so, the official sources do not admit it. In general, they preserve silence on the topic. In 1927, however, it was disclosed by a Member of Parliament that the Northern Ireland boys who had been transferred back to Malone from their English borstal did not find the meals there to their liking.[20] And again in recent years, there has been dissatisfaction with the food at St Patrick's, though not over quantity. In 1967 the rule

---

[19] It is no dead letter: there were 29 canings in 1971.
[20] H. C. Debates (N.I.), Vol. 8, col. 786: Mr Henderson.

was that on two days a week a boy got a stew with 6 oz. of meat in it; on others, the principal meal was corned beef or ordinary beef and vegetables, when the allowance was 8 oz. "What woman with a family", the governor asked, "could afford to give each of them eight ounces of meat every day?"[21] What the visiting committee began to complain about was an absence of variety. In 1969, it wrote:

> We are still awaiting the equipment promised to prepare chips, mash, and other variations in the basic diet. The introduction of eggs, cheese, salad, and fruit could be—for many—their first experience in a nutrition programme, to be carried over, we would hope, in their adult lives.[22]

The committee anticipated the end of the saga in 1971:

> It was difficult to appreciate the many explanations put forward for the unreasonable delays in the re-fitting of the kitchen—this was something long overdue. When the vegetable-preparation and wash-up areas have been attended to, all will be relieved to reach the end of a long road.

There is no culinary compliment equal to that paid by an anonymous inspector to the nuns who ran one of the Catholic reformatory and industrial schools in Northern Ireland:[23] the food was "abundant, appetising and well-served."[24]

Staff

James Watson, governor at Malone from 1927 to 1949,[25] left an indelible mark there but, of course, all governors and their staffs have been central to the life of their institution. As the men on the spot, it is they who have represented authority to the boys, and not the remote civil servant whose consent to discharge may be required, or the equally remote judge who will have been responsible for committal in the first place. The role of governors and their staffs has been decisive, but the problems faced by them in carrying out their work have not received as much attention as might have been expected. The *Reports*, it is true, commend

---

[21] "The Young Law-Breakers", *The Irish Times*, 3 July 1967.
[22] In the same paragraph, the committee wrote: "We are glad to record improvements in kitchen and dining-room. Already, the bread-slicer has eliminated waste and the more normal cutting must be a help, psychologically."
[23] St Joseph's reformatory and industrial school for girls, Middletown, County Armagh.
[24] *Home Office Services Report 1935*, p. 21.
[25] Mr Watson had previously been manager of the reformatory school at Malone.

them for their devotion[26], and especially warm tributes are paid to various people who have worked above and beyond the call of duty. In the South, there are tributes to two members of staff for organising boxing, to others for teaching carpentry classes and revising the educational programme, and to the first full-time chaplain at St Patrick's; in the North there is a fulsome tribute to a principal officer who had put heart and soul into life-saving instruction.

The *Reports* also pay particular attention to grievances over shortage of staff, especially the difficulty of hiring qualified personnel. Economies during World War I prevented the acquisition of an instructor for the band at Clonmel and in the nineteen twenties left the institution without an instructor in tailoring. Absence of money delayed the appointment of full-time tutors in the North during the nineteen sixties, and in the South there were long delays before money could be found to appoint the first welfare officer at St Patrick's, and again before the first fully qualified educationalist was selected. Difficulties in recruiting are rarely alluded to in the reports but an exception was 1927 when staff were being sought for the new Northern institution at Malone. The Ministry of Home Affairs regretted that as many as 75 per cent. of the appointees were ex-servicemen.

Staff members themselves have been concerned about the quality of their living quarters and general conditions of employment, and both matters receive attention in the reports, though whether as a mere matter of record or for some ulterior purpose is uncertain. The information is again sparse. In 1922, Kevin O'Higgins made it clear that a factor contributing to the selection of the Clogheen workhouse as a temporary borstal was the excellence of the staff accommodation. Thereafter, staff living quarters are only mentioned when improvements to them are recorded. At Cork, accommodation was constructed for the chief warder and his family. At Clonmel, the intern officers' quarters were included in a general renovation prior to the return of the institution in 1947, and these dwellings were reconstructed and renovated again in 1950. In the early nineteen fifties, hot water systems and baths were installed, and a sewer laid in the staff cottages at Clonmel. In St Patrick's the staff cottages were provided with new front doors and fuel sheds in 1962; fresh floors were laid in two of the buildings in 1965. There were staff houses, too, at the first Northern institution. It is likely that they were better appointed than those in the South since they were newly built in the grounds at

---

[26] Compare the position in earlier centuries. "We have yet to find in medieval art or literature a prison-keeper worthy to stand at the Judgment Seat beside Dr Primrose's gaoler or Dr Johnson's friend Richard Akerman": Ralph B. Pugh, *Imprisonment in Medieval England* (Cambridge: Cambridge University Press, 1968), p. 183.

Malone. At Woburn there are attractive staff houses in a crescent adjacent to the institution.

Before 1922 one extraordinary aspect of conditions of employment for borstal staff was discussed in Parliament. In a parliamentary question in May 1921, the Chief Secretary for Ireland was asked:[27] was it the case that the bachelor officers of the Clonmel borstal were denied a mess and, if so, was it not dangerous to expect them to eat food cooked by the inmates and objectionable in the present state of the country to force them to board out? Denis Henry, the Irish Attorney General, replying for the Chief Secretary, reassured the questioner. The practice, he thought, was neither dangerous nor objectionable and he had heard no complaints. In any event, Treasury rules stipulated that there must be a minimum of six bachelor officers before a mess could be established. At Clonmel, only two of the permanent officers were bachelors, and his information was that the two bachelor temporary officers were quite content to eat out.

In 1941, Fahy criticised conditions of employment at the Cork borstal. He thought that the working day was too long; at the time, the day extended, it seems, from early morning to final lock-up at night.[28] Improvements in pay and conditions have generally passed without notice but there were exceptions. In the North, the *Home Office Services Report* for 1930 welcomed the news that borstal staff had been placed on the same status, rates of pay and allowances as prison officers. An increase in the level of remuneration for staff at St Patrick's in 1964 drew a comment from the visiting committee: "This welcome trend should make the career more attractive for men of mature personality, to enter and to persevere in this vital service for the character formation of wayward youth."

The clothes worn by the staff may also tell us something about the atmosphere of the institution. Fahy, comparing in 1941 the position at Cork with that at Malone, reckoned that there was a connection. Cork, in his view, was authoritarian. The staff wore the dress of a prison warder, complete with belt and truncheon, and no distinction was drawn between the dress of training and discipline officers.[29] It was very different in Northern Ireland and has remained so. In the South at the present time, only the staff at Shanganagh and Loughan wear ordinary clothes.

The training and recruitment of custodial staff generally is now receiving belated attention in the Republic. The theme was mentioned by Desmond O'Malley, the then Minister for Justice, in 1970, when he supported the idea of pre-service training, but was forced to conclude that, in the short term, the introduction of any scheme was unlikely:

[27] *H. C. Debates* (5 series), Vol. 141, col. 1886, 11 May 1921: Mr Hirst.
[28] Fahy, "Borstal in Ireland", p. 83.
[29] ibid., p. 82.

". . . normally prison officers are recruited in small numbers at irregular intervals and this makes the organisation of pre-service training impracticable except at extravagant cost."[30]

[30] *Dáil Debates,* Vol. 247, col 105, 26 May 1970.

CHAPTER X

Borstal and Related Systems Assessed

But they never taught honour at the Grinders' School, where the system that prevailed was particularly strong in the engendering of hypocrisy. Insomuch, that many of the friends and masters of past Grinders said, if this were what came of education for the common people, let us have none. Some more rational said, let us have a better one. But the governing powers of the Grinders' Company were always ready for them, by picking out a few boys who had turned out well, in spite of the system, and roundly asserting that they could have only turned out well because of it. Which settled the business of those objectors out of hand, and established the glory of the Grinders' Institution.
Charles Dickens, *Dombey and Son*, chapter 38.

Reforms in the penal system excite, in the short term, an amount of overly enthusiastic support. So it was with borstal. In England, an early propagandist, R. F. Quinton, saw borstal fulfilling the same role as the reformatory school in helping stamp out the juvenile criminal gang. "The removal", he wrote in 1910, "of the heads, or of the leading spirits, to other spheres of industry at once damps the energies of the remainder and leads to the disbandment of the whole gang."[1] The original advocates of borstal had a different objective—they sought to reduce adult recidivism—and it was probably to attain this end that the Irish

---

[1] Richard Frith Quinton, *Crime and Criminals 1876–1910* (London: Longmans, 1910) pp. 124–25.

Prisons Board introduced the borstal system in 1906. For many years the Board was caution itself and only in 1915 did it express its firm belief in the wisdom of the initiative it had taken nine years before. Nevertheless, in the early months at Clonmel, committed voices were heard. The Church of Ireland chaplain wrote in his first report that he considered the borstal system "eminently qualified to help forward the reformation of these youths' lives."[2] The Catholic chaplain was less restrained. At a lecture he gave on temperance, every Catholic present had taken the pledge. Plainly affected by this response, he declared: "The extension of the Borstal system to this country . . . is a great blessing."[3]

A clergyman's opinion that borstal was a blessing did not make it one.[4] Nevertheless, for many years the position remained that much of the evidence adduced in favour of borstal consisted of little more than the expectations of clergymen and others. Information on success rates, it is true, was soon to be published, but however favourable the conclusions, they were drawn too quickly and, as a result, consciences were salved too easily. No fundamental inquiries into the borstal system were undertaken anywhere and no lead was provided in Ireland. As elsewhere, of course, there was tangible proof of apparent success: a borstal physically existed, the institution flourished and a variety of officials had grown accustomed to make use of it or even to earn a living from it. The question remained whether the system did any good, but some will have decided it was not worth asking. Others, while prepared to ask the question, will have thought the answer was provided by the conclusions to be drawn from the data on success rates.

Partition prompted the authorities to examine the *raison d'être* of the borstal system. In the South, the stimulus for an investigation was the crisis which overtook the institution in what had become the Irish Free State. Committals from Northern Ireland ended in 1921 and the numbers given in charge from within the Free State remained so low that, by 1925, the closure of the institution at Clonmel was seriously entertained.[5] This drastic step was not taken, at least for the moment, and a Southern borstal survived for another thirty years. In Northern Ireland the future of the borstal system was even more uncertain. In 1921 no local institution existed and at first nobody agitated for one to be opened.[6] In 1923, it is true, a majority of resident magistrates came out in favour of the borstal system,[7] and one spoke highly of what had been accomplished

---

[2] Quoted, *Prisons Board Report 1906–07*, p. 88.
[3] ibid.
[4] "I must be tolerably sure before I venture publicly to congratulate men upon a blessing, that they have really received one": Edmund Burke, *Reflections on the Revolution in France* (Harmondsworth: Penguin ed. 1968), p. 90.
[5] Above, chapter 4.
[6] Above, chapter 3.
[7] *Moles Report*, pp. 53 ff.

at Clonmel, but another R.M., Major Dickie, strongly disagreed with his colleagues. It was ill-advised, he wrote to the Moles Committee, to shut up boys at an impressionable age together with others of proven bad character in what amounted to a prison atmosphere. If boys were normal, Major Dickie continued, they would probably "steady down"; if not, no treatment he knew of would turn them into good citizens.[8] The Moles Committee was eventually to report in favour of the opening of a local borstal institution for Northern Ireland, but it needs to be recalled that it was under some pressure to do so: for reasons of constitutional law connected with the position of the Northern Ireland judiciary, the borstal system as such had to be retained, irrespective of what was done about the provision of a local institution.[9] Reasons of constitutional law differ from reasons based on conviction.

They are different again from economic considerations, which, for so long, prevented a borstal for girls being set up.[10] Before and after 1922, financial restrictions also determined official thinking on the operation of the borstals for boys, and were to lead in the South, in 1925, to the suggestion that the Clonmel institution should close, and in the early nineteen fifties to the decision to operate it as a joint institution for borstal detainees and young prisoners. In Ireland, from the outset, the force of the economic argument was exceedingly strong: the inmate population was always likely to be small. This factor, in one sense, put the Prisons Board on the defensive, but at the same time had the effect of galvanising it into action, for it set out to secure the public's acceptance of the value of what it was doing. The Board started to publish information on all facets of borstal in Ireland, and, in particular, on the people committed to borstal: their ages, their previous records, the crimes of which they had been convicted, their educational standards, their county of origin, even, on one occasion, their religious affiliation. Of still greater interest to the Board was any evidence suggesting that borstal was a success. In assessing the operation of borstal and of related custodial systems in Ireland, this kind of evidence which the Board and its successors managed to put together is of cardinal importance.

It consists, for the most part, of data on the reconvictions of borstal discharges occurring within three years of release (the period is shorter in some instances). The data was invariably presented in the form of a success rate. In the South, less information is available for recent years and the reasons may help to explain the comparative dearth of information for Northern Ireland.

Details for the years between 1906 and 1921 are far from complete

---

[8] At p. 59.
[9] Above, chapter 3.
[10] Above, chapter 6.

and facts are available only for the years from 1907 to 1910 and for 1914, 1915 and 1918. In the first full year, 1907, the success rate was reported to be 83 per cent.; thereafter, it fluctuated between 58 per cent. (1909) and 83 per cent. (1914). From 1914 to 1918 and, by implication, for a few more years as well, a minimum rate of 80 per cent. was maintained.

The only data for Northern Ireland to be preserved in an annual *Home Office Services Report* is that based on an early survey carried out by the visiting committee at Malone. The committee reviewed the cases of all boys released since October 1927, and published the results four years later. These showed that 65 per cent. had not got into any further trouble. Despite appearances to the contrary, the fate of the remaining 35 per cent. was no cause for concern either: any trouble that they had got into, the committee found, was of a trivial character and could not be classed as criminal (unfortunately, the sort of trouble is not specified).

Reasonably complete data is available for the Republic between 1924 and 1960 and there is also some data after 1960 for St Patrick's. Prior to 1934, statistics appeared at irregular intervals (1925, 1927, 1928, 1932 and 1933) but the *Prisons Report* for 1934 included comprehensive data on all discharges since 1924. The method used was a success rate based on a three-year follow-up for discharges in each of the years from 1924 to 1931. This rate never fell below 75 per cent. (the 1925 discharges) and was never more than 86 per cent. (the 1926 and 1928 discharges). The *Reports* for 1935 to 1938 presented similar information for those discharged between 1932 and 1935: the rate was highest (85 per cent.) for the 1932 discharges but it slumped to 61 per cent. for those released in 1935. The next *Report* to appear, that for 1944, omitted information relating to the 1936 discharges but provided it for all discharges between 1937 and 1941; the highest rate was found to be 86 per cent. for 1940 and the lowest, 64 per cent., for those discharged in 1939.

Bald success-rate figures are given in each of the years from 1945 to 1960 but it is clear both from the *Reports* and from the method of their presentation that these figures relate to all releases within the immediately preceding three years and not to each annual group of releases. The practice in earlier years was rather different, and it is unfortunate that, as a result of the change introduced in 1945, the figures for the years before and after are not easily comparable. It is some compensation, however, that the information reproduced since the end of World War II is more extensive than before. Percentages start to be kept of discharges who could not be traced, discharges committed to prison, and also those whose conduct had been unsatisfactory. From 1942 to 1960, the highest success rate is 80 per cent. (for the 1953–55 discharges, reported on at the end of 1955) and the lowest, 61 per cent. (for the 1957–59 discharges, reported on at the end of 1959).

Nineteen fifty-seven is the first year in which follow-up data is available for juvenile adults as opposed to borstal detainees. Such data is included in a number of the *Reports* in ensuing years, but lacks detail. The relevant *Reports* are content to give the total juvenile adults discharged within a certain period and the numbers known subsequently to have been re-committed to St Patrick's or sentenced to imprisonment; there are no percentages recorded.

After 1960 no official follow-up information for St Patrick's appears in the *Reports*. Not that the Department of Justice had lost interest, for in May 1970 during a Dáil debate, the then Minister,[11] Desmond O'Malley, referred to the fact that reconviction rates for Shanganagh releases were being compiled. (He went on to concede that these would not have any real significance until figures for a minimum follow-up period of two or three years were available). The *Prisons Report* for 1970 betrays some further special concern with discharges from Shanganagh: the cases had been reviewed of some 100 boys who had passed through Shanganagh, and 79 per cent. of these had not been in further trouble.

Unofficial studies have been made of boys discharged from St Patrick's. At the suggestion of the institution's chaplain, social science students from University College Dublin carried out a survey of boys released in both 1962 and 1963. The follow-up was for three years and the students found that some 28 per cent. of the discharged boys had got into further trouble and had been recommitted to St Patrick's or to Mountjoy Jail. A substantial proportion had emigrated to England.[12]

All this information is of value, but nonetheless suffers from certain defects. In the first place, the follow-up periods are not always of uniform length. The figures for the Clonmel borstal in 1907 clearly were based on a one-year period; those for the Malone borstal in 1927–30, for the Southern institutions in 1944–56, for St Patrick's in 1956–60, and for Shanganagh in 1968–70 were for anything from one to three years.

Nor are all the surveys equally concerned to identify a proportion of non-traceable releases who cannot be treated either as 'successful' or as 'disappointments'. A proportion is regularly supplied by the collator of the data for the South between 1952 and 1960 and the information is also available for certain of the earlier years (1925, 1927 and 1928, for example). The figure itself is not unimportant: eight per cent. of those under investigation in years as far apart as 1927, 1955 and 1959 could not be traced and the figure was even higher, at 11 per cent., in 1925. The *Prisons Report* for 1935 admits that figures relating to the subsequent history of discharged boys had decreased on account of increased emigration. Such a disclosure inevitably raises the question of the quality of

[11] *Dáil Debates*, Vol. 247, col. 96, 26 May 1970.
[12] *The Irish Times*, 3 July 1967; *Prisons Report 1965*, p. 21.

statistical data forwarded to the collator in the South. It can be assumed that the Garda Síochána will have cooperated in supplying information on reconvictions occurring in the twenty-six counties, but what happened where the reconviction occurred in England, as it could easily have done and where from time to time it certainly did? And how well-equipped were the employers, the clergymen and the agent for discharged prisoners (referred to in the *Prisons Report* for 1934) to supply the kind of information sought by the scrupulous civil servant?

Another difficulty with the statistics is that variations in prosecution policy can give a false impression if reconviction rates are looked at in the abstract. The point cannot be ignored. In 1936 the governor at Clonmel is reported to have remarked that in that year there was not more crime but more committals. People are aware of variations in sentencing practice; they need to be reminded of variations in prosecution practice too.

Nevertheless, with all their defects, the figures extrapolated from the *Reports* probably give a reasonably accurate impression of the proportion of discharged boys from borstal and St Patrick's who have subsequently got into further trouble with the law. It is now time to raise two critical questions. Does the information to hand enable any kind of qualitative assessment to be made? And has it ever?

A number of people have certainly thought that it has. In 1956, the visiting committee for the Clonmel institution, in reporting a disappointing success rate for 1954–56 discharges (69 per cent.), inclined to the opinion that curtailments in the training programme at Clonmel were responsible: if these had not occurred, the committee insinuated, the institution would have been able to prevent a higher proportion of offenders from relapsing into further crime on release. People in Northern Ireland have also thought that the data enabled a qualitative evaluation to be made. Sir Dawson Bates did, for a start. In the *Report on the Prisons in Northern Ireland 1926–27*, he wrote:[13] "The [Borstal] Institution is as yet in its initial stage, but I have little doubt that it will prove as valuable a factor in the redemption of lads from a life of crime as the similar institutions in Great Britain." So too did the Malone visiting committee. Convinced of the merits of the borstal system by its follow-up study of 1931, the committee drew this additional conclusion:

Having regard to their past history, and owing especially to unemployment difficulties, it is considered that if 65 per cent. of these lads can be turned into decent citizens, the system must be worthwhile. Given normal conditions of employment, the percentage would probably be higher.

[13] At p. 5.

In Ireland the largest claims ever made on behalf of the borstal system were put forward by the old Prisons Board on two occasions prior to 1922. We have seen that the Board was slow to express its views on the merits of borstal, but the favourable results of studies conducted during World War I encouraged the Board at last to speak its mind. The "very satisfactory results", the Board wrote in its *Report* for 1919, "are achieved simply by a blending of kindness with strict discipline and hard work, the object being to inculcate a spirit of manliness and self-reliance, approximating to that which obtains in public schools." Four years earlier, in 1915, in the wake of the favourable impression conveyed by another follow-up study, the Board had gone further. "It is more than probable", it wrote,

> that many of the habitual criminals who now cost the State large sums annually would not have continued in their criminal courses had they been afforded a thorough training in a well-equipped Borstal institution at an early stage of their career.

It has always been tempting to believe that, because a proportion of inmates of a penal institution invariably manage to avoid further brushes with the law, it is the experience of the institution itself which has been decisive. Previous generations succumbed to the temptation, but are entitled to be excused; even Dickens may have laboured in vain when he sought to disabuse his readers about the many accomplishments of that distinguished educational establishment, the Grinders' Company school of *Dombey and Son*. There are grounds for praising a penal institution, and there is the incentive for improving physical conditions and even experimenting with the régime, if the inmates' crime-free subsequent careers can be scientifically linked with their experience of the institution itself. Belief in the reality of the link may be an important item in the motivation of the staff member. Even so, it is clear that there is no necessary connection between an inmate's institutional experience and his later career. The institution may make a difference in a number of cases, but, equally, it may not, and it is naive to believe that a penal institution must take the credit in any case where the former inmate 'goes straight'.[14]

It is now acknowledged that a number of factors may determine whether or not the discharged inmate's later career is free from crime.[15] A young man may make a spontaneous recovery as a result of marrying,

---

[14] For awareness of this, see the speech of Mr O'Malley: *Dáil Debates*, Vol. 247, col. 96, 26 May 1970.

[15] See, conveniently, Nigel Walker, *Sentencing in a Rational Society* (Harmondsworth: Allen Lane, The Penguin Press, 1969), chapter 6.

growing older or, simply, in the phrase of the Northern R.M., Major Dickie, "steadying down". After-care may have been as important to the outcome as the experience of the particular institution. The institution may have some influence, but whether one kind of institution is likely to have been more successful than another is by no means obvious, nor whether some non-custodial sanction is to be preferred: published studies reveal similar 'failure rates' proportionate to the length of the criminal record of the offender. Of course, the length of record will always be critical, and this furnishes a reason for dismissing as unsound the Prison Board's euphoria over the Irish borstal system in both 1915 and 1919. The Board's enthusiasm grew out of follow-up studies published in the two years concerned, but at the time in question more than half of the boys being sent to Clonmel were first offenders. The Board did not ignore the point but neither did it choose to emphasise it. It was little wonder, then, that the success rate (at over 80 per cent.) was so high. The true teaching of the relevant follow-up studies needs to be appreciated: it may be not that borstal made any significant difference, but rather that those with a short or non-existent criminal record are not as likely as others to get into trouble again, irrespective of what the penal system has decided to do about them.

Statistics on the rate of reconviction are extremely useful and should be made easily accessible. But the rate can never say whether either borstal or St Patrick's is especially effective. The approach of the modern penologist to the value of reconviction rates is lucidly summarised in a paragraph from the British command paper, *People in Prison*,[16] which goes on to ask some fundamental questions on measuring the efficacy of any form of penal sanction:

> It must never be assumed that an offender who goes straight after release does so because of what happened to him in custody. Nor must it be assumed that an offender has gained no benefit from his treatment in prison or borstal because he again comes before the courts. His reconviction may be for a relatively minor and isolated offence as a result of which he may not return to custody and which may not prevent him from becoming an acceptable and useful member of society. Finally, because offenders, even those serving similar sentences, vary so widely in their temperaments, backgrounds, and criminal or non-criminal careers, an average reconviction rate may conceal such wide variations as, of itself, to be of little significance.[17]

---

[16] Cmnd. 4214, 1969.
[17] At p. 52.

Assessing the success of any penal treatment is not assisted by crude reconviction rates and, consequently, remains as difficult as before. Measuring the success of a punitive sanction, such as detention in borstal or in the modern St Patrick's, likewise remains extremely difficult—if not impossible. Roger Hood in his survey of borstal in England wrote: "If the borstal system is to be judged it must be assessed in terms of the vocational, personal and educational effects it has had on the boy."[18] Bottoms and McClintock employed experimental designs for Dover borstal to test such matters there. Future research in Ireland must adopt a similar approach. If this is not done, no proper assessment of the operation of borstal and related systems in Ireland will be possible.

---

[18] Hood, *Borstal Re-Assessed*, p. 200.

CHAPTER XI

Administration in Northern Ireland and the Irish Republic

For forms of government let fools contest;
Whate'er is best administered is best:
For modes of faith let graceless zealots fight;
His can't be wrong whose life is in the right:
In faith and hope the world will disagree,
But all mankind's concern is charity.
from Alexander Pope, *An Essay on Man*, Ep. iii, lines 303–308.

Administration in Northern Ireland and the Republic may be compared under three headings:
  (i) constitutional and legal framework;
 (ii) judicial sentencing practice;
(iii) day-to-day operation of the institutions.
Differences under the third heading are of the most interest, but those under the first two tell us much, not only about both borstal and related institutions North and South, but also about the penal systems of the two jurisdictions.

Constitutional and legal framework

From partition onwards, the Irish prison authorities were to operate within two distinct constitutional and legal traditions. In the long term, differences in statute law were to have the greater practical effect, but the impact after 1922 both of changes in constitutional status and of variations in constitutional law cannot be ignored.

For borstal in Ireland, December 1921 was the turning-point: the North ended committals to Clonmel and set about negotiating alternative arrangements for boys who were sentenced locally to borstal. In the twenty-six counties, the discontinuance of Northern committals to Clonmel raised at once the question of the future of the institution there.

Constitutional restrictions on its Parliament's legislative powers accompanied Northern Ireland's continuance within the United Kingdom, and one of these was to influence the future of borstal in the six counties. This was the prohibition of legislation affecting the new Northern Ireland Supreme Court of Judicature, embracing matters which have remained reserved ever since to the Parliament of the United Kingdom at Westminster. Any local legislation purporting to deal with the sentencing powers of the judiciary fell within this prohibition. This had two practical effects. It entailed, first, that provision had to continue to be made for a borstal system, irrespective of the views of the Northern Ireland government. The Moles Committee grasped the point in its report of 1923. There is no way of telling what might have happened, had the constitutional position been different.

Ironically, at the same time as the Northern Ireland government was moving towards its decision to open a local borstal, the government in the Free State was invited to consider a plan to scrap its existing institution which it had inherited from the British. Thus, from the outset, a critical difference in circumstances dictated policy. Northern Ireland was forced to establish a full borstal system and the Free State voluntarily decided to continue to operate one. The Free State government had greater freedom of action in the legal sense, but it is problematic whether it reaped any advantage.

A second consequence of the restriction on the powers of the Northern Parliament was that, for a number of years, it was debarred from enacting legislation on matters of procedure connected with borstal sentences and with appeals against them. A right of appeal was established in the Free State in 1924 and elaborated in 1928; Northern Ireland, however, had to wait until 1930 when a similar right was introduced, following enabling legislation enacted at Westminster. Even so, further legislation became necessary. The Free State legislature, in contrast, was supreme, but legislative supremacy on its own is no virtue, and the Oireachtas missed the opportunity to enact legislation which, in retrospect, appears to have been desirable. No change was introduced to enable a boy to appeal against a borstal sentence imposed by the Circuit Court, following his forwarding there by the district court. Legislation to meet this kind of contingency was enacted for Northern Ireland. Secondly, nothing was done to enable boys so forwarded for sentence to be granted bail in the interim. Conversely, in the North something was done, if not by the legislature: resident magistrates decided on their own initiative to admit to bail in such cases.

The fact that Northern Ireland remained part of the United Kingdom was to prove, to an extent, an administrative convenience. Authority for intra-United Kingdom transfers had been given by a provision of the Act of 1908, and, in circumstances which could not have been envisaged then, it was to solve the problem facing the Northern Ministry of Home Affairs from December 1921: where boys committed locally to a borstal were to be sent, in the absence of any local institution. The provision in the Act meant that they could be sent to an English borstal and, until 1927, this was what occurred. At a later period, the same transfer power was employed for girls, but in 1948 these arrangements broke down and the Northern Ireland government was forced, *faute de mieux*, to open its own borstal for girls. As chapter 6 relates, the institution did not thrive and was abandoned on the revival of the transfer power by Westminster legislation in 1961. This other experience of the consequences of membership of the United Kingdom had been more chastening.

Use of this 1961 legislation means that what Northern Ireland does with its older girl offenders can differ considerably from what happens in the Republic. Two questions arise, however, both of which need to be answered. Has the Republic been any the worse for lacking a female borstal or female equivalent of St Patrick's? And has Northern Ireland been better off because it can transfer its borstal girls to Britain to serve their sentences there?

The administration of the entire penal system in the Republic is being increasingly influenced by the Constitution of 1937. A major development is the encouragement it has afforded to the launching of habeas corpus applications by detained offenders. This has tended to mean that matters which in Northern Ireland would be handled by the executive—a magistrate misconceiving his sentencing powers, for instance—in the Republic would probably be dealt with by the courts.[1] This concentration by the judiciary on personal rights has brought some unexpected dividends. It is extraordinary, for example, that in recent years the habeas corpus application should have been the cue for such exhaustive

---

[1] This impression needs to be confirmed by further study. It appears probable, however, that the problem handled judicially by the Dublin High Court in *The State (Hanley)* v. *Governor of Mountjoy Prison*, 12 January 1973, would have been dealt with by the executive in Northern Ireland.

examination of the power of the executive to transfer a boy from St Patrick's to prison.[2]

Up till now in the Republic, the practice of judicial review has had little bearing on the administration of the institutions for young adult offenders. The courts have invalidated the power given by the Act of 1908 enabling the executive to order a transfer to prison to be made with or without hard labour, and the power to sentence summarily to St Patrick's for breach of the rules of a reformatory school.[3] Two forms of sanction, penal servitude and the suspended sentence, have escaped constitutional censure[4] and it is unlikely that any frontal assault on a sentence of detention in St Patrick's, if one could be launched (which is doubtful), could succeed. On the other hand, the rights of those detained in an institution like St Patrick's could one day present a constitutional issue,[5] as could the absence of a female equivalent of St Patrick's. Why, it might be asked, should a young woman of 19 have to be sent to prison when a young man of the same age can, in theory, be sent either to prison or to St Patrick's? Judicial interpretation of the guarantee of equality before the law by no means indicates that a constitutional challenge on the grounds of sex discrimination would succeed. But the argument is there to be made.[6]

In Northern Ireland the law on these matters is very different. Habeas corpus practice has not been developed to the same extent and similar possibilities of judicial review are not open to the Northern Ireland judges.

Legislative differences

Northern Ireland and the Free State inherited an identical code of statute law. Inevitably, variations were to develop, but those of importance were postponed until after World War II. In 1953, Northern Ireland altered the conditions that had to be met before a borstal sentence could be imposed; further reforms were introduced in 1968 when permitted lengths of sentence were changed and provision was made for the establishment of a different kind of young offenders institution. Legislative action came later in the Republic but was drastic in character: the Act of 1960 effectively ended the borstal system altogether. More recently, the Prisons Act 1970 enabled the maximum age of committal to St

---

[2] It may be asked whether other aspects of administration are worthy of equally detailed scrutiny.

[3] *The State (Sheerin)* v. *Kennedy* [1966] I. R. 379.

[4] *Application of Woods* [1970] I. R. 154 (penal servitude); *The State (P. Woods)* v. *Attorney General* [1969] I. R. 385 (suspended sentence).

[5] A separate but related development has been that human rights in prison have become increasingly important under the European Convention on Human Rights.

[6] The argument was made by counsel in the case in 1975 in which two Limerick girls were originally sentenced to detention in St Patrick's: *The State (two girls from Limerick)* v. *Limerick Circuit Court Judge*, *The Irish Times*, 23 January 1975.

Patrick's to be lowered and made possible the creation of further open institutions of the Shanganagh type.

At the present time, the legal frameworks within which the two principal institutions in the North and South function show marked differences. Northern Ireland has maintained a borstal system, though it has introduced changes in it as well (such as the provisions for shorter sentences and for keeping recidivists out), changes which have reflected comparable developments in Britain. The Republic has chosen to scrap its system altogether, substituting one principal and two subsidiary institutions, all with a legal foundation different from that which pertained for borstal. Of course, on close examination, purely legal differences may possess less practical significance than might be anticipated.

Judicial sentencing practice

In one area, parallel legislation was enacted: both jurisdictions conferred power on the lowest courts to sentence directly to the respective institutions. Northern Ireland gave this power to its resident magistrates in 1953 and the South to its district justices a few years later. Equivalent courts in England still lack such a power. In Ireland there has been a tradition of more extensive jurisdiction in the lowest court. The inconvenience, under the earlier law, of the practice of forwarding an offender to an intermediate court for sentence was recognised too. Both circumstances were sufficient to sweep aside any reservations in Ireland over the wisdom of so radical a change.

Radical it was, for the result has been that the majority of committals are now from the lowest courts. Arguably, control of the sentencer is needed and not merely that furnished by the existence of a right of appeal. Before the statutory changes were made, cases reported from both Irish jurisdictions showed that the intermediate courts were capable of ordering a borstal sentence where this was not appropriate. Plainly, the resident magistrate or district justice could not have been expected to evolve a sentencing record which would be free of criticism.

Pre-sentence screening is one answer, and in Northern Ireland legislation goes part of the way to ensure it. A section in the Act of 1953 stipulates that a copy of every official report which declares a boy to be suitable for borstal must be made available to him or his legal representative. There are, too, special provisions for remand. A further practical point is the high level of legal representation.[7] More general pro ection still will become available if and when the decision is taken to borrow the section in the English Criminal Justice Act 1972[8] which makes legal

---

[7] Desmond Greer, "Legal Aid for Summary Trials in Northern Ireland", *Northern Ireland Legal Quarterly*, XXII (1971), 431.

[8] Criminal Justice Act 1972, s. 37.

aid mandatory in any case where, *inter alia*, the imposition of a borstal sentence is likely.

A similar degree of protection does not yet exist in the Republic. No general rule requires that a report be presented before a boy is sent to St Patrick's. The Act of 1960 is silent on the matter and most committals now take place under it. While it is true that the Act of 1908 does envisage the preparation of a suitability report, in 1948 in *McMahon, Whelan, and others*, the Court of Criminal Appeal determined such a report was not a prerequisite for the imposition of a borstal sentence.[9] Nor is there any provision stipulating that the report has to be made available to the defence. At lowest court level, too, legal representation remains the exception rather than the rule. Entitlement to it has recently been more broadly defined[10] but the general position still compares unfavourably with Northern Ireland.[11] In fact, a curious sense of priorities on this question has been displayed in the Republic. The applicant for habeas corpus, who can present a plausible argument that his continued detention is unlawful, may receive free legal aid by way of administrative dispensation.[12] Some offenders could complain that it was more important to ensure general legal representation at trial level. Why the premium on argumentativeness?

As a result, the district justice in the Republic is subject to less checks than his counterpart in Northern Ireland; he also receives less assistance in arriving at his decision. Until recently, the position for boys in a younger age-group was much the same, but, today, the opening of a new assessment centre at Finglas and the increased use of social inquiry reports have improved matters.[13] As yet, such changes have had little obvious impact on the process of committing to St Patrick's, and a criticism voiced in 1969 by the visiting committee, though relating specifically to mentally disordered offenders, has not been attended to:

We are still concerned to find that, at the point of sentence, the

---

[9] *Irish Law Times and Solicitors' Journal*, LXXXIII (1949), 170.

[10] Criminal Procedure (Amendment) Act 1973, s. 3.

[11] See further Desmond Greer, "Legal Services and the Poor in Ireland", *The Irish Jurist (new series)*, IV (1969), 270. Further provision for legal aid in criminal cases is contained in the Criminal Procedure (Amendment) Act 1973.

It is noteworthy that when extradition arrangements between the Republic and Britain broke down in 1964, Lord Reid, in *R. v. Metropolitan Police Commissioner, ex p. Hammond*, raised the question of provision for legal aid in the Republic: [1965] A.C. 810, 826.

[12] See *Application of Woods* [1970] I.R. 154. The civil litigant has a grievance, too, in the absence of a state system of civil legal aid and advice. The deficiency has escaped constitutional censure (*O'Shaughnessy* v. *Attorney General*, 16 February 1971) but the entire matter is now under review by a government committee.

[13] Statement of John Bruton, Parliamentary Secretary to the Minister for Education: *Senate Debates*, Vol. 76, col. 138ff, 15 November, 1973. See too *First Interim Report of the Interdepartmental Committee on Mentally Ill and Maladjusted Persons: Assessment Services for the Courts in Respect of Juveniles* (Prl. 4688, 1975).

Courts have not available the advice of a forensic psychologist—
to grade more accurately, and prescribe for special treatment, border-
line cases of mentally-retarded boys.

Expansion of non-custodial sentences, of course, have an even earlier
call on available future financial resources.

Sentencing practice naturally invites more consideration than the
arrangements for sentencing themselves, but in Ireland, unfortunately,
this is a field where basic research has yet to be carried out. The subject
has attracted little notice in either the North or the South; in the six
counties, indeed, only one case connected with borstal sentencing has
found its way into the law reports. The particular case demonstrated
the unsatisfactory character of both judicial and executive screening for
potential committals, and there is more than one counterpart to it for
the South. However, the group of cases could be exceptional and any
satisfactory comparison on this aspect of sentencing in the two parts of
the island must await the research worker.

There are other tasks for such a worker to undertake. In the sentencing
of the young offender, the impact of variations in the rate of growth
of probation plainly needs to be assessed. Expansion in probation facilities
occurred earlier in Northern Ireland than in the Republic and, as a result,
the Northern boy could be expected to have usually experienced a longer
sequence of non-custodial sentences before being committed. The sudden
recent expansion of probation in the Republic[14] suggests that such a
pattern should emerge there too. A further task facing the researcher in
the Republic will be to examine any evidence indicating that the sentencer
is consequently being deflected from the earlier choice of a custodial
sentence, such as detention in St Patrick's.

Another topic calling for study is the effect on the Irish sentencer of
a lack of appropriate local custodial institutions for older girl offenders.[15]
The choice of sentence in these cases poses a problem common to sentencers
North and South, though not entirely peculiar to them: in recent years,
sentencers in England and Wales were placed in a somewhat similar
position until detention centres became available in each of the sentencing
catchment areas.

In the history of borstal in Ireland, one change in sentencing practice
had dramatic consequences. In the Republic the borstal system finally
died in 1960. Its demise was undoubtedly hastened by the refusal of the

---

[14] See Michael S. Roche, "Juvenile Delinquency and the Probation System", *Studies*,
LIX (1970), 180; "Welfare Service Expands", *Garda Review* (*new series*), I, no. 1, October
1973, 29.
[15] Above, chapter 6.

judges in the South to commit boys in sufficient numbers to the institution at Clonmel. How did this come about?

The decline in longer-term (i.e. borstal) sentences for youthful offenders was not without precedent. A similar trend was noticeable in the nineteen thirties and had been reversed only when district justices started to make use of their powers to forward offenders to the Circuit Court for sentence. In the nineteen fifties the trend emerged again and proved irreversible. The change in attitude of the judiciary cannot have been to the liking of governments. Considerable money and effort had been expended on the institution at Clonmel: the cost of refurbishing it prior to its reopening in 1947, the publication in the following year of the explanatory pamphlet, *The Borstal Institution at Clonmel*, and the visits organised at an official level. Yet, despite this expenditure and publicity, the number of committals kept falling and eventually the Department of Justice felt compelled to increase the use of its power to transfer young adult prisoners, so as to swell the inmate population.

The judiciary's change of attitude may be explained in a number of different ways. It is possible, first, that the judges began to believe that an unfair stigma attached to boys sent by them to Clonmel. As was pointed out in chapter 8, arguments over the question of stigma are difficult to assess. In order to offer an opinion, it would be essential to recapture the mood in official circles at the relevant time. This is not easy since there are only two slight pieces of evidence: first, in 1948, the change of name of the institution at Clonmel to St Patrick's; secondly, the continuing campaign of the visiting committee to secure the proscription of the term 'borstal'.

A second possibility is that the judiciary began to be influenced by the criticisms levelled at the régime in the Cork and Clonmel institutions. Edward Fahy and James Dillon, two principal critics, attempted to secure improvements there, but a possible side-effect, when coupled with the innuendos which the *Clonmel Notes* of 1948 were designed to answer, may have been that the judiciary's confidence in the administration of the borstal system had been undermined to some extent.

A third explanation may be that the judiciary began to doubt the achievements of the borstal system. This hypothesis, however, is unlikely: the annual *Prisons Reports* continued to publicise the results of the Department of Justice's follow-up surveys and these appeared reasonably satisfactory. The judiciary may have thought, nonetheless, that there was no evidence that the borstal system achieved anything *which some alternative form of custodial sentence could not equally achieve*. Even if the proof is slender, this is the most likely explanation for the judiciary's diminishing use of borstal and increasing preference for the short custodial sentence. The judiciary was certainly not to be discouraged from branching out in a fresh direction. In the nineteen forties, in the wake of general unemployment and of a spiralling rate of emigration, the special attention given to the after- care of borstal discharges all but vanished. At the same time, the Department of Justice, through its use of the power of transferring offenders, saw no objection to the practice of introducing short-term offenders into a borstal institution. Naturally, any remaining belief in the virtues of selectivity will have been torpedoed by this policy of mixing long and short-term offenders in the same institution. Furthermore, there was the argument that it was wrong to provide a privileged régime for a minority of young offenders; and this could have weighed with individual members of a new generation of judges.[16]

In other circumstances, two arguments might have received a sympathetic hearing and thus delayed, if not prevented, the closure of Clonmel. It could have been impressed upon the judiciary that it had a duty to the community to ensure a level of committals sufficient to enable the borstal to survive. At intervals, the executive has shown itself capable of applying pressure of this kind, the circumstances related by the nineteenth-century Dublin magistrate, F. T. Porter,[17] being remarkable only for the bluntness of the approach. In the case of the Clonmel borstal, however, there is no evidence whatsoever that such an approach was contemplated. By the nineteen forties and fifties, the implications of judicial independence were well understood and the executive will have known that any such approach would have been firmly resisted.

A second argument would have received even less support. Since the Irish penal system was modelled on the English, the judiciary might have been asked to copy English practice. In Britain, however, there was no precedent for ceasing to prop up the borstal system and it continued in existence. The implication, naturally, would have been that a borstal system should continue in the Republic. This second invitation would have been equally firmly rejected, as obnoxious to the nationalism lurking in the breast of the Irish administrator. Nationalist sentiment can enter into such things,[18] and could have influenced the decision to end the borstal system in the Republic. In a Dáil speech, Oscar Traynor, the Minister for Justice, explaining the proposal in the Criminal Justice Bill 1960 to abolish the term 'borstal', said:

Section 12 proposes to drop the term 'Borstal'. This term derives

---

[16] On the general background of Irish judges, see Paul C. Bartholomew, *The Irish Judiciary* (Dublin: Institute of Public Administration, 1971), chapter 2.

[17] See the quotation which introduces chapter 4 above.

[18] See the account of the reaction to Sir Thomas Molony's paper, "New Methods for Offenders", delivered to the Statistical and Social Inquiry Society of Ireland in 1940: *Journal of the Statistical and Social Inquiry Society of Ireland*, XVI (1937–42) (93 session), 49 at 59.

from the name of the English village in which the experiment of training young offenders was first tried. It has no native associations with this country: it invites comparison with the British system and the comparison is misleading because in Britain the numbers are very much greater and segregation into classes is possible.[19]

Chapter 1 is a refutation of Mr Traynor's third sentence but the passage ought not, perhaps, to be taken too seriously: his remarks are in the nature of a republican valediction of a kind at which, on the appropriate occasion, the Southern politician is peculiarly adept. There is no hard evidence at all that nationalist convictions precipitated the abandonment of the borstal system in the twenty-six counties. The probable explanation for this runs something as follows. The judiciary in the Republic entered a phase where they showed reluctance to impose longer sentences on younger offenders. To swell numbers at Clonmel, an increasing proportion of ordinary prisoners were transferred to it; a different kind of institution emerged as a result, but few people appeared to mind. Clonmel was not as convenient for visitors, or as attractive to staff, as a location in Dublin; so, slowly, the idea took root that the solution to the problem was the establishment of a larger institution for young adult male offenders in Dublin.

Day-to-day operation of the institutions

The inclusion of borstal in the English penal system was enough to ensure its survival in Northern Ireland. In matters of policy, England was again the yardstick. Before the Malone borstal opened in 1927, Sir Dawson Bates paid a visit to the English borstal at Feltham where inmates at the time included boys from Northern Ireland. On his return, Sir Dawson declared that the new Northern borstal would be "more or less on all fours with the Borstal institutions in England",[20] and the Ministry of Home Affairs was at pains to ensure that it remained so, at least in essentials.

In 1923, the Moles Committee rightly foresaw that the smallness of the local population would make impossible the development of special facilities which was to take place in England.[21] In nearly every other respect, the North's administrative experience was to be a carbon copy of England's: in the kind of accommodation, the type of régime, the emphasis on after-care, the institution of a reception centre, the concern with education, the revitalisation of training, the introduction of day release, even in the most recent legal changes. The similarity of the two

---

[19] *Dáil Debates*, Vol. 183, col. 563, 28 June 1960.
[20] *H. C. Debates* (N.I.), Vol. 7, col. 1204, 12 May 1926.
[21] Above, chapter 3.

systems is illustrated best of all in the nineteen thirties. Then Northern Ireland had its 'golden age' of borstal too: the scout troop, the camps and picnics, the handicraft classes and the whist drives. Indeed, there is evidence that Northern Ireland's golden age lasted rather longer than England's. In the North today, developments taking place in England are independently assessed prior to adoption locally, and any borrowing of ideas that eventuates is facilitated by the practice of appointing to governorships individuals with experience of English borstals (or at least the system)[22] and of encouraging the attendance of Northern Ireland governors at the governors' annual conferences in England.

Eyes were very rarely turned South. From 1922 to 1924, liaison between the two governments was needed to ensure the orderly release of persons who had been committed to penal institutions in Ireland prior to partition, but no further cooperation or exchange of views was to occur. A plan does appear to have been hatched under which, in the absence of a Northern borstal, Northern boys would again have been sent South but, even if this had been seriously considered, opponents would have been able to point out that the cost of maintenance in the Free State was marginally higher than in Britain.[23] In 1923, the Moles Committee reported adversely on the conditions then prevailing in the Southern institutions at Kilkenny and at Clonmel, and that settled the matter.

The South, for its part, was not over-eager to look North. Recent innovations in the Republic's penal system, such as day-time employment release and the inauguration of open institutions, owe much to developments in Britain, but direct North-South contact, at least until recently, has been negligible.[24] A precedent for official visits was finally set by the Kennedy Committee on Reformatory and Industrial Schools Systems which, in the course of its investigations, inspected the training school at Rathgael, near Bangor in County Down, and made a number of recommendations, clearly traceable to what it saw there.[25]

It has already been observed that in one area of borstal administration Northern Ireland has chosen to differ, not only from the Republic, but

---

[22] There are no straightforward transfers between the two prison services, but a successful English candidate for any post in the Northern Ireland service would normally have his pension rights transferred.

[23] In 1923, Northern Ireland boys cost £121 per head per annum to maintain in England, and £123 per head per annum to maintain in the Free State: *Moles Report*, p. 26. In 1924 one Northern boy was costing £125 in the Free State and others £109 each in England: *H. C. Debates (N.I.)*, Vol. 4, col. 644, 9 April 1924.

[24] A smattering of civil servants and governors, North and South, have made the acquaintance of their counterparts across the Border. Otherwise, contacts in the area of the administration of justice appear to have been largely confined to the police. In 1936, for example, members of the Garda Representative Body visited the Royal Ulster Constabulary depot at Enniskillen, and compared it favourably with their own depot: Séamus Breathnach, *The Irish Police* (Dublin: Mercier Press, 1974), p. 131.

[25] "Reformatory and Industrial Schools", *The Irish Jurist (new series)*, V (1970), 294.

also, atypically, from England: its system provides for the infliction of corporal punishment. The obvious explanation for this discrepancy— a different attitude North and South to corporal punishment—has already been rejected, as being not in accordance with the facts. Another explanation is that in the North corporal punishment has been tolerated because it is viewed as a 'school' punishment and the Northern borstal is seen more as a school than a prison.

The argument is not wholly convincing. In the first place, when the legislation on corporal punishment in borstal was under consideration, Nationalist and other non-Unionist MPs did not hesitate to condemn beating as degrading, even though by then the régime in the North was recognisably based on that of a school. Moreover, the mere fact that the borstal régime is so modelled is no guarantee that corporal punishment will be available: in English borstals, after the early nineteen twenties, it was not practised.

The argument implies that the régimes in the South—first, of borstal and then of St Patrick's—have been based on that of prison, rather than that of a school. The assumption is not warranted. Before 1922, the Prisons Board certainly said that the régime at Clonmel was modelled on that of the public school, and after Independence the claim was to be repeated: in the *Clonmel Notes* of 1948, for instance, the impression that the institution was being compared with school is unmistakable. On the other hand, Fahy clearly suggests that the courts in the South treated borstal as prison.[26] In recent years it is also worth noticing that, whereas for legal purposes a Northern Ireland court was not prepared to equate borstal detention with imprisonment,[27] for constitutional purposes a court in the Republic was willing to equate detention in St Patrick's with imprisonment.[28] The evidence remains contradictory: St Patrick's closely resembles a prison, but the organisation of the new institutions at Shanaganagh and at Loughan is plainly different.

The true explanation for the existence of corporal punishment in the Northern borstal system may lie in the character of the school on which the parliamentary majority in the nineteen thirties sought to model that system: it was Eton or Harrow, not, as it might now be put, some secondary modern.[29] And as a one-time headmaster of Harrow, E. C. Welden, later Bishop of Calcutta, noticed, there is the "curious paradox" that the upper classes submitted to chastisement which the lower resented and resisted: "It is far easier to flog a peer's son than a pauper's."[30]

[26] Fahy, "Borstal in Ireland", p. 85.
[27] Above, chapter 3.
[28] *The State (Sheerin)* v. *Kennedy* [1966] I.R. 379.
[29] Yet smoking was permitted from 1940; smoking was only allowed in the Southern borstal in 1948.
[30] Quoted in Cyril Pearl, *Victorian Patchwork* (London: Heinemann, 1972), p. 23.

The atmosphere of the institutions North and South is not easy to compare, but on custodial conditions and aspects of administrative practice, the advantage has recognisably lain with the North. The conclusion is supported both by official sources and by Edward Fahy. In Fahy's opinion, conditions at Malone in 1941 were far superior to those at the Southern borstal then at Cork.

> If . . . training has not been given, if in fact the only aim is to engage the cogs of the machine between the hours specified in a timetable and to lock them safely away on the chime of a clock or the blast of a whistle, then it is futile to expect promising results from employment on discharge.[31]

Conditions were to improve at Cork and again when the borstal returned to Clonmel, but both then and later, when St Patrick's opened in Dublin, the quality of accommodation and the provision for education, vocational training and after-care were superior in Northern Ireland.

The better facilities in Northern Ireland can be attributed to more money and more official concern. Evidence to corroborate the view that greater finance has been available is neither easy to find nor to evaluate, but the facts unfolded in chapter 3 suggest that this has been the case. Greater official interest in the administration of its institutions might have been anticipated from Northern Ireland's wish to keep pace with Britain. Hard proof is again difficult to come by but a valid approach is to compare the occasions on which borstal or its equivalents have been the object of study by government committees North and South. In the North there was the Moles Committee in 1923 and the Lynn in 1938, though their reports touch on other matters besides. In contrast, institutions for young adult offenders are barely mentioned at all in reports from the South—just a passage on borstal for girls in the *Cussen Report* of 1936 and the paragraph on St Patrick's in the *Kennedy Report* of 1970. Naturally, it can be argued that an absence of attention from government committees betokens the underlying health of an area of administration, but while this may be true in other Irish contexts, it is unlikely to apply in the present one.

In historical perspective, then, greater interest has been displayed in Northern Ireland, but it is necessary to be cautious about the position today because, at the present time, more detailed information is provided in the average annual report from the South. A further feature of these reports in recent years is the space devoted to the remarks of the various visiting committees: there is no equivalent practice in the case of the

[31] Fahy, "Borstal in Ireland," p. 84.

annual *Home Office Services Reports*. Once again, an absence of detail
(this time relating to the North) ought not necessarily to invite unfavourable comparison, but the prominence afforded the views of visiting
committees in the Republic deserves welcome. The coverage given to
affairs at Shanganagh in the *Prisons Report 1972* is particularly interesting.
In a later section of the *Report*, the visiting committee lists a number of
criticisms in its survey for the year;[32] several of these are replied to
in the official section which precedes it.[33] The *Report* thus shows that
dialogue is taking place within the establishment.

All this signifies greater general interest, as does the existence of groups
pressing for reforms in the penal system, an offshoot of what F.S.L.
Lyons has termed "a preoccupation with social justice"[34] in the modern
Republic. Of importance, too, is a matching development in Northern
Ireland—the founding of the Northern Ireland Association for the Care
and Resettlement of Offenders (though this organisation does not yet
shoulder any responsibilities for the welfare of borstal discharges).

The principal harbinger of change will be government itself. Neither
North nor South has government as yet established any purpose-built
institution for the 16 to 21 age-group. But within the resources at their
disposal, experiments have been tried and, doubtless, more will take place.
Under-capitalisation and an absence of local research remain indictments
but, to look at the other side of the coin, there are the institutions at
Woburn, Shanganagh and Loughan, and these, in varying fashion,
represent progress.[35] As it happens, Shanganagh and Loughan represent
something else in the South: a departure from the idea of the single
custodial institution, St Patrick's, and a return to the philosophy which,
historically, has underlain the classical borstal system.

A development which is likely in the future is the adoption of a com-
posite sentence embracing institutional custody and supervision in the
community.[36] Whether this in turn is labelled as loyalty to a tradition
will matter little. In the penal system, the remarks of Alexander Pope
are particularly appropriate: "Whate'er is best administered is best."

---

[32] *Prisons Report 1972*, pp. 24–27.
[33] ibid., pp. 11–12.
[34] *Ireland Since the Famine* (London: Fontana, 1973), p. 692.
[35] Improvements within the closed institutions are not to be ignored either.
[36] Such a sentence, if proposed for the Republic, would of course have to run the
gauntlet of constitutional approval.

Bibliography

A. Parliamentary debates

1. Irish Republic
Dáil Debates; Senate Debates.

2. Northern Ireland
H.C. Debates (N.I.); Senate Debates (N.I.).

3. United Kingdom
H.C. Debates (5 series); H.L. Debates (5 series).

B. Official reports

1. Irish Republic
Appropriation Accounts (annual).
Annual Reports of the General Prisons Board Ireland (1920–21 to 1927–28).
Annual Reports on Prisons (1928 to 1971).
Annual Reports on Prisons and Detention Centres (1972 to —).
Report of Commission of Inquiry into the Reformatory and Industrial School System. P. 2225, 1936.
Report of Committee on Reformatory and Industrial Schools Systems. Prl. 1342, 1970.
Report of Commission on the Status of Women. Prl. 2760, 1972.
First Interim Report of the Interdepartmental Committee on Mentally Ill and Maladjusted Persons: Assessment Services for the Courts in Respect of Juveniles. Prl. 4688, 1975.

2. Northern Ireland
Reports on the Prisons Northern Ireland (1921–23 to 1926–27).

Reports on the Administration of Home Office Services (1928 to —).

Report of the Departmental Committee on Industrial and Reformatory Schools in Northern Ireland. Cmd. 14, 1923.

The Protection and Welfare of the Young and the Treatment of Young Offenders: Report of the Committee Appointed by the Minister of Home Affairs. Cmd. 187, 1938.

The Protection and Welfare of the Young and the Treatment of Young Offenders. Cmd. 264, 1948.

Report of a Public Inquiry into the Proposal to acquire Kiltonga House, Newtownards for the establishment of a training school and remand home. Belfast: H.M.S.O., 1973.

3. United Kingdom

Fifth General Report on the District, Criminal and Private Lunatic Asylums in Ireland 1851 (C. 1387), H.C. 1851, xxiv.

Second Annual Report of the Directors of Convict Prisons in Ireland 1855 (C. 2068), H.C. 1856, xxxiv.

Reports of the General Prisons Board Ireland (1877–78 to 1919–20).

Reports of the Royal Commission on Prisons in Ireland 1884, Vol. II, Minutes of Evidence (C. 4233–1), H.C. 1884–5, xxxviii.

Report from the Departmental Committee on Prisons 1895 (C. 7702), H.C. 1895, lvi.

Report of the Departmental Committee on the Supply of Books to the Prisoners in H.M. Prisons and to the Inmates of H.M. Borstals 1911 (Cd. 5589), H.C. 1911, xxxix.

First Report of the Northern Ireland Special Arbitration Committee. Cmd. 2072, 1924.

Report of the Departmental Committee on the Treatment of Young Offenders. Cmd. 2831, 1927.

Report of the Interdepartmental Committee on the Business of the Criminal Courts. Cmnd. 1289, 1961.

Residential Provision for Homeless Discharged Offenders: Report of the Working Party on the Place of Voluntary Service in After-Care. London: H.M.S.O., 1966.

The Place of Voluntary Service in After-Care: Second Report of the Working Party. London: H.M.S.O., 1967.

Detention of Girls in a Detention Centre: Interim Report of the Advisory Council on the Penal System. London: H.M.S.O., 1968.

Report of the Advisory Council on the Penal System: The Regime for Long-term Prisoners in Conditions of Maximum Security. London: H.M.S.O., 1968.

People in Prison. Cmnd. 4214, 1969.